BROOKLANDS BOOKS

The
LAND ROVER
STORY

Part One	1948-1971

Written and compiled by
James Taylor

ISBN 1 85520 3391

Published by
LRO Publications Ltd.

D1261786

Distributed by

BROOKLANDS BOOKS LTD.
P.O. BOX 146, COBHAM,
SURREY, KT11 1LG. UK

A-LRS1

Printed in Hong Kong

INTRODUCTION

The articles reproduced in this book appeared in Land Rover Owner magazine over a period of 31 months, between June 1991 and December 1993. They were written with the full co-operation and approval of Land Rover Ltd, but all parties concerned knew that there were bound to be gaps in the information available. As a result, every article was accompanied by a request for information on upcoming subjects or for corrections to what had already been printed. Additional material appeared as "Updates" accompanying later articles.

This admittedly unusual method of gathering information proved extremely successful. "The Land Rover Story" generated a great deal of correspondence, unearthing information which might otherwise have remained lost or forgotten. Many people were only too pleased to pass on their recollections of what had really happened, to add information or to query accepted assumptions. It all made the business of writing "The Land Rover Story" much more enjoyable, and it ensured that - in the end - the story itself was that much more accurate.

This book not only gathers together the original articles, but also incorporates corrections, additions and other improvements. My sincere thanks go to all those who provided additional information, but it would be arrogant to imagine that this book contains the final word on Land Rover between 1948 and 1971. New information is surfacing all the time and - who knows? - perhaps this book will prompt those who can add a little detail here and there to pass it on to me through Land Rover Owner magazine.

At the time of writing, "The Land Rover Story" is still appearing in Land Rover Owner magazine, and the series is very far from over. Rest assured that there are plans to re-issue these later episodes in book form in due course!

James Taylor

COVER ILLUSTRATIONS

Front - 107 inch Station Wagon
Back - Top Left - 80 inch
Back - Top Right - Series II 88 inch
Back - Bottom - Series IIa 109 inch One Ton

Distributed by

Brooklands Books Ltd., PO Box 146, Cobham, Surrey KT11 1LG, England
Phone: 01932 865051 Fax: 01932 868803
Brooklands Books Ltd, 1/81 Darley St., PO Box 199, Mona Vale, NSW 2103, Australia
Phone: 2 999 78428 Fax: 2 997 95799
CarTech, 11481 Kost Dam Road, North Branch, MN 55056, USA
Phone: 800 551 4754 & 612 583 3471 Fax: 612 583 2023
Motorbooks International, Osceola, Wisconsin 54020, USA
Phone: 715 294 3345 & 800 826 6600 Fax: 715 294 4448

Printed in Hong Kong

BROOKLANDS BOOKS

CONTENTS

Land Rover -the company

*WHAT sort of company is Land Rover? Where has it come from? In this first instalment of our complete Land Rover history, **James Taylor** establishes a few basics.*

TODAY'S Land Rover company can trace its origins right back to the last quarter of the nineteenth century, when J. K. Starley Ltd., of Coventry, branched out from the business of sewing-machine manufacture into the new and profitable market for bicycles. The Starley cycles sold so well that, by 1896, they had completely eclipsed the firm's original business.

In that year, Starley's therefore went into voluntary liquidation, and the firm's directors formed a new company to take over the bicycle manufacturing business. Borrowing the evocative name first given to an 1884 Starley tricycle, they called it the Rover Cycle Company.

Like many other cycle manufacturers, the company turned to cars at the beginning of the new century. Its first model appeared in 1904 and, a year later, the word "Cycle" was deleted from the company's name. Cycles (and motorcycles) continued to figure in Rover sales catalogues until 1926, but after that date the company made only cars.

However, the late 1920s were not good times for Rover. The company tried unsuccessfully to break into the big-volume small car market and rapidly ran into financial difficulties. Not until 1933 did a change of managing director and financial director bring about a new manufacturing policy and a complete change-round in the company's fortunes.

The Wilks era

That new policy put the quality of the Rover product above the quantities in which it was produced. New managing director Spencer Wilks had also persuaded his fellow-directors that the company should aim its products specifically at the well-to-do middle-classes. Rovers soon became known for being well-made, well-appointed, discreet rather than flashy, and just a little bit more sprightly than average. They became cars for the bank manager, the doctor, or the solicitor; and they sold extraordinarily well.

So well did they sell that the company was once again on a sound footing by the mid-1930s, and in 1936 was asked by the Government to take on the management of a new "shadow" factory near Birmingham. This was one of many being built to "shadow" or duplicate the production capacity of the country's military aircraft manufacturers at a time when war with Germany was looking increasingly likely. The major car manufacturers were asked to look after them and so to gain experience in aircraft manufacture before their own assembly plants were requisitioned for war work.

Three years after work had begun on the first factory, the Rover Company was asked to take on a second and much larger one at Solihull. Building began in 1939 just before war was declared and, by the autumn of 1940, the Solihull plant was pro-

△ *Land Rover's Solihull factory as it is today, and, right, the first Rover.*

ducing its first aero engines.

The move to Solihull

After the war, it was almost inevitable that Rover should move its car production to the Solihull factory. The company's original premises in Coventry's Helen Street had been severely bombed by the Luftwaffe and were in need of major renovation.

Secondly, the terms of its contract with the Government gave Rover the right to take over the shadow factories it had been running when these were no longer needed for the war effort. The Rover directors took the decision to move in principle in 1944 and the company relocated at Solihull in 1946.

Rover's main concern at the end of the 1940s — and, indeed, for the first few years of the new decade — was to obtain the raw materials with which to build enough cars to survive. The British economy had been shattered by the war, and it took several years for normal trading and supply con-

ditions to resume.

The Government encouraged motor manufacturers to simplify their ranges and to earn currency from abroad by exporting the greater part of what they produced. These policies — sensible enough in themselves but much-disliked at the time — gave rise to some cars which were unlike anything British manufacturers had built before. Among them was the Land-Rover, which made its commercial début in April 1948.

Enter the Land-Rover

The Rover board sanctioned production of the Land-Rover in the hope that it would keep the company afloat by earning export orders until normal trading conditions returned. But, by the end of 1948, it was clear that it would achieve much more than that: while export demand for Land-Rovers was enormous, the cars on which the company had built its reputation were not selling well overseas. As a result, the company

had to reverse its production priorities and to start planning to build twice as many Land-Rovers as cars from the end of 1949.

This unexpected expansion in the Land-Rover field was the first step in a gradual division of the Rover Company into two camps during the early 1950s. One side became concerned with cars while the other side looked after Land-Rovers.

After 1956, that division was formalised, and each side of the business was given its own assistant chief engineer who reported to a chief engineer with overall responsibility for the company's products. At the same time, major components (such as engines and transmissions) were designed by departments which worked for both the car and Land-Rover sides of the company, so that the two product lines could use common components wherever possible.

During the 1960s, the heads of the car and Land-Rover sides of the business were elevated to chief engineer status. Apart from this, however, things remained fundament-

THE LAND ROVER STORY

△ *This aerial photograph of Solihull dates from the mid-1960s and shows the original aero engine factory in the background. Lode Lane is at the bottom right of the picture. In the foreground new building work is already beginning on the 200 acres of farm land surrounding the factory site which the Rover Company had prudently purchased in the 1930s.*

Solihull's "face" — the imposing facade of No. 1 block in the mid-1940s. The building remains largely unchanged and now houses the Press Office, among other departments, but you won't see cars like those parked outside any more!

ally unchanged until the advent of British Leyland in 1967.

There then followed a period of 11 years during which the Land-Rover business seemed to be in a constant state of flux. A great deal of confusion reigns about the exact sequence of events affecting the company's ownership and structure during those 11 years — the Leyland era — and it is worth examining in some detail what happened.

The Leyland era

A series of mergers and take-overs within the British motor industry during the early 1960s saw two major groupings form — one centred on the Leyland truck and bus company and the other on the old BMC organisation. Rover belonged to neither, with the result that BMC's purchase of the independent Pressed Steel company, which produced all Rover's bodyshells, left it with a problem. Whether it stayed with Pressed Steel or turned to the Leyland group for its

bodyshells, it would in effect be using a rival company as a major supplier.

Choosing to negotiate from a position of strength while they still could, the Rover board entered in the closing months of 1966 into talks with the Leyland Motor Corporation. The conclusion they reached was that a merger would be in the interests of both parties, and so in the early part of 1967 the Rover Company was absorbed into Leyland.

A year later, the Leyland Motor Corporation itself merged with British Motor Holdings (the old BMC group, plus Jaguar), and the new conglomerate called itself the British Leyland Motor Corporation.

Within what had been the Rover Company, however, the division into car and Land-Rover activities remained unchanged. Rover proved to be one of the few successful components of the BLMC empire, and was therefore left to get on with its own business in relative peace. At first, the only real difference was that its board was

supplemented by two directors from the BLMC main board.

Things began to change in the early 1970s, however. BLMC had begun to grow uneasy about the overlaps between the Rover and Triumph saloon car ranges, and by the beginning of 1971, there were plans to resolve this duplication of product lines by merging the two still largely independent companies.

Initially, there was a certain degree of co-operation on the engineering side, none of which affected Land-Rovers; but in 1972 this co-operation was formalised when Rover and Triumph were combined within the Specialist Cars Division of British Leyland. In the new division with them, most reluctantly, was Jaguar, and somewhere in there, rather bewildered but trying to hold its head high, was the Land-Rover side of the old Rover Company.

BLMC's operations went from bad to worse, however, and at the end of 1974 it turned to the Government for financial

△ *Name plate on a seven-seater Series One.*

Is this a Land-Rover, a Leyland Cars Land-Rover or a British Leyland Land-Rover? Actually, it's a 1976 Series III, built when Land-Rovers were a product of Leyland Cars, itself a subsidiary of British Leyland Ltd.

Who has owned the Land Rover name?

1947-1967 The Rover Company.

1967-1968 The Rover Company (as a subsidiary of the Leyland Motor Corporation).

1968-1972 The Rover Company (as a subsidiary of the British Leyland Motor Corporation).

1972-1975 Rover-British Leyland UK (a company within the Specialist Cars, Division of the British Leyland Motor Corporation).

1975-1978 Leyland Cars (a subsidiary of British Leyland Ltd).

1978-1988 Land Rover Ltd (an autonomous company within British Leyland Ltd, which was renamed as the Austin Rover Group in 1982 and then as the Rover Group in 1986.)

1989-present Land Rover Ltd (a subsidiary of the Rover Group).

help. The first outcome was nationalistion; the second was the appointment of industrial adviser Sir Don (later Lord) Ryder to look into the company's affairs.

His report recommended greater centralisation and so, from November 1975, Rover and Land-Rover manufacture fell to the new Leyland Cars subsidiary of what was now called British Leyland Ltd. Once again, Land-Rovers sat rather uncomfortably within it.

The restructuring did not cure BL's troubles. Many of the Ryder Report's recommendations were quickly discredited — particularly its suppression of the long-established marque identities in favour of a corporate centralistaion — and Michael (later Sir Michael) Edwardes was appointed as chairman of BL to sort out the mess in October 1977.

Ryder had, in fact, recommended separating Land-Rovers from the luxury cars division of BL in his 1975 report, and plans for this were well advanced by the time Ed-

wardes arrived. The plans were allowed to continue unchanged and, in July 1978, Land Rover Ltd was set up as an autonomous company within British Leyland.

It was the first time that Land Rovers had been completely separated from Rover saloons (and also, incidentally, the first time that the hyphen was officially dropped from the Land Rover name). At the end of 1982, Rover car assembly was moved out of Solihull, and the plant was given over completely to Land Rover Ltd.

From the beginning, Land Rover Ltd was given its own managing director, and the company enjoyed a considerable degree of independence over the next ten years. During that period British Leyland was reorganised first as the Austin Rover Group (in 1982) and then as the Rover Group (in 1986), all without major change at Land Rover.

Government plans to sell Land Rover Ltd to the private sector in 1986 came to nothing. However, two years later the Rover

Group was sold to British Aerospace, and Land Rover went with it.

One almost immediate result of the change of ownership was a major organisational reshuffle. With effect from January 1989, Land Rover Ltd lost its independence as Rover cars were re-integrated into a single organisation under a single managing director.

Some of the engineering departments of the Rover car business and the Land Rover business also began to work together once again. At the time of writing, Land Rover's own most senior management figure is its commercial director (whose job was confusingly retitled "Managing Director, Land Rover (Commercial)" in January 1991).

But those who know the history of Rover cannot have failed to recognise how much the developing situation parallels that of thirty years ago, when Land Rovers and Rover cars depended on common design departments.

Plus ça change, plus c'est la même chose!

Land Rover - the people

△ Maurice Wilks, father of the Land Rover.

▽ Gordon Bashford, designer of the original Land Rover chassis.

OF THE MANY men and women who have worked for the Land Rover company and its predecessors over the years, only a small number have been in a position to exercise a powerful influence over the products. Their names will occur over and over again in future instalments of the Land Rover Story, so **James Taylor** *has compiled a dictionary to help sort out Who was (and is) Who.*

BACHE, David ... served his apprenticeship with Austin at Longbridge, and then moved to Rover in 1954, where he was put in charge of the newly-created Styling Department. His first work on Land-Rovers was the restyling of the Series I to make the Series II in 1958. He tidied up the original Range Rover styling for production in 1970, and continued to have oversight of all Land-Rover styling until he left what was by then the Austin Rover Group in 1982 to become a freelance styling consultant.

BARTON, Tom ... was involved with Land-Rovers for 33 years, and had earned the nickname of "Mr Land-Rover" by the time he retired in 1980.

He was one of five section leaders in the Rover Drawing Office who were asked to sketch up the Land-Rover in 1947, and his task was to adapt the existing Rover gearbox to take the four-wheel-drive transfer box. In 1954, he became Chief Development Engineer, and 12 years later Land-Rover Chief Engineer, which job was retitled Director of Product Engineering on the formation of Land Rover Ltd in 1978.

BASHFORD, Gordon ... joined the Rover Company at the beginning of the 1930s, and by the middle of the decade was involved in the design of Rover saloons. After the War, he was one of the five section leaders who sketched up the Land-Rover: his was the core task as he was charged with drawing up the vehicle's overall layout. In the early 1950s, he was asked to look after design research for all future vehicles. With Spen King, he drew up the initial plans for the Range Rover in the late 1960s. At the end of the 1970s, he took on a new research job at the Gaydon proving ground, from which he retired in 1981.

BOYLE, Robert ... joined the Rover Company in the 1930s, and became Chief Design Engineer and Maurice Wilks' right-hand-man. By the time the Land-Rover was being drawn up, he was the most senior engineer in the company after Wilks himself, and he remained in this position right up until his retirement in 1963.

BROADHEAD, Mike ... joined the Rover Company in the late 1950s and almost immediately became involved with the Land-Rover side of the business. He worked his way up through the ranks to become Chief Engineer and to take over from Tom Barton on the latter's retirement in 1980. He left the company in 1985 and now runs a car dealership in the north of England.

CULLEN, John ... was in charge of development under Arthur Goddard in the late 1940s and was responsible for testing the first prototype. He was head-hunted by David Brown Industries to take charge of their planned 4x4 vehicle, and left Rover in 1954. The David Brown 4x4 did not materialise.

Second part of James Taylor's history of the Land Rover

△ *Time for a celebration in March 1966. Personalities pictured with the first of Land-Rover's second half-million include Peter Wilks (extreme left), William Martin-Hurst (at the wheel), Tom Barton (in the centre seat), A. B. Smith (in the passenger seat), Bernard Jackman (standing beside A. B. Smith), and Gordon Bashford (far right).*

DONOVAN, Mike ... joined the newly-formed Land Rover Ltd in 1978 as a Product Planner. In the early 1980s, he became involved with the ground-up survey of Land-Rover products and markets initiated by Managing Director Tony Gilroy. Out of that came his appointment as head of the Project Jay team which drew up the Discovery. At the end of the 1980s, Donovan moved to the Rover Group as a Regional Director, and earlier this year took up a new appointment with Rolls-Royce.

DRINKWATER, Joe ... was one of the five section leaders who drew up the original Land-Rover. His particular responsibility was the engine, on which task he reported to Jack Swaine.

EVANS, David ... is currently Chief Designer, Land Rover Product Design; essentially, his responsibility is for styling.

FARMER, George (later Sir George) ... became Rover's Commercial Director in 1953. In 1956, he was appointed Joint Managing Director of the Rover Company with Maurice Wilks. He became Deputy Chairman in 1960 and retired in 1963.

GILROY, Tony ... had been in charge of manufacturing at BL's Longbridge plant and then reorganised the Freight Rover van operation before joining Land Rover Ltd in 1983 to take over from Mike Hodgkinson as Managing Director. It was he who created the modern Land Rover company, by initiating the far-reaching review of products and markets which led both to the Range Rover's redevelopment for the US market and to the development of the Discovery. Gilroy left the company in January 1989, after a management reshuffle.

HODGKINSON, Mike ... was Land Rover Ltd's first Managing Director, appointed by Sir Michael Edwardes on the company's formation in 1978. His motor industry career had started with Ford, but by 1969 he was a financial analyst with BL, and was one of the team which recommended that the Range Rover project should go ahead. At Land Rover, he implemented the £280 million investment which led to the rationalisation of the company's manufacturing resources, the Stage I V8 and 90/110 Land Rovers, the first In

Vogue limited-edition Range Rovers and the four-door Range Rover. He was succeeded by Tony Gilroy in 1983.

JACKMAN, Bernard ... was a long-standing Rover man whose father, Len, had designed the bodies for the very first Rover cars in 1904. Jackman succeeded A.B.Smith as Managing Director of what was by then known as Rover-Triumph, which also encompassed Land-Rovers. However, his appointment lasted only two years, as his job was abolished in the 1975 Leyland Cars reshuffle.

KING, Spen ... is a nephew of the Wilks brothers who joined Rover initially to work on gas turbine engines. When the company ceased experimenting with these in the early 1960s, he moved into mainstream engineering, working mainly with Gordon Bashford on new vehicle concepts. The two of them drew up the original plans for the Range Rover. King moved to Triumph as Chief Engineer, became Chief Engineer of the combined Rover-Triumph companies in 1971, and moved up to become Director of Engineering and Product Planning for Leyland Cars in 1975. He retired in 1985.

THE LAND ROVER STORY

THE LAND ROVER STORY

△ It isn't all big names, of course. This picture of the Project Jay (Discovery) Team shows how many individuals may be involved in the design of a vehicle. Standing on the extreme right, with hands behind his back, is the project's co-ordinator, Mike Donovan.

◁ The modern era — Chris Woodwark, now Land Rover Ltd's Managing Director.

The 1991 limited-edition Range Rover CSK was so named in his honour (his full name is Charles Spencer King).

LLOYD, John ... was a Triumph man of long-standing who was made Technical Director of Rover-Triumph in 1974. As such, he also had overall responsibility for Land-Rover engineering. When Leyland Cars was created in 1975 and the individual marque identities were submerged, Lloyd's job ceased to exist.

LOKER, Harry ... was Chief Body Designer under Maurice Wilks in the late 1940s, and was therefore responsible not only for body design but also for translating Wilks' ideas on styling into metal. He was later succeeded by his assistant, Sam Ostler.

MACKIE, George ... was Rover's European representative in the late 1940s, left the company briefly to build the Rover-based Marauder sports car with Spen King and Peter Wilks, and took on responsibility for sales technical data and press releases back at Rover when the Marauder venture foundered. In 1957, he was appointed head of the

Land-Rover Special Projects Department (initially known as the Technical Sales Department), in which job he remained until his retirement in 1981.

MANTON, Stan ... is currently Director of Product Engineering at Land Rover.

MARTIN-HURST, William ... was related to the Wilks family by marriage. He joined Rover as Production Director in 1960, but took over from Maurice Wilks as Managing Director in 1962. During his seven years in office, he discovered and acquired for Rover the General Motors V8 engine.

MATURI, Roland ... was involved in product planning until his appointment as the head of the Special Vehicle Operations division in 1985. He has since been responsible for the complete transformation of the custom-building work which used to fall to SVO's forerunner, the Special Products Department.

MORRIS, Bill ... took over from Mike Broadhead as Land Rover's Director of Product Engineering in 1985. He over-

saw the development of the Range Rover for North America. He was succeeded by Stan Manton.

OSTLER, Sam ... was one of the five section leaders in the Drawing Office who drew up the original Land-Rover. His responsibility was body design. Ostler later took over from Harry Loker as Chief Body Designer at Rover.

POGMORE, Jack ... joined the Rover Company in 1958 to co-ordinate certain aspects of Land-Rover work. He had the title of Land-Rover Administration Manager.

POOLE, Tony ... was a fitter in the gas turbine department until he demonstrated a talent for styling in the mid-1950s. He became a senior stylist at Rover and, subsequently, Land Rover Ltd, and was in charge of Land Rover new projects styling until he retired in 1989.

POPPE, Olaf ... was in charge of Production Engineering at Rover in the late 1940s. It was he who proposed the original method of building Land-Rover chassis without expensive tooling by

△ Tony Gilroy, managing director from 1983 to 1989.

◁ Spen King, with Gordon Bashford he drew up the original plans for the Range Rover.

David Bache, a designer, he restyled the Series One into the Series II. ▷

welding four strips of flat metal together to make a box-section member.

SHAW, Frank ... was one of the five section leaders in the Drawing Office who sketched up the Land-Rover in 1947. He later took charge of gearbox design at Rover and subsequently moved on to Rolls-Royce.

SMITH, A.B. ... joined Rover as a buyer in 1925 and worked his way up through the company. In 1969, he was appointed Managing Director; in 1973 he became Non-Executive Chairman; and he retired two years later as Divisional Chairman of Rover-British Leyland UK Ltd.

STEPHENSON, Alex ... came from Perkins to Land Rover in May 1989 as Director of Component Engineering. In December that year, he was appointed vehicle Director to manage the MoD contract and the introduction of new models. Since April 1991, he has been Managing Director (Powertrain) with responsibility for both Land Rover and other Rover Group products in this area.

SWAINE, Jack ... was in charge of engine design at Rover from the 1930s until his retirement in the late 1960s. He designed the IOE petrol engines and the original diesels, and oversaw Rover's adaptation of the General Motors V8 in the mid-1960s.

THOMSON, George ... is currently senior stylist for Land Rover.

WHITTAKER, Derrick ... was Managing Director of Leyland Cars between 1975 and 1978, in which role he had a hand in securing the funds for the major investment scheme which Land Rover Ltd implemented after 1978.

WILKS, Maurice ... was the father of the Land-Rover. Chief Engineer at Rover since 1930, he was the man who suggested producing a vehicle similar to the Willys Jeep. From 1947 until his death in 1962, he was in charge of all Rover and Land-Rover engineering, although he delegated much of the direct responsibility to others after 1956. In that year, he was appointed joint Managing Director of the Rover

Company with George Farmer, and between 1960 and 1962 he held that post alone.

WILKS, Peter ... was another nephew of the Wilks brothers, and a cousin to Spen King. In the later 1950s, he became Robert Boyle's deputy, and in 1963 he succeeded Boyle as the senior Rover design engineer, taking the title of Technical Director. Ill-health forced him to take early retirement in 1971, and he died a year later.

WILKS, Spencer ... was the elder brother of Maurice. He was Rover's Managing Director from 1933 to 1956, its Chairman from 1956 to 1962, and retained his seat on the Rover Board until 1967. He then retired, becoming the company's President. He died in 1971.

WOODWARK, Chris ... was Land Rover's Commercial Director between 1989 and 1991. His position was retitled Managing Director (Land Rover Vehicles) in April 1991 and he remains Land Rover's most senior figure.

By James Taylor

Origins of the Land Rover

WHY EXACTLY did Rover need to manufacture anything other than their elegant and expensive saloon cars in the late 1940s? How did they decide that a light utility 4x4 would meet that need? And how original was their idea? James Taylor looks into the circumstances of the Land-Rover's birth.

The 1939-1945 War completely changed the comfortable, complacent Britain of the 1920s and 1930s. So heavy was the country's debt in 1945 that, without American aid, Britain would have been bankrupt. Overseas trade, too, had been seriously disrupted and the favourable terms of trade which had buoyed up Britain's worsening performance in export markets during the 1930s had gone for ever. Between 1945 and 1951, the terms of that trade actually turned more and more to Britain's disadvantage.

The Government therefore had no choice but to minimise the imports which took money out of the economy and to put a new and heavy emphasis on exports. To effect these policies, it relied upon rationing. Thus, the need to import a commodity such as petrol was controlled by limiting the amount any individual could buy. Similarly, as the greater proportion of home-produced goods was earmarked for export, rationing of the remainder was used to control demand at home.

For the motor industry, this emphasis on exports caused some quite serious problems. British manufacturers had traditionally been very insular in their outlook, taking the general view that there was no need to cater for overseas markets when they could make a healthy profit by concentrating on the domestic one. Some British motor vehicles were shipped abroad, but there was no real attempt to design or modify vehicles to suit conditions outside Britain.

In this respect, the Rover Company was typical of British manufacturers. It had built its reputation on well-made, conservative cars for the British professional middle classes during the 1930s, and it had never produced any left-hand-drive vehicles at all. Nor did it have an overseas dealer network, and it was only in 1945, when the War ended, that it set up an Export Department.

Rationing of raw materials supplies caused further problems for the motor industry. A particular difficulty was caused by the Government's policy of rationing sheet steel, which was vital to motor manufacturers and to many other industries.

Without steel, there could be no cars; but the Government arranged things so that allocations of steel were dependent on a manufacturer's export success. By today's standards, these policies seem positively draconian, but they were necessary as the country teetered on the edge of bankruptcy.

△ If this had gone into production, there might never have been a Land Rover. The M1 was Rover's attempt at producing a high-class Minor (though the Minor itself would not appear until two years later), and featured the new 10E engine in 699cc form.

Rover's plans

The Rover Board had actually started planning for the future as early as 1944. The tide of the War had begun to turn in the Allies' favour and it was once again becoming possible to think of the peacetime future.

There was no point at first in discussing exactly what the company should produce when the wartime restrictions were lifted: as there had been no opportunity to draw up new models or prepare for their manufacture, the only option was to put the 1940 models back into production.

But Managing Director Spencer Wilks considered that the economic climate after the War would probably lead to a demand for smaller and cheaper cars - just as it had led to the cyclecar boom after the 1914-1918 War.

Several months before the War was over, on 18th January 1945, he advised the Rover Board that the company should aim to expand its output, "and that to achieve this we should not look primarily to our pre-War models, but that we should add to our range by the introduction of a 6hp model".

He proposed that the company should produce 5,000 examples of this a year, plus 15,000 examples of the larger cars with which it had been associated before the War. The figures made sense. Rover had the space to make that many cars now that it had moved into the factory at Solihull and, indeed, if post-War demand lived up to most thinking people's expectations, those figures would prove to be on the conservative side.

So it was that Maurice Wilks, Rover's engineering chief, set his designers to work

on the design of the new 6hp car immediately after VE-Day. The vehicle came together quite quickly under the guidance of senior designer Gordon Bashford and, as production of the revamped 1940 models was just getting under way at Solihull in 1946, the first prototype of the M1 (the M was for "Miniature") took to the roads.

The details of the M1 design are fascinating in themselves, but some of them were to have particular relevance to the later Land-Rover project. Firstly, the car was very different from previous Rovers, which suggested that the company was fully prepared to produce something radically new if necessary. Secondly, it was powered by a small (699cc) version of the new engine with inlet-over-exhaust valve layout and sloping cylinder head joint face which Rover planned to use in its larger models later on. And thirdly, although steel

was used in its manufacture, its body and platform-chassis were made entirely out of aircraft-type light alloy.

The great advantage of this was not just that it saved weight, but that it was more readily available than the sheet steel traditionally used in car manufacture. Its only disadvantage was cost - but Rover customers were used to paying a little more than the average man for their cars, anyway.

However, circumstances conspired against the M1. As Maurice Wilks told Harold Hastings in an interview for The Motor of 10th August 1949: "First, we found that we could not get adequate supplies of steel for the planned production of the existing range, let alone for an additional model. Then there came the Government call for rationalisation - you know, the one-maker one-model cry - coupled with an official emphasis on medium-sized cars in the belief that such models represented post-war requirements in the export field.

"These political influences, backed by the changes in the taxation scale which took place, all tended to reduce the empha-

sis on the really small car. In the face of so many external influences, we reluctantly decided that the place which we had foreseen for the M1 in the post-war market would not materialise."

So development of the M1 was abandoned at the prototype stage, probably early in 1947.

That left the company with a serious problem. Plans were well advanced for the next full-size saloons, and even for the models which would eventually succeed them, but it was becoming painfully apparent at Solihull that the current models were too old-fashioned to sell well in overseas markets, particularly those which had been exposed to the latest advances in American styling.

The latest Government requirement of the motor industry was that it should export 75% of everything it manufactured, and manufacturers unable to comply were faced with the threat of having their already inadequate supplies of steel cut or stopped altogether. For Rover, the unspoken question was whether sales of their current models would hold up well

enough to merit the supplies of steel they needed to get the new ones into production at all.

To be sure of their future, they needed a product which would sell abroad - and they needed it quickly.

Why the Land-Rover?

As demobilisation proceeded in the years immediately after the War, a large number of former military vehicles came on to the civilian market. Among these were many thousands of the American-built Jeeps which the British Forces had used during the conflict, and Maurice Wilks bought one for his private use early in 1947.

He had a simple but compelling reason for wanting a Jeep. The first months of 1947 saw Britain gripped by Arctic weather conditions which left the country covered in snow for weeks on end. Conditions made it impossible to drive an ordinary car up the long sloping drive which led from the main road to the house at Blackdown Manor, Wilks' home near Kenilworth. The drive presented no hazard to a four-wheel-drive

After the war, the Rover Company put its 1940 models back into production. Excellent though they were, like this 1947 Rover 1t Sports Saloon, they had a limited appeal in export markets and Rover had to come up with something else to sell. The Land Rover was the result

Jeep, however, so Maurice Wilks decided he must have one.

He soon pressed his new toy into use for snow clearance at Blackdown Manor, too, and home movies still owned by his family show it with a snow plough attached to the front. Not long afterwards, when severe gales on 16th March brought down a number of trees in the long drive, the Jeep was hitched up to a trailer and Wilks used it to clear the fallen trees.

The Jeep's value as a multi-purpose vehicle must therefore have been firmly implanted in Maurice Wilks' mind by early April, when he took his family to Anglesey for part of the Easter school holiday period. Although he had recently bought a property there, it was in need of renovation and so the family stayed at a hotel called Wern-y-Willan, close to Red Wharf Bay.

It was while on the nearby beach that he came up with the idea that Rover should build a Jeep-type vehicle to meet the increased demand for mechanisation by farmers both at home and abroad which had resulted from the War. After all, he

must have reasoned, Standard had done very well with the Ferguson tractors which they had been building under licence since July 1946, and had even managed to secure a special ration of sheet steel to make them.

From that point on, things moved very quickly indeed. Wilks no doubt discussed his new idea with his brother Spencer when he returned to Solihull after the holiday in Anglesey, but before long he had instructed a number of staff in the Drawing Office to sketch up plans for the very first Land-Rover. The Jeep, meanwhile, was still in use: on 11th June, it was registered as FWD 534, and Wilks later took it to Anglesey. Nevertheless, home movies recording this event give no hint that he might have been evaluating the vehicle as well as using it for recreation.

Origins of the idea

The idea that Rover should design and build a Jeep-type vehicle was entirely Maurice Wilks'; whether he already knew that Willys Overland were producing adaptations of their wartime Jeeps for agri-

cultural purposes is less clear. He may well have done.

The "peacetime" CJ2-A Jeep had been announced nearly two years earlier, in July 1945, and its specification included a number of items which were not part of the wartime vehicle and which eventually found their way into the Land-Rover. Most notable among these was a rear-mounted power take-off, which could be used to drive machinery.

There had been other indications that the Jeep would have a peacetime role in agriculture, and Maurice Wilks might have come across any or all of these, too. A feature in Life magazine for July 1942 reproduced some paintings commissioned by the Chairman of Willys Overland which showed the Jeep being used for agricultural applications in peacetime.

The US Department of Agriculture and a number of State agricultural departments conducted studies during 1944 to look into the Jeep's versatility; and the Agricultural Experiment Station of the State College of Washington actually produced a small booklet called "The Jeep as a Farm Truck-Tractor for the Post-War Period", in which were illustrations of the military version being used for agricultural purposes.

Lastly, H.W.Wade's famous book, Hail to the Jeep! was published in 1946, and related several stories of Jeeps in use in US agriculture, where they had showed up very well against tractors.

It would be reasonable to suppose that the Rover designers made efforts to obtain these publications once the Land-Rover project was under way, if they had not already seen them.

None of this in any way diminishes the importance of Maurice Wilks' idea. Not the smallest element in its significance was that it put Rover well ahead of the game. Although other car manufacturers did design Jeep-type vehicles in the late 1940s - Fiat, Alfa Romeo, Delahaye, Peugeot and the Nuffield Group in Great Britain all tried their hand - each one of these was designed as a purely military vehicle which would duplicate the role of the original Jeep.

Outside Willys Overland, it was only Rover which aimed a vehicle at the civilian market; and that would remain so until the early 1950s, when Toyota, Nissan and Mitsubishi in Japan began to manufacture Jeep-type or Jeep-based vehicles for civilian use.

In the difficult circumstances of the late 1940s, it was availability which counted and, thanks to Maurice Wilks, the Rover Company was able to make available the vehicle which thousands of people wanted all over the world.

Quotations from Rover Company Board Minutes are used by kind permission of the Rover Group and BMIHT.

The information about Maurice Wilks and his Jeep comes from original research carried out by John Smith of the Land-Rover Register, and I am most grateful for his permission to use it.

By James Taylor

The very first Land Rover

The first Land-Rover prototype was half-Jeep and half-Rover, and had its steering wheel in the middle. James Taylor tells its story.

There are no documentary records to tell us exactly when Maurice Wilks initiated the Land-Rover project, but memories and logic both suggest it was some time in late April or early May 1947. It was not a moment too soon - poor overseas sales and materials supply difficulties had already led to production cutbacks at Solihull, and on 1st May the Board meeting noted that car production had been restricted to four days a week on alternate weeks.

Wilks selected five section leaders in the Drawing Office as the team who were to turn his idea into reality. He entrusted the overall layout of the new vehicle to Gordon Bashford; he asked Sam Ostler to sketch up the body; Joe Drinkwater was charged with engine design; and Frank Shaw and Tom Barton took on transmission design.

In theory, each of them reported to Wilks through Project Engineer John Cullen, Assistant Chief Engineer Arthur Goddard and Chief Design Engineer Robert Boyle, but in practice Wilks seems to have been much more closely involved than that chain of command would suggest. The new vehicle was,

after all, his idea, and he was well-known for the boyish enthusiasm with which he tackled new projects.

Although each one of the five section leaders had a specific task to perform, each one was also well aware of the overall design brief for the vehicle. That brief was very simple, as Tom Barton once told author Graham Robson:

"Maurice Wilks wanted us to design a vehicle very like the Jeep," recalled Barton, "but it had to be even more useful to a farmer. That was the point - it was to be a proper farm machine, not just another Jeep. He wanted it to be much more versatile, much more use as a power source.

"He wanted it to be able to drive things, to have power take-offs everywhere, and to have all sorts of bolt-on accessories, and to be used instead of a tractor at times. It had to be able to do everything! .... We had a very broad brief, nothing detailed, except that we were asked to make a vehicle similar to the Jeep."

What Barton left out of that account was the urgency attached to the project. Wilks wanted his new vehicle up and running as soon as was humanly possible, and he was prepared to take all sorts of short cuts to achieve that end.

Wherever possible, he wanted to use existing Rover car components; and he

instructed his designers to design a body which could be built by hand so that the company could save time and money by managing without body press tooling.

Aircraft-style aluminium alloy was easy to work by hand, and was the material he chose for this body; it was also readily available, whereas steel was not (although it was also three times as costly as steel); and it was corrosion-resistant, which would be particularly important in an agricultural vehicle.

Other items which were not already to hand would have to be designed; but the design should be as simple as possible consistent with good engineering practice and the likely hard use to which it would be put.

If the new vehicle was going to be like a Jeep, it was obvious that the designers were going to have to study a Jeep to see what made it tick, and Gordon Bashford recalled some years ago that one of his first tasks was to visit an Army surplus dump and purchase a pair of Jeeps for Rover to take apart and study.

At the same time, Solihull's own design work got under way. But Bashford remembers how influential the Jeep was on Rover's work. The fact that the first Land-Rovers had an 80-inch wheelbase was purely because that was also the wheelbase of the Jeep he was studying!

Apparently just completed, the centre-steer prototype posed on 15th October 1947 with its hood erected and a dummy capstan winch on the front bumper.

Although the paper design of the Land-Rover was probably well under way by the time of Rover's traditional two-week summer shutdown at the end of July, any sort of running prototype was still a long way off. Once work resumed in August, everyone at Solihull apart from the few directly involved in the Land-Rover project was fully occupied in preparing for the introduction of the new P3 saloons, which would take place in February 1948.

Getting prototype parts made up must therefore have been a nightmare, particularly in view of the ever-present difficulty of getting the raw materials from which to make them.

Effectively, this meant that the design team would have to wait until the beginning of 1948 before they could get a proper prototype of the Land-Rover built up. That represented a delay of five months, which was totally unacceptable on a project of such urgency.

No-one now remembers who took the next important decision, but that decision was to build a "mule" vehicle by grafting those Rover parts which did exist or could be cobbled up quickly on to a Jeep. This hybrid could then be used to gather valuable test data while further design went ahead, so that the proper Land-Rover prototypes which could be built at the beginning of 1948 would need correspondingly less development work to

make them suitable for production.

Meanwhile, decisions were also being taken at Board level. Up to this point, the Land-Rover had simply been Maurice Wilks' brainchild, and no policy decision had been taken on its future. Wilks had secured the support of his brother Spencer, but as far as the rest of the Rover Company was concerned, the Land-Rover was still nothing more than an idea.

It was Spencer Wilks who got things moving, as the minutes of the Rover Board meeting held on Wednesday, 4th September 1947 show. This was in fact the first time the Land-Rover project had been formally explained to the Board (although some of the Directors may well have been told informally what was going on), and it was presented as part of a review of future product strategy:

"Mr. Wilks said that of the various alternatives that had been under consideration, he was of the opinion that the all-purpose vehicle on the lines of the Willys' Overland Post-War Jeep was the most desirable.

"The P3 engine, gearbox and back axle could be used almost in their entirety; little additional jigging and tooling would be necessary, and body dies would

not be required, as facilities had already been provided in our Shops for the necessary body pressings. Considerable research had been carried out on this vehicle by our Development Department.

"It was, therefore, agreed that this should be sanctioned for production."

It says a lot for Spencer Wilks' powers of persuasion and for the trust which the Board placed in Maurice Wilks to turn his bright idea into the winning product the company so badly needed that the Board approved the Land-Rover for production *before the first prototype had even been built!*

What was it like?

No documents survive to tell us when construction of the first prototype began, but the earliest pictures of it (now lost, unfortunately) were taken on 23rd September 1947. Further pictures followed a week later, showing details of its engine, chassis and tyres, and on 30th September, the assembled but still unpainted vehicle was photographed in the Jig Shop at Solihull. The finished and painted vehicle was first photographed on 15th October, and it is rea-

△ This picture was taken on 19th January 1948, after the centre-steer prototype had been in use for just over three months. There are signs that the seat back support had been repositioned, and the front bumper had been altered slightly. Otherwise, in appearance, it differed not at all from when it was built.

◁ Probably also taken on 19th January, this picture shows the curious dashboard layout of the centre-steer vehicle.

sonable to suppose that it had been completed on or very shortly before that date.

Unfortunately, these pictures are the only surviving evidence of this first Land-Rover prototype, and consequently its story has to be reconstructed by means of deduction and guesswork. What is quite clear, however, is that much of the design work which had already been done was not incorporated in the prototype, for the simple reason that there had not been time to get the new components manufactured.

To Tom Barton and Gordon Bashford, we owe the knowledge that the vehicle was built up on a suitably modified Jeep chassis. Several pictures of this chassis were filed at Rover on 30th September 1947, but all the negatives are now missing from the archives now held by BMIHT at Gaydon.

The engine installed in the Jeep chassis was a step in the right direction, but it was not quite what Rover's designers had in mind for the longer term. Their plan was to fit the Land-Rover with the new four-cylinder P3 IOE engine, which in saloon form gave the same 60bhp as the Jeep's much larger Continental side-valve engine.

Unfortunately, the need to build up supplies of new engines to get the P3 into production was paramount, and the Land-Rover project team seems to have been denied the use of even a single

engine for this reason! As a result, the prototype started life with the 1389cc OHV four-cylinder engine from the 10hp saloon, a time-expired design which was due to go out of production within months and, with only 48bhp, can never have been considered man enough for the job.

Why the larger-bore 1496cc version from the Rover 12hp with its extra 5bhp was not used remains a mystery. Perhaps supply shortages meant that there simply were no spare examples available.

As for the gearbox, that in the 10hp car had been redesigned when car production re-started in 1945 and would be carried over for the P3 models. It was this which the Land-Rover team planned to use in production vehicles, but they also intended to use a transfer box of their own design.

This was not ready in time for the prototype, and so Tom Barton had simply modified the main gearbox - taken, like the engine, from a 10hp saloon - to mate up with the Jeep's original transfer box. Presumably, the gearbox had been fitted complete with its freewheel device, a traditional Rover feature since the 1930s and one which would be retained for the Land-Rover in order to overcome the problem of axle wind-up in a four-wheel-drive vehicle.

The Rover designers had also come up with their own body. As this was designed to be made by hand from easi-

ly-worked aluminium alloy, it had been possible to get one ready for the prototype, and it was this which was fitted to it when it was pictured in the Jig Shop on 30th September.

Also in evidence in that Jig Shop photograph was the prototype's most distinctive feature: its centrally-positioned steering column. The actual component seems to have been a modified Rover saloon item, connected by chain and sprockets to the Jeep's original Ross steering box. This novel layout was primarily intended to avoid the additional cost and complication of making both RHD and LHD vehicles.However, Maurice Wilks may also have been thinking that the farmers he wanted to buy his new vehicle were familiar with the central steering position from tractors and would therefore appreciate the same feature in the Land-Rover.

On trial

The centre-steer prototype seems to have been put on test straight away. On 15th October, it was pictured with a dummy capstan winch at the front, and later the same day it was photographed undertaking various agricultural duties on the farmland which then surrounded the Solihull plant and was rented to tenant farmers by the Rover Company. A day later, the Rover Board approved the name "Landrover" (it would always be

Later in the day on 15th October, 1947, the vehicle was set to work in the fields. Here it is driving a Massey-Harris conveyor by belt from its rear PTO. Agricultural tasks like this would normally have been carried out by a tractor, or possibly even by a steam traction engine. ▷

◁ *The last known pictures of the centre-steer vehicle were taken on 28th January 1948. Appropriately, it was still plugging its way through the mud.*

written as a single word until the launch in April 1948) for the new vehicle.

The centre-steer prototype spent the next three and a half months clawing its way through the muddy fields around Solihull and at nearby Packington, and acting as a stationary power source for all manner of belt-driven agricultural machinery. It was John Cullen who was in charge of this test programme, and the information which he was able to feed back to the designers contributed greatly to the redesign which had taken place by the time the first pre-production models were made.

The vehicle also put in an appearance at Blackdown Manor, Maurice Wilks' home. To George Middleton, who was then carrying out some building work at the house, we owe the knowledge that this historic prototype was painted grey.

However, the centre-steer prototype's life appears to have been relatively short, and the last known pictures of it are dated 28th January 1948. Whether it was tested to destruction or simply cannibalised for parts is not clear, but it certainly was broken up. Stephen Wilks, Maurice Wilks' son, remembers his father showing him a heap of body parts in a corner of the factory and telling him that they were the remains of the first Land-Rover.

There have been suggestions that there was more than one centre-steer

Land-Rover prototype, and estimates of the numbers built have varied between four and seven. However, Gordon Bashford recently stated that "there was only one prototype made with centre steering wheel" and the late Ralph Nash, who was foreman in the Development Shop when the prototype was built, remembered only one being built out of the two Jeeps which had been bought.

Certainly, the time-scale of the whole operation and the makeshift nature of the centre-steer prototype make it very unlikely that more than one would have been made.

Tom Barton, however, believes that more than one prototype was made out of a combination of Jeep and Rover parts, and only recently commented that this explained why the Rover engineers nicknamed the new vehicles "Rovers in Jeep's (sheep's) clothing".

The company certainly seems to have bought some more Jeeps on which to experiment - Gordon Bashford recently recalled that "several vehicles were obtained, mainly to get axle units" - and it may be that some of these were used as test-beds for the running-gear Rover intended to use in its production models.

Thanks to Gordon Bashford and Tom Barton for their time and help; to John Smith for permission to quote from his researches; to John Craddock for the loan of photographs; and to Tony Hutchings for starting it all.

Extracts from the Rover Board minutes are quoted by kind permission of the Rover Group and BMIHT.

LOST - SOME VITAL INFORMATION

All the photographs of the centre-steer vehicle were taken on glass-plate negatives, and over the years many of these have disappeared, possibly through breakage. Fortunately, a master-list exists, and it is this which provides the dates and information used above. However, it is not possible to match all the existing negatives with the numbers in the master-list, as many have been removed from the storage bags on which the numbers were written.

Prints taken from these negatives generally had the negative number written on the back, and these can now help us to reconstruct the defective archive. If any readers have prints of the centre-steer prototype other than number 228937 (which is a later re-print), we would be pleased to hear from them with details of the neagtive numbers. We will pass any information we receive to BMIHT, who have custody of the remaining negatives.

It should go without saying that we would also love to hear from anyone who has any further information about the centre-steer prototype!

THE LAND ROVER STORY

By James Taylor

△ RO1 in restored condition

Pre-productio

THE FIRST Land-Rover prototype had been a hybrid; the next 48 closely foreshadowed the production models. James Taylor looks at their design, construction, and use.

EVEN THOUGH the Rover Company was under pressure to get the Land-Rover into production as quickly as possible, it was not prepared to compromise its reputation for doing things thoroughly. Before putting its new vehicle into full production, it planned to build no fewer than 50 pre-production examples for evaluation and testing.

These would be based on the design drawn up in the summer of 1947, but modified in the light of experience gained from the testing of the hybrid centre-steer prototype. In building them, the company would be able to train its assembly-line workers, to discover production problems, and to determine the best layout for the main production line and its sub-assembly feeder lines.

Some Land-Rover histories claim that 25 of these pre-production vehicles were sanctioned at the end of 1947 and a further 25 early in 1948, but it is clear that the company in fact planned to build 50 right from the beginning. As early as 16th October 1947, Spencer Wilks informed the Rover Board that "a pre-production batch of fifty was already in progress, and the first prototype was at present on test."

Wilks' remark about progress was more than a little premature, because vital parts for the pre-production vehicles did not become available until early in the New Year and the first pre-production Land-Rovers were not completed until March 1948, nearly five months later.

The design

Yet perhaps the Rover Board welcomed any glimpse of light at the end of what then must have seemed like a long and dark tunnel. Certainly, Wilks thought it prudent to make more encouraging noises at the next Board meeting, on 12th November. The minutes of this record that "Mr Wilks informed the Board that work on the pre-production batch was proceeding." No doubt his intention was not to mislead the Board, but the work he referred to can have been nothing more than design of preliminary sub-assembly work.

Meanwhile, the designers continued to refine their plans on the basis of what they learned from testing of the centre-steer vehicle. It is impossible now to say how much they had to alter their original ideas, but a number of quite major features certainly were changed.

The prototype showed up the impracticality of the centre-steering layout, and so the designers reworked their plans to allow for conventional right-hand or left-hand drive. It was probably also experience with the centre-steer vehicle which prompted a redesign of the rear body: certainly, the flat panels adopted on all subsequent vehicles would have been easier to hose down and less prone to catching on the undergrowth than would the projecting sections of the centre-steer's body.

However, it was probably the production engineers who requested a change to the sweeping front wing style of the centre-steer, and the designers came up with a stubby type — eventually adopted for production — which must have been easier to fabricate by hand than the originals.

None of these plans appears to have been translated into production-ready hardware until assembly of the P3 saloons was safely under way in January 1948.

models

Opposite page: The first pre-production Land-Rover (chassis no. R.01) was bought back into Rover Company ownership in 1954 and restored early in 1956 by Land-Rover apprentices.
Above: This picture was taken on 28th June 1948 and shows the final pre-production Land-Rovers being assembled. Alongside, the proper production line is still being installed.

After that, the new Land-Rover components began to appear, one by one. Photographic records now held by BMIHT suggest that the body was the first of these to become available, and the redesigned type was pictured for the first time on 29th January. A new grille was ready by 19th February, and the chassis frame followed on 24th February.

Experimental frames had been built up long before that date, of course. From the beginning, designer Gordon Bashford had wanted to use a box-section frame instead of the open channel-section type found on the Jeep, and the first experimental frame was made in the summer of 1947, "immediately after Maurice Wilks had asked me to lay out the package for a very simple vehicle", as Bashford told author Graham Robson some years ago.

However, it took some time to get the design right. That first frame was made from 12swg steel with 4½ inch deep side members, but it twisted too much in stress tests. A second frame with 6 inch deep side members of 12swg steel proved too rigid.

At the third attempt, however, the Land-Rover team got it right, and all subsequent frames had 6 inch side members made of lighter 14swg steel. Somewhere along the line, a decision was also taken to galvanise the frames to protect them against corrosion, and the one pictured on 24th February had been so treated. All the pre-production chassis which followed would be galvanised, although the process would not be adopted for production Land-Rovers.

In the summer of 1947, the Land-Rover designers also had to solve a knotty manufacturing problem. Although there was no doubt that Gordon Bashford's box-section frame was necessary to provide the strength they wanted, such frames required expensive press tools and jigs, and Maurice Wilks wanted the absolute minimum of new tooling to get the Land-Rover into production.

It was Chief Production Engineer Olaf Poppe who found a way out of the dilemma. Working closely with Bashford, he proposed to make the box-sections out of four flat pieces of steel. Any twist which occurred while welding one edge would, he reasoned, correct itself when the opposite edge was welded in turn. With the addition only of a simple jig (nicknamed the "Christmas Tree" because of its shape), Poppe's method was adopted for produc-tion. So well did it work that all short-wheelbase Land-Rover chassis were made in this way until the demise of the Series III models in 1985.

Assembly begins

A temporary assembly line was set up in a corner of the factory at Solihull early in 1948, and work got under way on the first pre-production vehicles at the end of February or the beginning of March. The first vehicle to be finished, chassis number R.01, was booked into the Despatch Department at Solihull on 11th March, which was probably also the date on which it had been completed. R.02 followed on 15th March. On 23rd March, the Board meeting minutes triumphantly recorded that the "the first prototypes of the Landrover are now on test, and the Directors made a personal inspection of one of these".

Assembly was painfully slow at first, and the third, fourth and fifth vehicles were not completed until 27th March, followed by two more on the 28th March. But it was important to announce the vehicle's avail-ability and attract some orders, even if in practice deliveries could not be made for

◁ *R.08, restored to original condition by its owner, LRO technical editor Robert Ivins.*

All the pre-production vehicles had galvanised chassis frames and many (probably the first thirty or more) had front bumpers integral with the chassis. The design was later changed for the more practical bolt-on type which was fitted to all production vehicles. This detail is of R.20. ▷

some time yet. So it was that, on 20th April, *The Times* had the distinction of being first with the story of Rover's new product, now hyphenated as the Land-Rover.

The press announcement was one thing, the public introduction quite another. The Rover Company really wanted to give its new product the best possible send-off by putting it on display at a prestigious international Motor Show, but the obvious choice of Geneva in March was ruled out because the Land-Rovers were simply not ready. The next show on the calendar was to be held at Amsterdam from 30th April to 9th May, and Rover plumped for that one. Board minutes reveal that the show vehicles left Solihull on Wednesday, 28th April.

The absence of records causes an irritating gap in the Land-Rover story here. No pictures of the Rover stand, on which the Land-Rover would have been shown alongside the new P3 saloon models, have yet come to light, and it is not certain even how many Land-Rovers went to Amsterdam. According to *The Motor* of the 28th April, Rover planned to send two vehicles, one "equipped with an arc welding unit driven

by vee belts from the centre take off."

Military vehicle historian Bart Vanderveen remembers visiting the Amsterdam Show as a boy and seeing at least one vehicle on the Rover stand inside the exhibition hall and a left-hand-drive demonstrator outside which had trouble with a sticking clutch. This latter could well have been L.05 (the fifth vehicle), which did have left-hand-drive and had been fitted with welding equipment in time to go to Amsterdam.

The second Amsterdam vehicle must have been another of the first eight pre-production vehicles. Whether it had right-hand-drive or left-hand-drive remains a mystery, however. More information about the Amsterdam Show would be welcome.

The Rover Company continued to promote its new vehicle at agricultural shows over the next few months, even though full production had not yet begun. Three pre-production Land-Rovers were on static display at the Bath and West Show, held in Cardiff from 26th-29th May, and three more at the Royal Ulster Show in Belfast, held over the same dates. Two were probably displayed by the local Rover agent

at the Highland Show in Inverness from 22nd-25th June, and two more at the Royal York Show from 6th-9th July.

Orders had already begun to come in from abroad, and the company now knew it had a success on its hands: as early as 28th April, Spencer Wilks had reported to the Rover Board his satisfaction "that there was a considerable demand both at Home and Overseas for this vehicle," and by 21st July he was able to say that "it was becoming more and more apparent that there was a very extensive demand for the Land-Rover both at Home and Abroad, and that the export orders and firm enquiries on hand at the moment amounted to approximately 8,000 of these vehicles."

Not surprisingly, the specification of the first fifty pre-production Land-Rovers evolved as the vehicles were being built. Records suggest that only 48 complete vehicles were actually made, and there is more than one theory to account for the "missing" two. It may be that the centre-steer prototype was counted as one and that one of the experimental chassis frames accounted for the other; or perhaps two Land-Rover "sets" were used as some kind

△ *One of the last few pre-production vehicles pictured on tilt-test on 21st November 1948. Just visible painted on the left-hand dumb-iron is the number 46, indicating that this is vehicle number L.46.*

of spares float for the others. Evidence to support either theory is lacking.

No fewer than 22 of the 48 pre-production Land Rover-Rovers were built with left-hand-drive (and these had chassis numbers prefixed 'L', whereas RHD models had and 'R' identifier). Some had permanent four-wheel-drive with a freewheel to prevent axle wind-up while others had selectable four-wheel-drive, still with a freewheel and with controls through the bulkhead rather than on the floor as would be the case with the production models.

The first 40 were painted in a light green which was the same colour as was used in wartime aircraft cockpits and was probably available in quantity at Solihull as a result of Rover's involvement with airframes during the war. The last eight were in "No.2 Green", a darker colour also used on Rover cars at the time. Mirrors were wing-mounted on the first vehicles but windscreen-mounted on the later ones, while the door stop rubber originally fitted to the door itself later ended up on the wing. The first vehicles also had

front bumpers integral with the chassis-frame, but the final ones had the bolt-on type used for production. Some vehicles were used for experimental or development work at Solihull and were modified in use; some went to senior employees for evaluation; and others were actually sold to customers who placed early orders.

The last few pre-production Land Rovers were probably completed at the beginning of August, but by then a proper production line had been set up and was operating, if a little erratically. The first production Land-Rovers were made in July 1948 and with them began Solihull's post-War success story.

I am grateful to John Smith of the Land - Rover Register for permission to quote from his researches into the development of early the Land Rover chassis. Readers interested in the pre-production Land Rovers might like to buy Tony Hutchings' books on the subject ("Land-Rover: the early years") and to join the Land-Rover Register 1947-1951 (contact Frank Mell at 10 Rowan Mount, Wheatley Hills, Doncaster, South Yorkshire

DN2 5PJ). Quotations from Rover Board minutes are used by kind permission of the Rover Group and BMIHT.

Early Land Rover Chassis

John Smith's researches for the Land Rover Register suggest that the chassis pictured in the first Land Rover sales brochure is actually the experimental one with 4.5-inch side members; presumably photographs of production types were not available when the brochure was being put together.

John also has a theory to explain why only 48 pre-production Land-Rovers were built. He believes that the centre-steer prototype counted as "number 1" (though it was not actually numbered) and that the rolling chassis with 4.5-inch side members counted as "number 2". It was therefore necessary to build only 48 more vehicles to meet the total of 50 prototypes which the Rover Board had asked for. What, though, of the over-rigid chassis number 3? Was it perhaps used for one of the 48 pre-production vehicles?

By James Taylor

THE LAND ROVER STORY

△ *Pictured at Solihull in February 1949, this left-hand drive vehicle went to President Peron of Argentina. Note the silver-painted chassis, the early strap-type hood fixings on the body sides and the optional semaphore trafficators on the windscreen pillars. The flag staff and the high-mounted windscreen hinges were special fitments. On the right is Spencer Wilks, Rover's Chairman.*

The 1.6 litre m

Spartan and noisy it may have been, but the early Land-Rover was an enormous success. James Taylor looks at the vehicle which established the Land-Rover tradition.

The Land-Rover went into production in July 1948, nearly three months after its launch at the Amsterdam Show. In Britain, it cost £450, although only small numbers had been sold before the price was increased to £540 in October.

The first production Land-Rovers were very similar indeed to the pre-production models which had been built earlier in the year. The main differences were that the chassis was no longer galvanised, the aluminium body panels were of a lighter gauge, and (after the first hundred or so vehicles had been built) the seat backs were crudely sprung against the rear body instead of fixed.

Rover had planned to charge extra for doors, sidescreens, a canvas cab roof, the passenger seat, the starting handle, a spare wheel carrier, and the spare tyre, but all these items were included in the basic price by the time the first production Land-Rovers went on sale.

Nevertheless, the vehicle was still extremely spartan. In "basic" form, it had two individual seats in the front and a rear pick-up bed capable of carrying 1,000 lbs. The doors had no external handles but were opened by reaching through a flap in the sidescreen to operate the internal release.

The simple canvas tilt was stretched over metal sticks and held down by straps, while the canvas cab roof and sidescreens did very little to protect driver and passenger, who suffered from draughts, water leaks and high noise levels. Instrumentation was minimal, there was no floor covering at all, and the only paint colour available was green. A heater, a third passenger seat, and even the PTOs on which Maurice Wilks had insisted, were all extra-cost options.

Under the bonnet, the 1595cc Rover P3 engine had been detuned from its saloon application - mainly so that it would run on the very poorest of fuel then available in some export territories - and gave just 52bhp. Yet that was enough for a road speed of around 55mph, slow by modern standards but in fact very high for an agricultural vehicle in the late 1940s, when small family cars could muster no more than 60mph.

△ This cutaway of a 1948-9 Land Rover shows the drive arrangements for the rear PTO, which is here powering a sawbench. The lever under the trapdoor in the centre (numbered 20) controlled the PTO. Note the early type of spade-shaped spring rear seat backs.

Among the options was the centre PTO. This sales brochure dates from November 1949. ▷

odels

Torque of 101 lbs/ft gave the Land-Rover excellent towing abilities and could of course be multiplied by using the low range in the two-speed transfer box. Four-wheel-drive was permanently engaged, but there was a freewheel in the transmission to allow for axle wind-up, and this could be disengaged manually.

At £540 in the latter part of 1948, the Land-Rover was a considerable bargain in Great Britain. For that price, the only other new vehicles available were 8hp and 10hp saloons, the equivalents of today's small family hatchbacks. However, the Land-Rover was not competing for sales with these, because its only real rival as a dual-purpose vehicle was the ex-military Jeep. At Army Surplus dumps all over the country, these could be bought for around £120, which was less than a

quarter of the Solihull product's cost.

At first sight, then, the Land-Rover looked like an expensive option for British customers who wanted nothing more than a working vehicle. But the choice was not that simple, for the Jeep had a number of drawbacks. That all Jeeps were second-hand (and often extremely well-used) was the least of these.

The Jeep had a 6-volt electrical system, which meant that many of its electrical components were not compatible with those commonly available in Britain. It also had poor lighting, a poor handbrake, no sidescreens and came only with left-hand-drive.

Spares were relatively hard to come by, because specialists were few and far between and Army Surplus spares invariably came in the sort of quantities needed by a field workshop

and not the small quantities wanted by an individual user. And lastly, there were no optional extras: a Jeep came "as seen" from the Army Surplus dump.

Against these disadvantages, the Land-Rover was a clear winner. It had standard 12-volt electrics, good road lighting, right-hand-drive, a handbrake which worked, sidescreens to keep out the worst of the weather and numerous optional extras. Better still, it was made by a well-established and highly-regarded manufacturer which had outlets all over the country, with the result that spares and servicing expertise were readily available.

The cachet of the Rover name helped a great deal, and the Land-Rover was certainly regarded as very much superior to the Jeep. Farmer Stuart Hibberd remembers that some

△ *By January 1950, when this left-hand drive example was pictured, there were rope-type hood fixings and a green-painted chassis. On pre-production models, the exhaust had been on the left. Note the Land Rover badge, always on the opposite side to the steering wheel.*

of the bigger farms in Wiltshire and Dorset ran both Jeeps and Land-Rovers, but that the Jeeps would be given to the farm hands while the farmer himself would drive a Land-Rover.

Outside Britain, in the markets which were crucial to the Land-Rover, the Jeep hardly figured at all. Many countries had seen Jeeps during the hostilities, but the vehicles had gone back to America and Britain with the Allied Armies and were simply not available on the second-hand market outside those two countries.

The Land-Rover arrived in time to capitalise on the interest which the wartime Jeep had already aroused, and it found no competition. It could thus hardly have failed.

Optional extras

From the beginning, Solihull offered the Land-Rover with a number of extras. These were, of course, purely utilitarian, unlike many of the luxury add-ons available for today's Land Rover products. In the beginning, there were centre and rear PTOs, both of which were supplied with an engine speed governor and hand throttle.

Customers could also specify detachable-rim wheels in place of the standard disc type, 7.00 x 16 tractor-tread or Dunlop "Fort" tyres instead of the standard 6.00 x 16 type, and a bonnet-mounted spare wheel carrier. A rather crude cab heater became available, together with semaphore trafficators, a radiator chaff guard, and a windscreen ventilator.

Propshaft UJ gaiters and an Army type pintle hook (presumably to allow owners to tow Army-surplus trailers) were also on the options list by July 1950. And later that year, an oil cooler, coolant thermometer and oil gauge were introduced, mainly for use with the PTOs.

Demand soon led to the introduction of larger "extras". During 1949, Rover introduced a 15cwt trailer, designed by Brockhouse to be exactly the same width as the Land-Rover and to share its wheels and tyres so that there was no need to carry an extra spare. A removable metal hard top arrived in February 1950, which also provided a cab roof and a certain amount of welcome insulation from the elements for driver and passenger. Then in October that year, a front PTO became available in addition to the existing centre and rear types.

Nor was it long before companies working independently of Rover began to produce useful extras for the Land-Rover. The aftermarket suppliers were nothing like as widespread or as numerous as they have become since, but two examples illustrate how the trend began.

In 1950, Chilmark Garages, the Wiltshire Land-Rover franchise holders, introduced their "Wilbrook" wooden partition, which divided the cab from the load area and could also be used in place of the rear tilt curtain.

At about the same time, Messrs J and L White of Leeds introduced longitudinal bench seats with back rests to fit the rear of both current and earlier models. At this stage, Rover did not

△ This 1951 model shows the 'shovel' seat backs adopted early in 1950, which lacked the spring mountings of the earlier type.

Larger options included the Brockhouse trailer. This sales brochure, which probably dates from 1950, shows that the then-current 15cwt type cost £75. The trailer was, of course, finished in Land Rover dark green as ▷ standard.

15 CWT. BROCKHOUSE TRAILER FOR

The

LAND ROVER

offer such seats on home market models, although folding rear seats were optional on export 80-inch models and came as standard on Land-Rovers delivered to the British military through the Ministry of Supply.

Evolution

Although many of the minor production changes made during the three years of the 1.6-litre Land-Rover's life are now of interest only to restorers, others help to give an idea of how the vehicle developed. It had probably always been Rover's intention to fit the 4.7:1 axle of the P3 saloon, but the first 1300 or so Land-Rovers used up stocks of the 4.88:1 units fitted to 10hp and 12hp cars which had gone out of production at the end of 1947.

Experience with the first vehicles lay behind the changes from five-leaf to six-leaf road springs and from a body-mounted gear lever to a gearbox-mounted one in December 1948, after 1500 vehicles had been built.

In October came the Welder and Station Wagon models, although in practice neither of these was available until the end of the year. 1949 then saw Solihull begin exporting Land-Rovers in kit form (known as CKD, or Completely Knocked Down, vehicles) for local assembly in order to meet certain countries' import regulations.

In the spring of that year, body-colour green replaced the silver paint used on chassis frames and, in June, rope fixings for the canvas tilt replaced the strap type and the tailgate side cappings were modified.

At the end of 1949, the ring pull freewheel control was changed to a yellow knob and the Land-Rover took on the new P4 car gearbox with its taller third gear - a clear indication of the 4x4's continued dependence on saloon-car engineering.

Shortly after the removable metal hard top became available in February 1950, the seat back design changed from the "spade" shape to a "shovel" shape. May then saw the introduction of a new grille which exposed the headlamps for the first time.

For the last year of 1.6-litre Land-Rover production - the 1951 model-year which ran from August 1950 to July 1951 - the freewheel and permanent four-wheel-drive were replaced by a selectable four-wheel-drive system, which would be used on every Land-Rover until the Stage I V8 reintroduced permanent four-wheel-drive in 1979.

The last noteworthy change to the 1.6-litre models came in spring 1951, when the sidelamps moved down from the bulkhead to the wing fronts. That autumn, Rover replaced the 1595cc engine with a more powerful 2-litre type.

THE LAND ROVER STORY

The 4-wheel drive all-purpose vehicle

We were lucky to get a Land-Rover, and it has certainly proved to be a worthwhile purchase. With its 4-wheel drive and eight forward speeds, it earns its keep in a variety of ways, towing heavy trailer loads of castings from foundry to machine shop, liaison service between works and office, relieving the two-tonner of many small, uneconomical delivery runs and with its power take-off (belt or shaft drive) providing power for portable generators, compressors, pumps, etc. No wonder they all call it 'Britain's most versatile vehicle!'

LAND ROVER

Britain's most versatile vehicle

DEALER'S

NAME AND ADDRESS

MADE BY THE ROVER CO. LTD., SOLIHULL, BIRMINGHAM, ENGLAND

CVS-46

Land Rover dealers could obtain this advertisement 'blank' from the factory during 1950, add their own details in the space provided and use it in the local press. This advertisement stresses the vehicle's uses in light industry.

Building and sellin

IN SPITE of constant production difficulties, Rover somehow managed to keep most of their customers satisfied. James Taylor looks at the background to sales of the 1.6 litre Land Rovers.

IT WOULD be all too easy to imagine that the enormous demand for the Land Rover had solved all of Rover's problems at a stroke. Unfortunately, that was far from being the case.

For the first few years of production, foreign politics and shortages of raw materials made life a constant nightmare for those who were trying to build and sell Land Rovers. At the same time, the British Government's export policies ensured that only small numbers were available to satisfy customers at home.

Production difficulties

When the Land Rover stumbled into production during July 1948, the Rover Company already had enough orders and firm enquiries to keep its assembly lines busy for two years at the planned production rate of 100 vehicles per week. Nevertheless, it would be some months before even that production rate was achieved.

Records now held by BMIHT show that no more than six complete vehicles passed to the Despatch Department during July (of which one was earmarked for King George VI) and that only 24 did so during August. By September, however, things were looking better, with well over 100 vehicles passing into Despatch, and production continued to increase thereafter.

Long before that original target of 100 vehicles per week had been achieved, it was clear that it was going to be inadequate. At the Rover Board meeting on 21st July, Spencer Wilks acknowledged that there were already plans to build 150 vehicles a week by December that year, but he urged the Board to give serious consideration to building no fewer than 500 a week in order to be in a position to satisfy the potential demand that there was for this type of vehicle, and also with a view to reducing costs, so that they might be in a position to meet competition which he felt they might have to face from other manufacturers.

The Rover Board approved Wilk's recommendations in principle, but took no immediate action. By September, however, the Company had been informed that its steel allocation for the last quarter of 1948 had been reduced - presumably a poor export performance earlier in the year had been the cause - and this made the expansion of Land Rover production more urgent than ever.

Wilks recommended that the Company should take steps immediately to increase Land Rover production to 250 a week, but pointed out that it would first be necessary to raise £100,000 in order to finance this. To go to 500 vehicles a week (plus 200 cars a week) would cost a further £1 million.

By the time of the October Board meeting, steps were in hand to increase Land Rover production to 250 a week by early 1949. This would be achieved on existing financial resources, but in order to reach the figure of 300 a week by the end of 1949, the company would need to raise extra share capital.

By the time of the February 1949 meeting, production was running at over 200 a week, and a figure of 250 a week was in view. The extra capital was raised during 1949 and, by June 1950, around 350 Land Rovers a week were rolling off the production lines. That represented an increase in production capacity of 250% in just under two years!

Part seven: By James Taylor

Another 1950 advertisement 'blank', this time stressing the Land Rover's versatility on the farm. The 'working for prosperity' slogan perfectly reflects the preoccupations of a post-war Britain bent on economic recovery through trade.

the early models

THE LAND ROVER STORY

All the time, however, the expansion of Land Rover production was inhibited by materials shortages and other problems of the immediate post-War era. Steel supplies were rarely sufficient to meet the Rover Company's hopes: thus, although its allocation for the first quarter of 1949 was slightly up on that for the last quarter of 1948, it was still only enough to allow for 100 Land Rovers a week at a time when the company was planning to make two and a half times that many.

For the next few years, production rates had to be juggled constantly in order to meet the export targets set by the Government. For a time at least, Rover coped by restricting P3 saloon production in order to use the steel available to build a correspondingly greater number of Land Rovers (which, of course, had less steel in them than did the cars).

As late as February 1951, the Board was discussing materials shortages which might restrict output while, despite an excellent export performance, Rover's steel allocation for the second quarter of 1951 was going to be 10% down on that for the first quarter.

The market situation was also extremely unstable. In spite of bulging export order books, Land Rovers could sometimes simply not be shipped to their intended destinations. New Zealand, for example, was "closed" to imports for a time during 1948-1949, and no Land Rovers could be sold there. During 1950, the massive export drive by all of Britain's industries led to a shortage of space on cargo vessels so that in December of that year, the Rover Board was obliged to debate whether it should restrict its production and exports of CKD vehicles.

Yet in spite of these problems, Land Rover production had outstripped Rover car production by two to one within three years of its introduction. Rover's Chairman, E. Ransom Harrison, had told the company's shareholders in December 1948 that there were signs the Land Rover would prove to be much more than the stop-gap Maurice Wilks had originally envisaged. By 1951, few people at Solihull can have imagined how life would continue without it.

The customers

No-one knows exactly how many Land Rovers were sold on the home market in the first few years of production, but it is clear that most people who aspired to one could do no more than dream about it. The vehicle had been intended primarily for export and indeed, the vast majority of Land Rovers always would be sold abroad. The figure of 85% exports of May 1949 mentioned at the Board meeting on 31st of that month was exceptional, but exports would absorb 75-80% of Land Rover production for many years to come.

At a time when total Land Rover production was between 750 and 800 a month, figures like these meant that no more than 200 new Land Rovers a month would be available throughout the British Isles. There were certain complicated schemes under which export models could be sold on the home market, but these did not materially increase the numbers available, and it was only towards the end of the 1.6 litre model's production run that Land Rovers really became available in any quantity in their home country.

Most of the Land Rover's initial customers were probably the farmers and other outdoorsmen for whom Maurice Wilks had mainly intended it. Yet its versatility soon made it attractive to a wider market.

An early Land Rover in its natural habitat. HAC 943 is actually the 53rd production vehicle, and still survives. Present owner Guy Pickford discovered it some 15 years ago at a Land Rover specialist less than than a mile from where the Land Rover Story is now being written

In export territories like Africa, it soon proved its value as a general means of transport, because it was tough enough to survive on what passed for roads. Perhaps even more importantly, its simplicity of construction meant that repairs could be quickly effected by the local blacksmith.

Back at home, its dual-purpose nature also added to its appeal. Although farmers were buying it primarily for use as a working vehicle, it was perfectly acceptable as a road vehicle - at least, for relatively short journeys. However, many farmers were using their Land Rovers in place of conventional saloon cars, and this led to a problem.

The Land Rover was classed as a commercial vehicle in Britain, which meant that it was exempt from the Purchase Tax levied on private cars and could be run on non-rationed "commercial" fuel. There were stiff penalties for those who used commercial petrol in private cars and, in order to enforce the law, commercial petrol was dispensed from separate pumps and was stained red so that it was easily identifiable.

So, was a farmer who used his "commercial" Land Rover like a private car not breaking at least the spirit of the law?

It must have been considerations like these which led the Chancellor of the Exchequer to review the Land Rover's commercial-vehicle status in the spring of 1950. Petrol rationing had, in fact, ceased on 26th May, but the Land Rover could still be subjected to Purchase Tax and there must have been a few anxious weeks at Solihull while the Chancellor deliberated.

Only some fast talking by Spencer Wilks seems to have saved the day. The Land Rover retained its commercial vehicle status, and a relieved Rover Board "congratulated Mr Wilks on the successful outcome of his negotiations" at its meeting of 11th July.

Farmers were certainly not alone in using Land Rovers, of course, and the vehicles were also selling to builders and for other light industrial uses. Nevertheless, Solihull's first attempt to produce a specially-adapted Land Rover for light industry - the Land Rover Mobile Welding Plant - was not a success.

A further attempt to broaden the range, in the shape of the coachbuilt Station Wagon, introduced in 1948, also failed to attract customers, and was abandoned after three years of low-volume production. Land Rovers equipped as fire tenders also never sold very well, although they were available throughout the period of the 1.6-litre model's production, and fire engine conversions are still a part of the Land Rover scene today. More significant in sales terms appear to have been bulk orders from the AA, which took its first Land Rovers as patrol vehicles during 1949; and from the Post Office, which took a number with the optional hard top (introduced in February 1950) as telephone lines maintenance vehicles.

However, undoubtedly the most important bulk orders came from the British Army, which took delivery of its first Land Rovers through the Ministry of Supply in 1949 and has remained loyal to the marque ever since. The story of these and of the other non-mainstream Land Rovers built between 1948 and 1951 will be told in future instalments of the *Land Rover Story*.

1.6 litre production

The Rover "model-years" changed in the middle of each calendar-year so that improvements could be introduced at the annual Motor Show. In principle then, a 1950 model was available between October 1949 and September 1950.

However, an exception was made in 1948, because that model-year's sanction of 3,000 vehicles was not completed until late in the year and so 1949 models did not

Australia's economic problems were similar to Britain's and the Land Rover's exemption from Sales Tax there paralleled its exemption from Purchase Tax on the home market.

become available until the very end of 1948.

1948 Models
Chassis numbers beginning
R86. or L86...   Total: 3,000

1949 Models
Chassis numbers beginning
R or L866. (Basic models):   4,920
R or L867. (Station Wagon):   70
R or L868. (Welder):   10
                    Total: 5,000

1950 Models
Chassis numbers beginning
R or L061 or 611. (Basic & CKD):   15,439
R or L062... (Station Wagon):   480
R or L063... (Welder):   30
071 (2-Litre prototypes):
                    Total: 15,999

1951 models
Chassis numbers beginning
161 (Basic models):   13,359
162 (Station Wagon):   100
163 (Welder):   20
166 (CKD, Basic models):   2,401
                    Total: 15,880

Grand Total
(1.6-Litre models):   39,829
(Plus 50 2-Litre prototypes = 39,879)

(These figures are taken from the Rover Company despatch records currently held by BMIHT and are used by kind permission. They differ considerably from financial-year figures previously published, e.g. by Graham Robson and in my own book, *The Land Rover, 1948-1988*.)

THE LAND ROVER STORY

△ *The prototype Station Wagon was built by Tickford on L.20, a left-hand-drive pre-production chassis. It was later converted to right-hand-drive. Note the split windscreen; production examples had a single-pane type. The fake wooden framing pressed into the side panels was a direct crib from the Jeep Station Wagon.*

Something extra

In this third instalment of our look at the 1.6 litre Land Rovers, James Taylor discusses how Solihull created a wide variety of models from the single basic design.

ALTHOUGH the Rover people recognised that the Land Rover might appeal to a much wider customer group than just the farmers for whom it had originally been designed, they had no precedent to follow in marketing it. On the agricultural side, they chose to follow the lead set by the manufacturers of the primary agricultural vehicle – the tractor – and to offer the Land Rover as a basic vehicle onto which the customer could bolt the equipment he needed to adapt it to its intended tasks. This made sound sense, as it would have been uneconomical to build for stock ready-equipped examples of all possible varieties of the Land Rover.

Just as the tractor manufacturers confined their activities to making tractors and left the specialists to make the machinery and implements with which they would be used, so Rover stuck to what they knew best – making cars. The company was prepared to supply certain extras from the factory, like different wheels and tyres, extra seats, and the PTOs because these were closely connected to the vehicle's drivetrain. For specialist equipment, however, it was decided early on to turn to the specialists.

No records exist to explain exactly what happened, but it was probably early in 1948 that the Rover Company approached various manufacturers of agricultural equipment to see if they were interested in developing adaptations of their products to fit the Land Rover. It would have been difficult to make much progress until the first pre-production Land Rovers became available in March, and no doubt some companies elected to defer a decision until they could see how Land Rover sales went.

Others, however, agreed to work with Solihull to produce a Land Rover "fit" for their equipment right from the beginning. Among these were Dorman's of Cambridge, who manufactured crop-spraying equipment. Over the summer of 1948, the Rover company lent them pre-production Land Rover R.17, and this eventually became the company's demonstrator and figured in their sales literature.

Agricultural applications of the Land Rover were one thing; light industrial applications were quite another. It was fairly clear that the Land Rover would be useful for general runabout and load-carrying duties in the difficult conditions of a large construction site, but there was no British market precedent for a vehicle which was permanently equipped as a power source for light industrial uses. Welders, compressors, generators and the like were traditionally either trailer-borne or stand-alone units carried on the back of a small truck.

In the USA, the civilian CJ-2A Jeep could be bought ex-works with two sizes of compressor, a generator and an arc welder as optional equipment. Rover decided it should offer similar facilities for the Land Rover, and accordingly approached several suppliers of specialist equipment. Among those who responded positively were Bullows, makers of compressors, and Lincoln, who made welding equipment.

During 1949, it became possible to buy the Bullows 2A 5000 three-cylinder compressor mounted in the load-bed of a standard Land Rover. The compressor was driven by V-belts from the centre PTO; an engine governor was of course standard; and the complete vehicle cost £995 in

△ *The prototype Welder was on pre-production chassis. L.05. The standard vehicle was equipped for arc welding only, and the gas bottles shown stored here were designed to demonstrate how oxygen and acetylene cylinders could be carried if necessary. Oxy-acetylene welding equipment could be fitted in place of the arc welding gear, if required.*

December 1949. No sales records have survived, but the package does not appear to have sold well.

The Welder

Standard practice with these adaptations for the agricultural and light industrial markets was for Solihull to provide a basic Land Rover off the production line and for the equipment manufacturer to modify the vehicle as necessary before delivery to the customer. It was a system which caused numerous headaches for the Technical Service Department, which was responsible for overseeing it. Nevertheless, it minimised the Rover Company's direct involvement in the production of low-volume adaptations and was thus, broadly, cost-effective.

There was a single exception to this standard practice, however. The Land Rover Mobile Welding Plant, to give the Lincoln-equipped vehicle its full title, needed certain production-line modifications before it was sent to the equipment manufacturer's works. In consequence, it became the only specially-equipped Land Rover variant to have its own chassis numbering sequence.

The Mobile Welding Plant was announced at the Commercial Motor Show of October 1948, although a prototype (on pilot-production chassis L.05) had been demonstrated at the Amsterdam Show when the Land Rover was first announced that April. This vehicle would, in fact, remain the only left-hand-drive Welder until 1951, for sales of the production model both at home and abroad would always be slow.

According to a sales brochure dated January 1950, the Mobile Welding Plant was:

"A complete travelling welding workshop which can be taken just where it is needed more speedily and readily than any other form of welding equipment previously designed. The vehicle is the well-known go-anywhere Land Rover fitted with a centre power take-off from which the drive is taken by the belts to the Lincoln SA.150 Arc Welding Generator carried in the body. The generator is capable of a current capacity of 30-200 amperes producing direct current suitable for all types of welding electrodes, ferrous and non-ferrous and also permits the use of carbon arc welding or cutting."

The brochure further claimed that the Welder would be:

"Invaluable to emergency repair engineers in all branches of industry and is equally useful in agriculture for the repair on the spot of farm machinery."

No doubt all this was true, but at £825 on the home market without the gas welding equipment which most customers probably wanted, the Welder was an expensive option. Only ten were made during 1949, of which the majority were shipped abroad to the Anglo-Iranian Oil Company. Records now held by BMIHT show that 30 more were made in the 1950 model-year, but only 20 in the 1951 season. Although production did continue after the 2-litre Land Rovers arrived in autumn 1951, it was still in penny numbers and the Welder was dropped as a separate model two years later when the 86-inch Land Rover replaced the 80-inch models.

Fire engines

Once again probably inspired by Willys, whose Fire Jeep version of the civilian CJ-2A model became available in 1946, Rover experimented from very early on with a Land Rover Fire Engine. The first example

△ *An early right-hand-drive Welder at work inside the Solihull factory in April 1949. In the background are P3 car bodyshells.*

was built on pre-production chassis R.06, and had been completed by 22nd September 1948, when it was photographed for Solihull's archives.

It seems to have served as a demonstrator, and probably also as a works fire engine at Solihull, until it was rebuilt in 1950–51 and fitted with a pre-production 2-litre engine. In this form, it was then sold to Dewar's of Calcutta, Rover's Indian importers.

In later years, the Land Rover fire engine would be a big success. For public Fire Brigades whose areas contained woodland, commons and heaths, and in towns where narrow thoroughfares denied access to full-size appliances, it became an essential vehicle.

Similarly, it gained acceptance as the ideal appliance; for factories and other industrial complexes with their own Fire Brigades. However, sales of the early vehicles were very slow, perhaps because of the ready availability of cheap, ex-government, war surplus fire engines at the time.

Nevertheless, a few Brigades did take delivery of these early Land Rover fire engines. One notable example was the Derby Fire Brigade, which took a number in November 1949. Inevitably, the amount of equipment which could be incorporated in the relatively small load-bed was limited, but the specialist suppliers managed to find room for hoses (in boxes along the sides), a water tank (in the load-bed itself), a ladder (supported on stands above the load-bed) and a water pump (mounted at the rear and driven from the rear PTO).

The Station Wagon

In the USA, Willys had not been slow to recognise the sales potential of a station wagon body for the CJ-2A Jeep, and introduced just such a vehicle in 1946. Sitting on an extended wheelbase of 104 inches, and fitted with rear-wheel-drive only (until 1949), the Jeep Station Wagon had an all-steel body which was nevertheless pressed and painted to look like the wooden bodies which were then universal on other station wagons.

These Station Wagons were unobtainable in Britain, but a number of small concerns developed broadly similar vehicles by extending the chassis of ex-military Jeeps and fitting wooden bodies onto them. One example, built by John Burleigh Automobiles Ltd of Kensington, London, was reported on favourably by *Country Life* magazine in its issue of 6th February 1948.

Vehicles like this might well have been the catalyst which set Maurice Wilks and his designers on the road to drawing up the Land Rover Station Wagon, which was announced at the Commercial Motor Show in October 1948 alongside the Welder. Like that vehicle, it was different enough from the standard vehicle to merit its own chassis numbering sequence.

As for its market, a sales brochure dated September 1949 claimed that it had been:

"Designed specially to cater for a wide variety of uses…Station Wagon, Estate Car, Shooting Brake, Service Vehicle, Family Runabout, School or Hotel Bus, it fills all these and many other requirements."

The history of the Station Wagon is a little obscure, but the first prototype seems to have been built over the summer of 1948 on pre-production chassis number L.20. Construction of the body was farmed out to Salmons and Sons of Newport Pagnell (soon to be renamed Tickford after their most famous style of bodywork), the company which had supplied drophead coachwork on Rover car chassis during the later 1930s and would also build some prototype drophead bodies on post-War car chassis.

The Land Rover body was quite unlike anything Tickford had done before, for their expertise lay in building elegant drophead coachwork by traditional methods. That meant using metal panels on an ash frame, and indeed they employed the same construction methods in the Station Wagon body, albeit using a more durable wood which was probably mahogany. This immediately meant that the price would be high; and it was rather at variance with the rugged, utilitarian nature of the standard Land Rover.

△ *The first fire engine was built on pre-production chassis R.06 in 1948*

△ *Pilot-production vehicle R.17 went to Dorman's for conversion into a crop-sprayer and remained as the company's demonstrator until the 1960s. It still survives, and is owned by enthusiast Nigel Withers.*

Styling must have been a problem, and whether Tickford themselves discovered inspiration in the Jeep Station Wagon or Rover pointed them towards it is now uncertain. What is clear, however, is that the Tickford body owed a strong debt to the Jeep design, even though the latter was built on a much longer wheelbase than the Land Rover.

One look at the decorative pressings on the side panels of the two vehicles, or at the distinctive two-piece windscreen (which was found only on the prototype Land Rover; production bodies had a one-piece screen) is enough to confirm the relationship.

The Station Wagon body was arranged to seat seven, with the individual seats in the front and four inward-facing seats at the rear. The cushions of these seats could be folded away or removed entirely to leave the rear body clear for luggage or goods. On production vehicles, flaps pro-vided access to storage areas under these seats, but the prototype offered no such access.

There has been some controversy over the production Station Wagon, and various writers have suggested that either Mulliner (at Bordesley Green) or Abbey Panels (in Coventry) built them. However, it is now beyond doubt that all the production vehicles were built by Tickford themselves.

The Station Wagon proved a slow seller. Its coachbuilt construction meant that the basic retail price was £750 in September 1949, when the standard Land Rover still cost £540. On top of that, the Station Wagon incurred £209 1s 8d Purchase Tax because it was a passenger-carrying vehicle and not an exempt commercial like the standard Land Rover. That inflated its total cost on the home market to £959 1s 8d - far too much to attract many customers.

Even export markets did not take to the Station Wagon, perhaps because of its cost and perhaps because its construction was considerably less rugged than that of the standard Land Rover. A bulk order from UNICEF helped to inflate the production figure for the 1950 season, and a large number went out to Poland, Yugoslavia and Finland between February and August 1950, in support of the charity's work in those countries.

However, sales slumped during the 1951 season to just over a fifth of the previous year's total, and Rover stopped production on the Station Wagon before the 2-litre Land Rover arrived that autumn. Only 650 examples, plus one prototype, had been built in three years.

Thanks to Peter Galilee, John Smith, Nigel Withers and Ian Gough for help of various sorts with this episode of the Land Rover Story.

THE LAND ROVER STORY

△ *The first batch of Land Rovers for the British Army leaves Solihull in December 1948.*
The RAF also ordered Land Rovers. This one, pictured at Solihull on 11th May 1950, was
probably among the first to be delivered. It has inward-facing seats in the rear load-bed. ▷

Early military

The Land-Rover had been designed as a civilian utility vehicle, but the military authorities soon recognised its potential, too, writes James Taylor.

When Maurice Wilks had conceptualised the Land-Rover, his very clear aim had been to build a vehicle which would sell to agricultural users abroad. Even though the design used a military Jeep as its springboard, it was therefore never specifically intended to meet military requirements.

Nevertheless, someone at Solihull must have recognised the Land-Rover's military potential at a very early stage. At the Board Meeting on 23rd March 1948, Managing Director Spencer Wilks reported that Rover had received an enquiry about Land-Rovers from the Indian Army. As that meeting was held before the Amsterdam Show and before the Land-Rover had become public knowledge, the Indian Army could only have known that there was such a thing as a Land-Rover if someone at Solihull had told them, presumably in the hope of gaining an order.

Perhaps that same person also told the British War Office about the new vehicle; or perhaps the military authorities found out about it in the same way as the general public. One way or another, the War Office very quickly expressed an interest through

its ordering agency, the Ministry of Supply. As a result, two pilot-production vehicles (L.29, with left-hand-drive, and R.30) were supplied in June 1948 to the Fighting Vehicles Research and Development Establishment at Chertsey, for evaluation.

The first military order

The War Office was clearly impressed. Not long afterwards, Rover received an order for 20 Land-Rovers. By military standards, this was not a large order, but the War Office was presumably treading cautiously. The first of that batch of 20 were despatched in December 1948, and were photographed in a group at Solihull to commemorate the occasion. The picture makes clear that they all had standard silver-painted chassis, plus optional semaphore traffictors mounted on the windscreen frames. As was the practice at the time, they had no registration numbers but, instead, had military serial numbers painted in white on the bonnet sides. These serial numbers ran from M6279781 to M6279800.

Exactly what the Army did with its Land-Rovers is not clear, but no doubt it distributed them around various units to see how they performed in as wide a vari-

ety of situations as possible. As the wartime Jeeps were gradually wearing out and their purpose-designed FV 1800 (Champ) replacement was still a long way from entering production, no doubt the Army saw its Land-Rovers as a convenient stop-gap. The other Armed Services also saw merit in the vehicle, and the Royal Navy put in its own order, probably taking delivery of its first Land-Rover in February 1949. In due course, even the RAF would order Land-Rovers, though the first of these was probably not delivered until May 1950.

The 20 Army vehicles must have created a favourable impression. Rover Board Meeting minutes suggest that the War Office began discussions with Rover about further deliveries of Land-Rovers in March 1949, and Spencer Wilks reported to the Board at the end of that month that there was the prospect of an order for 1,800 vehicles. As steel was still being rationed, the Rover Company would be made a special allocation to enable it to build these Land-Rovers. When the order finally materialised - on 2nd May, under contract number 6/V/3659 - it was for 1,878 vehicles. Spencer Wilks reported the good news to his Board the day after.

On 19th July 1949, the Rover photographers once again pictured a batch of mil-

Land Rovers

itary Land-Rovers ready for delivery. Whether these were the first to be delivered under the new contract is not clear. However, what little evidence survives suggests that they were, and that their chassis numbers began somewhere around 8667260.

Also unclear is whether these vehicles were originally delivered with white-painted W.D. serial numbers on their bonnets or had registration numbers from the beginning. The new system of military registrations appears to have been introduced in 1949 and the numbers allocated to the Land-Rovers were 00BC01 to 18BC78, inclusive. (Under this new system, the two letters recorded the class of vehicle and the four numbers made up the serial number: thus 18BC78 was the 1,878th vehicle in the BC series.) The original batch of 20 Land-Rovers also received new military registrations in place of their W.D. numbers: R860756, for example, became 90YJ00 in the series reserved for re-registered vehicles.

The 81-inch

Although the military authorities were impressed with the Land-Rover, they did have some firm ideas about how it might be improved to suit their needs. No doubt

Rover did not welcome the thought of non-standard specifications, even on large batches of vehicles such as the War Office usually ordered, for Solihull was still busily trying to keep up with demand for the standard Land-Rover. However, building what the War Office wanted was likely to lead to large repeat orders, and so Rover listened carefully to the first of the War Office's bright ideas.

This first bright idea was to fit a small trial batch of Land-Rovers with an engine belonging to the Rolls-Royce B-series family, on which the British Army intended to standardise. The reasoning behind it was that spares supplies could be simplified if all Army vehicles used variants of the same engine. Thus, smaller vehicles would be fitted with the four-cylinder B40, larger ones with the six-cylinder B60, and larger ones still with the eight-cylinder B80.

So it was that 33 vehicles were added to the May 1949 order for 1,878 Land Rovers, and these were to be fitted with the 2.8-litre Rolls-Royce B40 engine for evaluation purposes. A further block of registration numbers- 39BC02 to 39BC34 - was also allocated, although this was not reserved for the B40-engined vehicles which were dotted about throughout the BC series numbers.

As Rover was far too busy to carry out the conversions at Solihull, it sub-contract-

ed the work to Hudson Motors of London, supplying complete vehicles to them and receiving the redundant engines back at Solihull after the modifications had been carried out. All 33 vehicles were probably built in the autumn of 1949, and the last one was completed that November. Chassis numbers were in the range 06104400 to 06104650.

The modifications made by Hudson Motors proved quite extensive. The B40 was a much bigger engine than the 1595cc Rover unit, and it would fit into the Land-Rover engine bay only after the chassis cross-members had been modified, the battery had been moved from the engine bay to under the passenger seat, and the bonnet had been raised on rubber buffers to give extra height. In addition, the bodywork had to be modified around a bell-housing which had been enlarged to accommodate a 10-inch instead of a 9-inch diameter clutch, a larger radiator had to be fitted (with a filler cap which projected through the bonnet), and the cooling system had to be pressurised to 10psi as compared to the 5psi of the normal 80-inch model.

There were changes, too, to the clutch and brake linkages, to the front propshaft, and to the positioning of the front bumper, which had to be mounted 1¹/₂ inches higher so that its starting handle hole lined up

△ *The British Army asked for a small batch of Land Rovers to be fitted with Rolls Royce engines in 1949. This survivor, originally registered 12BC00, was photographed by owner Andrew Cross. The flashers below the bumper are of course a modern addition.*

with the dog on the end of the B40's crankshaft. The rear springs and shock absorbers were moved back by an inch - with the result that these vehicles have always been known familiarly as "81-inch" models - and the transfer gears had to be changed to kep the tractive effort roughly the same as that of a 1595cc Land-Rover. There were sundry other minor modifications.

With 50% more power and 75% more torque than the standard Land-Rover, the 81-inch model was capable of much higher on-road speeds. 50mph was a comfortable cruising speed and maximum speed was around 80mph, despite an overall weight increase of some 2 cwt. Nevertheless, the vehicle did not prove a success. In trials conducted at the Army proving ground in Chobham during 1950, a B40-engined Land-Rover was bested by a standard 1,595cc vehicle (which also, incidentally, proved a better vehicle than a prototype Champ). The great plan for the Army to standardise on the B-series engine also evaporated soon after this, but the 81-inch Land-Rovers remained in service as long as their standard brethren, being sold off in the late 1950s and early 1960s. Only a handful survive with their

In action

Meanwhile, events were in motion which would give the British Army's Land-Rovers their first taste of action. On 25th June 1950, North Korean troops advanced into South Korea. Two days later, President Truman secured the agreement of the UN Security Council to send US troops to support South Korea and to protect Formosa. Britain soon became embroiled in the UN efforts and, on 6th September, the first British troops went into action in Korea under the command of General MacArthur, Commander-in-Chief of the UN forces.

The Land-Rovers - Rover Mk.1s in Army parlance - which went to Korea with the British troops performed extremely well. Not only did they prove able to duplicate the roles of the Jeeps which the British Army was still using, but they were also able to stand in for its car-derived pick-ups. They offered better weather protection than the Jeeps, and greater versatility than the purpose-designed Champ promised, for this had been designed as a strict four-seater with minimal load capacity. The Korean experience also showed up a number of short-

comings and, in due course, the Army would persuade Rover to make appropriate modifications to the vehicles it bought.

The Champ project was nevertheless still forging ahead. Basing itself on American experience with the Jeep, the Ministry of Supply had always intended that manufacture should be entrusted not to a single company but rather spread among several. So it was that, in June 1950, Spencer Wilks reported to the Rover Board that the Company had been asked by the MoS to tender for the manufacture of 15,000 Champs.

Never one to miss an opportunity, Wilks went to talk the issue over with Sir Archibald Rowlands, Permanent Secretary to the Ministry of Supply. On 11th July, he reported to the Board that "he had told the Ministry that he was prepared to supply a modified version of the Land-Rover at a net overall saving to the Ministry of approximately $4^{1}/_{2}$ to 5 million pounds on the Contract." Possibly, the vehicle he had in mind was the 81-inch Land-Rover; but equally possibly, Wilks had simply expressed a willingness to modify the Land-Rover to meet whatever requirements the Ministry cared to lay down.

The proposal met with some interest at the MoS, but the Rover Board agreed at

△ *The Rolls Royce B40 engine was physically much larger than the Rover 1.6 litre.*
This picture, by Ian Sparks, shows the engine in situ.

its July meeting that Wilks should also tender for the manufacture of the Champs specified in the original invitation to tender. In the event, Rover secured neither contract, but the prospect of massive savings which Wilks had held out to the Ministry of Supply as bait must surely have acted in the Land-Rover's favour when the Army next came to order light utility vehicles in quantity.

Meanwhile, contract 6/V/3659 had been extended by 33 vehicles to replace those 33 of the original 1,878 which had been fitted with Rolls-Royce engines, and this second batch of 33 was delivered during 1950. Registration numbers were 39BC02 to 39BC34 and chassis numbers (probably) 06107647 to 061097679. It also looks as if at least one more batch of Land-Rovers was ordered by the British Army during 1950 or 1951, because several 1951 models are known to have had registration numbers in the later BD series. Some late 1951 models also acquired ZC registrations, which suggests they had been re-registered for some reason. The details of these vehicles will become clearer when research currently under way by The Road Transport Fleet Data Society is completed.

Foreign military orders

The British Army was by no means the only one to buy Land-Rovers. The 1948 enquiry by the Indian Army has already been mentioned; though whether it was ever followed up is not clear. By November 1949, Land-Rovers were certainly being prepared for delivery to the Netherlands Army and, during the preceding month, Spencer Wilks had fielded an enquiry on behalf of the French military authorities.

This enquiry actually came from Automobiles Talbot, and it looks from surviving evidence as if the company's intention was to compete for a contract to supply light utility vehicles to the French military authorities and to the military authorities in the French Colonies generally. Talbot's proposal was to manufacture the Land-Rover under licence, presumably at its Suresnes factory. In due course, Spencer Wilks had discussions with Talbot, and on 28th March 1950, he reported back to the Rover Board that the company did not yet have a firm contract with the French authorities. If it secured one, however, it would need to build vehicles to a specification which differed from standard, and it would wish to badge them as Land-Talbots. In the event, Talbot never did get the contract.

Just over a year later, a similar enquiry came in from Minerva in Belgium. On 2nd May 1951, Spencer Wilks told the Board

that Minerva had asked if Rover would be willing to supply "major Land-Rover components" for vehicles to be built up by Minerva and supplied to the Belgian Army. By June, it was apparent that 2,500 vehicles would be wanted, and that the Land-Rover was in competition with the Willys Jeep for the contract. In August or September, the Belgian Government insisted that Minerva should also be allowed to sell its Land-Rovers to other European countries of the Atlantic Pact. To all this, Rover agreed, and the Minerva order was confirmed by Monsieur Van Roggen of that company on 9th October 1951. By then, however, the 2-litre Land-Rover had entered production, and the Minerva Land-Rovers - very special vehicles, which will be dealt with separately - entered production with these enlarged engines.

The Road Transport Fleet Data Society can be contacted at 18 Poplar Close, Biggleswade, Bedfordshire SG18 0EW. It already publishes nine booklets covering registration details of the 'BC' vehicles and of several 1960s and 1970s military registration series.
Material from the Rover Board minutes is used by kind permission of the Rover Group and BMIHT.

An instant recognition feature of the 1952 models (and therefore the 2-litre Land-Rovers) was the external door handle. The lower panel the sidescreen, of course, lost its canvas flap at the same time. Standard tyres were Dunlop Trakgrip.

The 2-litre 80

CUSTOMER PRESSURE persuaded Rover to introduce a more "torquey" 2-litre engine for the Land-Rover in 1951. The original 2-litre Land-Rover lasted just two years. James Taylor tells the story.

EVEN THOUGH Land-Rovers outsold Rover saloons by two to one during 1951, the Rover Company still thought of itself primarily as a manufacturer of saloon cars in the early 1950s. The Land-Rover, after all, had been introduced as a temporary measure to keep the company afloat until trading conditions returned to normal and Rover could once again sell its elegant and refined saloons in quantity. For that reason, when feedback from Land-Rover customers made clear that a more powerful engine would be a welcome improvement, the development of that engine was closely tied up with developments on the saloon car side of the Rover Company.

The need for a new engine must have been apparent as early as 1948, when the P4 saloon then under development looked like becoming a much heavier car than the P3s then in production. The single-carburettor six-cylinder engine in the P3 was just not up to the job of giving a P4 the sort of performance it needed, and the four-cylinder type (which was also used in the Land-

Rover) was out of the question. So it was that only six-cylinder P4s appeared in 1949, and the four-cylinder P3 was not replaced. In public, Rover argued that this was a concession to the Government's pressure on manufacturers to minimise production overheads by building single-model ranges. The reality, however, was almost certainly rather different!

Even the twin-carburettor six-cylinder engine adopted for the production P4 75 was a disappointment. At Solihull, the engineers knew very well that a well-tuned P3 75 could outrun the new model, and so their thoughts turned to ways of getting more power out of the six-cylinder engine. as six-cylinder saloon and four-cylinder Land-Rover engines were based on a common design, it was obvious that the most cost-effective solution would be to draw up a modification of that design which would suit both derivatives.

Maurice Wilks was not keen on multiple-carburettor layouts, for the simple reason that he thought they would present maintenance problems in some of Rover's more backward export markets. So he agreed with his chief engine designer Jack Swaine that development should go ahead on a big-bore block. For the four-cylinder engine, Swaine's team took the capacity as

close to 2 litres as they could get, with a 77.8mm bore and the existing 105mm stroke. For the six-cylinder, a slightly smaller enlargement of the bore took capacity up to 2638cc.

Agreement on the design seems to have been reached late in 1949, and prototype batches of both engines were made early the following year. This was an unusual approach: generally, two or three prototypes had sufficed, but the experience of the 48 pilot-build Land-Rovers in 1948 had left its mark. This time, Rover built 50 prototype 2-litre Land-Rovers and 30 prototype 2.6-litre saloons. Both were given their own special chassis number sequences and both took to the roads in the first half of 1950, the first Land-Rover appearing some four months before the first saloon.

However, the big-bore block solution was something of a compromise, because it meant that there was no longer room for water passages between all the bores. From the beginning, Jack Swaine had warned that this might lead to problems, and he was vindicated when one of the prototype saloons returned to Solihull with scuffed bores after some prolonged high-speed work. As a result, the enlarged six-cylinder engine was held back until the block could be redesigned with water-

Nothing had changed inside the vehicles, though. This shows a very early 1952 model.

inch models

ways between all the bores. In the Land-Rovers, however, no such problems showed up, mainly because the engines were simply not subjected to long periods of high-speed running. The "siamese-bore" four-cylinder engine was therefore sanctioned for production.

In production

The new 2-litre Land-Rovers were announced in August 1951 for the 1952 model-year. In development, Swaine's team had aimed primarily for low-speed torque rather than additional power (these priorities had of course been reversed in the saloon engine), and the new engine gave some 26% more torque at lower rpm than its predecessor. It also had an extra 2bhp, which made no discernible difference to the Land-Rover's top speed. This was fortunate because Rover would otherwise probably have had to improve the vehicle's brakes as well.

"The more powerful 2-litre engine has been designed primarily to produce high torque at low rpm," read a Rover Company announcement. "This is to give the Land-Rover increased 'slogging' power at low engine speed, particularly for agricultural work and towing operations.

"Other features of this new engine are an

increase on occasions in economy of fuel consumption due to useful working power now being obtained at low rpm and, as a result of this latter characteristic, the necessity for gear-changing is reduced when the Land-Rover is performing heavy duties."

These alone were welcome improvements, but the 2-litre Land-Rovers also incorporated a number of modifications elsewhere. The chassis frame had been strengthened with two transverse bracings and outrigger supports and – a change which aided recognition of the new models – there were now proper exterior door handles. There was also a new optional extra in the shape of a detachable truck cab, which could also be fitted to earlier vehicles. The truck cab consisted of an aluminium alloy roof and rear panel which clamped to the windscreen frame and the forward hood stick sockets. Its ribbed roof section was shared with the optional hard top, while the rear panel incorporated a sliding perspex rear window. Unless to special order, the truck cab was always painted cream in order to cut down heat absorption inside. Clearly, Rover's thinking was geared to tropical climates rather than the British one!

The model range, of course, remained the

same as it had been for the last of the 1.6-litre models in the 1951 model-year. The basic 2-litre Land-Rover was an open vehicle, which could be supplied with or without a canvas tilt. There were truck cab and hard top options, but the Station Wagons were no more, and the closest approximation to one was available only for export. In this, inward-facing rear seats could be fitted in the load bed, together with the so-called "window hard top", which added a single fixed window in each side of the metal hard top. The Mobile Welding Plant remained available, and still had its own special chassis-number series, but examples would never be numerous.

Production and sales

By the end of January 1952, according to the Rover Board Minutes, Land-Rover production was running at 400 vehicles a week, an increase of 50 a week since June 1950. This expansion in production had not been as rapid as the expansion from 100 to 350 a week in the first two years of Land-Rover production, but it was certainly not for want of orders, which continued to exceed Solihull's ability to build the vehicles. Further expansion of production would need more factory space and more capital, and the Rover Board turned its

The truck cab could be fitted to earlier vehicles and, in this sales catalogue shot, it clearly was! Note the canvas flap in the sidescreen and the absence of door handles.

attention to securing both during 1952.

There was barely time to draw breath for those involved in Land-Rover production. A small celebration was held on 15th January 1952 when the 50,000th Land Rover came off the lines, and a single minor production change was made shortly afterwards: the finger-hole in the perspex side screens was deleted and replaced by a knob. Anything much more complicated that that would probably have disrupted production too much!

Of course, it was not all plain sailing for the Land-Rover at this time. On 18th June 1952, Spencer Wilks reported to the Rover Board that "we were feeling the effects of the closing of various Export Markets, particularly Australia, New Zealand and Brazil." The main reason for this was that such countries were trying to protect their domestic economies against a flood of imports. In due course, many countries would ban the import of fully built-up vehicles but would approve the sale of vehicles imported in kit form and built up using local labour and sometimes also a degree of locally-sourced parts. Thus it was that the numbers of Land-Rovers exported in CKD form mushroomed in the early 1950s.

Fortunately, the supply difficulties which had so drastically affected Land Rover production in the early days were now easing. The Government still pursued policies which encouraged exports, however, and at the June Board Meeting, Spencer Wilks reported on the latest easing of the restrictions.

"The Ministry," he reported, "had increased the Home Quotas for Cars and Land-Rovers for the calender year 1952, and in view of this . . . we should be able to maintain our output of 600 vehicles, plus spares, at least until the end of the present calendar year." That figure, of course, represented Rover's weekly output of saloons and Land-Rovers , and the Home Quotas were the numbers of vehicles the company was allowed to sell in the home market.

Looking at the production figures for the 1952 and 1953 seasons, the only two during which the 2-litre 80-inch Land-Rovers were available, it is possible to detect certain trends. For the 1953 season, production totals of the basic models were some 20% down on 1952, and these reductions affected both home and export models. 1953 saw more success in export markets which took right-hand-drive vehicles than 1952, but poor performances elsewhere kept the total low. The Welder continued to be a very small-volume model and, although the 1952 season was better than 1951, 1953's figures dropped to former levels. Totals were in any case insignificant: there had been 20 welders in 1951; 1952 saw 31 made, and 1953 saw only 22.

However, 1953 was a better year overall than 1952 as far as Land-Rover production was concerned, and that solely as the result of a massive increase in the export of left-hand-drive CKD kits. Right-hand-drive CKD kits had meanwhile dwindled to nothing (though the markets were not lost and would pick up again when the 86-inch and 107-inch models came on-stream for 1954).

The LAND-ROVER FIRE ENGINE

is a practical, self-contained fire-fighting appliance, particularly useful for cities and villages with narrow streets, rural areas, forestry service, factories, large estates, etc. Its powerful four-wheel drive and its compactness will take it almost anywhere—over fields, through mud, sand or scrub—and enable it to approach nearer to the fire than the larger fire engine. The same Rover 4-cylinder, 52 b.h.p. engine drives the vehicle and the Pegson 200 gallon per minute self-priming pump, which apart from supplying the twin full-sized delivery hoses, also supplies the 120 ft. first-aid hose reel from a self-contained 40-gallon tank. The front driving compartment accommodates driver and crew of two. The metal cab is an optional extra.

FIRE

PUMP MOU
member and dr

DRIVE. The
centre power ta
step-up gearbo
ratio of 1.678 t
chassis cross-me

CONTROL O
By engine gove
mounted on the
limits the engin
which results in
in top gear in th

ENGINE OIL
mounted immed

STANDARD
FIRST-AID W.
main pump via s
FIRST-AID W
tank, capacity ap
wheel arches. T
main pump succ

Fire Engine to reach trou
ground clearance make it
vehicle capable of operatin

The fire tender as it looked in a 1953 sales catalogue.

Fire Engines and Military Land Rovers

Fire engines remained available after the 2-litre engine had been introduced, although they appear to have sold in the same small numbers as their 1.6-litre predecessors. A May 1953 sales brochure for the Land-Rover Fire Engine shows that an engine speed governor and oil cooler were standard equipment from the Rover options list. The specialist fire-fighting equipment consisted of a 40-gallon tank in the load bed, with a 120-foot first-aid hose stored on a reel above that. There was a Pegson 27H 200gpm pump fitted at the rear and driven from the centre PTO through an extra step-up gear box mounted behind the centre crossmember. The pump had its own control panel, also mounted at the rear.

There were suction hose cradles on the front wings and bumper, but Rover did not supply the hose itself because requirements varied from one Fire Authority to another. The complete vehicle cost £905, plus £25 11s 0d if the optional truck cab was specified.

The War Department continued to take Land Rovers too. Contract number 6/V/7008 called for 600 Land-Rovers, of which the second batch of 200(registered as 36BD05 to 38BD04) were the first 2-litre models to enter military service. They were known as Rover Mk2s, to distinguish them from the 1.6-litre Mk1s and, under the new military vehicle type classification system, they also acquired the code of FV 18001.

Next came a further order for 1,900 2-litre models, under contract number 6/V/7711 of 11th January 1952, and these entered service in 1953 as 00BH01 to 19BH00. A smaller number of vehicles, ordered under separate contracts, also went to the RAF and Royal Navy, and these had the usual AA and RN registration letters respectively.

Many thanks to John Smith and to Pete Jarman of the Road Transport Fleet Data Society for help with this article. Quotations from the Rover Board Minutes are used by kind permission of BMIHT and the Rover Group.

2 Litre 80-inch Production

1952 models
Chassis numbers beginning

261 (Basic models):	15,607
263 (Welder):	31
266 (CKD, Basic models):	3,077
Total:	18,715

1953 models
Chassis numbers beginning

361 (Basic models):	12,742
363 (Welder):	22
366 (CKD, Basic models):	7,268
Total:	20,032

GRAND TOTAL	38,747
(2 Litre 80-inch)	

(Note: the 50 2-litre prototypes built in 1950 were included in the 1950 build figures).

These figures are taken from the Rover Company despatch records currently held by BMIHT and are used by kind permission.

Above: Although the first series of Road Rover prototypes were all broadly similar, the design did develop over the years. This is the fourth prototype, built in 1952, with half-width rear door and external spare wheel.

Right: Did this vehicle have four-wheel-drive? If not, why does it have all terrain tyres (all the others had saloon car tyres), and why has the number plate been repositioned above the bumper if not to improve the approach angle? This is RR11, built in 1954.

What shall

IN THE early 1950s, Rover could still hardly believe that the Land Rover was selling so well. Planning perhaps for a worst case, they developed new vehicles which could have filled the gap if Land Rover sales had collapsed, James Taylor explains.

AS EARLIER episodes of the Land Rover Story have shown, exporting vehicles was something of a nightmare in the late 1940s and early 1950s. Not only were there complications at home — Government pressure to export and supplies shortages, to name just two — but there were also political complications abroad. Those working in the export department at Solihull were quite likely to arrive for work one morning to discover that the country to which they had been hoping to send a batch of Land Rovers had suddenly banned the import of foreign vehicles in order to protect its domestic economy. Or, because the British Government would not guarantee credits, that there was no money to pay for the vehicles due to be sent abroad that day. Most of the time, things ran smoothly, but problems of this sort arose often enough to keep the Rover Company permanently on edge about its dependence on Land Rover

exports.

The minutes of the Rover Board meetings are too emotionless to reflect this kind of preoccupation, but the evidence of what was going on in the Engineering Department provides a reliable pointer to the way things really were. The first idea for a potential Land Rover replacement seems to have surfaced towards the end of 1951. "The aim," as Gordon Bashford explained many years later, "was to produce a road car based to some extent on Land Rover body structuring." There are references in one of Bashford's own notebooks to layouts for a Utility Car drawn up in September 1951, and it seems pretty certain that this was the vehicle in question.

The idea had come from Maurice Wilks. Convinced that there was a market for a simple passenger-carrying utility vehicle, and undaunted by the failure of the original Land Rover Station Wagon (which had gone out of production in the summer of 1951), he had perhaps turned once again to the Willys Jeep for inspiration. Willys had been building two-wheel drive Station Wagons ever since 1946 on long-wheel-base versions of the Jeep chassis, and it was clearly this sort of vehicle which Wilks had

in mind for his new project.

Right from the beginning, the Utility Car seems to have been conceived as a hybrid, using existing Rover components to produce a new vehicle as quickly and cheaply as possible. The list of layout drawings in Gordon Bashford's 1951 notebook shows that all kinds of schemes were under consideration, some using Land Rover bodies on P3 and P4 chassis frames, and others using new "utility body" styles with Land Rover or car chassis. Among the ideas were frameless construction (Bashford was then actively investigating chassisless structures for the saloon cars) and front-wheel-drive, and it looks as if the idea of an Army Staff Car was also being mooted, because one layout is described as a "Land Rover Staff Car on modified P4 chassis." Perhaps the idea behind the experimental Land Rover Army Staff Car built the previous summer (see *Dead Ends* in the December 1991 *LRO*) was still kicking around at Solihull.

By November 1951, Gordon Bashford was involved in detail design for the new vehicle, and his notebook contains calculations for the handbrake installation on what he was still calling the Utility Car. Meanwhile, Maurice Wilks had begun

we do if...

work with his chief body designer, Harry Loker, on full-size mock-ups of the vehicle. Exact dates of the mock-ups are no longer available, but surviving pictures were probably taken at the end of 1951 or early 1952.

These mock-ups were translated into reality during the first months of 1952 and, on 8th April, the first prototype of the new vehicle was registered as MAC 162. "I remember the very first vehicle to run was nicknamed the 'greenhouse' because of its slender framework and the amount of glass used," Gordon Bashford recalled, many years later. By now, however, the Utility Car had acquired a proper name: Road Rover.

According to Rover's company vehicle records, the first Road Rover (chassis number RR1) was built on the chassis of a 1952-model export P4 75 saloon, though this had presumably been modified with a shortened wheelbase. Dimensions are not available, but later Road Rovers had a 97-inch wheelbase and there is no reason to think that this one was significantly longer or shorter. Its engine was also recorded as bearing the number RR1, which does not help in identifying what it was; but later Road Rovers had prototype "spread-bore" 2-litre engines of the type intended for the

P4 60 saloon and also introduced with the 86-inch and 107-inch Land Rovers in autumn 1953, so it might well have been one of these.

On 20th May 1952, Spencer Wilks presented to the Rover Board a plan for the company's future expansion which included the Road Rover. At this stage, he stated that £30,000 would be needed for development purposes. Three more prototypes were put on the road before the end of the year, and these were presumably all similar to RR1.

However, what had started out as a very simple method based on existing production components was already beginning to get more complicated. During January 1953, front-wheel-drive was again under consideration, and so was a 2.25-litre version of the V6 engine with which Jack Swaine's engine designers were experimenting. Nothing seems to have come of these ideas, however, and the fifth and sixth prototypes, which appeared in February and March that year, seem to have been substantially similar to the first four.

Six prototypes would normally have been enough for a new model. Indeed, things seem to have been going well with

the Road Rover project because Spencer Wilks formally proposed that it should be adopted for production at the Board Meetings on 15th April. The Board agreed, and allotted a further £60,000 for the purchase of the necessary jigs, dies and tools, although it is interesting that no production date was mentioned.

Perhaps problems began to show up on prototypes, because the development engineers felt it necessay to build a seventh vehicle, which was put on the road in July. Then, at the Board Meeting on 23rd July, Road Rover production was postponed. No reason was given, although the coincidence of timing with the appearance of the seventh prototype does reinforce the idea that the project had run into unforeseen snags. However, at this stage, things presumably did not look too serious, because the Board agreed that production would go ahead "about June next year."

June 1954 came and went without any further reference to the Road Rover project at Board meetings. Prototypes numbers 8 and 9 had meanwhile been built, but after November 1953 there would be a pause in the prototype build programme until June. Presumably there were still problems and

By the time of the twelfth and final prototype in this first series, built in 1955, a one-piece rear door was fitted and the spare wheel was stowed horizontally below the rear floor. Note the ingenious arrangement of the jump-seat, which folded away into the floor when not in use. This vehicle is preserved in the BMIHT Collection ▷

A nice touch: RR12 has a Land-Rover combined instrument dial, which has been neatly "doctored"… ◁

some redesign work was under way. Certainly, Gordon Bashford was once again examining the possibility of front-wheel-drive, and by the end of May he was sketching up front suspension details for such an installation in the Road Rover.

Prototype build resumed that summer, number 10 being put on the road in June and number 11 in July. But the development engineers must still have been calling for new ideas, because a whole series of further schemes were under consideration during July. In addition to front-wheel-drive, four-wheel-drive had come into the picture, and there was some possibility that the vehicle might be offered in three different versions, with rear-wheel, front-wheel and four-wheel-drive! Some consideration was also being given to a three-speed gearbox, double-reduction axles for the front-wheel-drive and four-wheel-drive versions, a double-wishbone independent front suspension with inboard brakes, a magnetic or friction clutch and, on the rear-wheel-drive version, disc brakes like those then in the early stages of development for the P4 saloon.

Gordon Bashford commented much later that the Road Rover "finally got itself so over-sophisticated that it was killed off."

He was in fact referring to the final ver-

sions, built in the later 1950s during the second phase of the project, but from the evidence of the ideas being kicked around for the project during 1954, the tendency to become over-sophisticated had already risen! In fact, none of these more outlandish ideas ever got off the drawing board, and the twelfth and final Road Rover prototype from this era, put on the road in June 1955, was very similar indeed to those which had gone out before it.

Was a four-wheel-drive Road Rover ever built? Pictures of the eleventh prototype show that it had Land Rover wheels and tyres (all the others had saloon wheels and tyres), and it is just possible that a four-wheel-drive system lurks under the boxy body. The timing is right: prototype number 11 was put on the road in July 1954, when four-wheel-drive was being considered for the Road Rover and, a month later, Gordon Bashford's notebooks show that he was calculating spring rates for "no. 2 Road Rover, 4WD", which seems to imply that one four-wheel-drive prototype already existed. However, both Tom Barton and Spen King are adamant that no four-wheel-drive Road Rover was ever made.

If there ever was a four-wheel-drive Road Rover, it came too late to be of any benefit

to the project as a whole. By summer 1953, a seven-seat Station Wagon on the 86" Land Rover chassis was in preparation and a ten-seater on the 107" chassis was in preparation. Between them, these vehicles took care of any market there might have been for a 4WD Utility Car. By 1954, it must also have been much clearer at Solihull that, despite the vicissitudes of overseas trade, Land Rover sales were not going to collapse overnight. Who, then, was going to need Maurice Wilks' Utility Car, whether it had four-wheel-drive or not?

In fact, the Road Rover project did not die out. Revamped in 1956, it staggered on until 1959; but the story of the Series II Road Rover belongs at a later point in *LRO's* Land Rover Story.

If the Road Rover had indeed originally been intended as a potential Land Rover replacement, it had certainly acquired a life of its own by the end of 1952 and was being viewed as a third product line alongside the P4 saloons and the Land Rover itself. So it was that the engineers associated with the Land Rover decided to draw up a second new vehicle which Rover might produce, "should the Land Rover not be successful in holding sales," as Tom Barton put it recently. The exact start date of

△ The unique Land-Rover tractor prototype, with John Cullen at the wheel.

this project is impossible to establish, but all the evidence points to late 1952.

The new vehicle was a farm tractor, although it was sufficiently different from the tractors then in production to be of considerable interest. The inspiration had probably come from two sources: firstly, from the Land Rover itself, which had of course been designed primarily as an agricultural vehicle, and secondly, from the discussions which senior members of the Rover Company had conducted in autumn 1952 with Harry Ferguson, whose lightweight "grey Fergie" tractor had been enormously successful in the immediate post-War years. The talks, which involved some sort of collaboration between Ferguson and Rover, eventually foundered; but they must have left their mark.

The new tractor was drawn up by John Cullen and Tom Barton, who were then the two most senior Land Rover engineers. The single prototype had a very simple rectangular frame with a Land Rover petrol tank at the rear, a 1595cc engine (probably P3 car engine if the air cleaner arrangements in surviving pictures are anything to go by) and four-wheel-drive. For manouevrability, Cullen and Barton also provided it with four-wheel steering and, in order to give it maximum rough-terrain ability, they developed a system of gears in the wheel assemblies by means of which the vehicle could be raised an extra 10 or 12 inches.

What Rover might have called this remarkable vehicle if it had ever gone into production is not clear, but the name of Land Rover Tractor would certainly have been appropriate. However, the project did not prosper. Gordon Bashford remembered that there were "some misgivings in relation to safety, including the danger of tipping over under extreme lateral conditions.' and Tom Barton now says that "we did not put the tractor into production because the Land Rover had become so successful that we could not cope with a completely new vehicle." Exactly when the tractor project was dropped is not clear, but it certainly did not continue beyond 1954, when John Cullen left Land Rover to become Director of Engineering at David Brown Industries, themselves manufacturers of farm vehicles.

I am grateful to Tom Barton OBE, for his help in the preparation of this episode of the Land Rover Story and for the loan of the picture of the Tractor prototype. Quotations from the Rover Board minutes are used by kind permission of Rover Group/BMIHT.

THE LAND ROVER STORY

△   86 inch wheelbase Series One with canvas tilt

Longer

For the 1954 season, Rover introduced its new 86-inch and 107-inch models. James Taylor explains the background.

THE ROVER Company made quite a splash with its 1954 models, announced in the autumn of 1953. On the saloon car side, there were two new models – the 60 and 90 – and a number of valuable revisions to the existing 75. On the Land-Rover side, the existing 80-inch wheelbase model was replaced by two new models, both with longer wheelbases. And on the shorter of these new Land-Rover chassis, there was a new seven-seater Station Wagon, which Rover presented as an addition to its passenger car range.

To introduce five new models all at once was a major event, and Rover celebrated the fact by holding its first post-War meeting for U.K. dealers and distributors at its Grosvenor House offices in London's Park Lane on 23rd September 1953. Each guest was presented with a special souvenir booklet, which opened with a statement on "Rover Policy and Purpose" from Managing Director Spencer Wilks.

"I am pleased to announce a considerably improved version of the existing Land-Rover,' he wrote, 'together with an entirely new addition to the range in the shape of the Land-Rover Pick-Up. The improved Land-Rover has a longer wheelbase than its predecessor and, whilst maintaining all the maneouvrability and performance of the previous model, has 25% more carrying capacity in the rear compartment. In addition, many improvements of detail are offered, evolved in the light of five years' experience in the design and manufacture of four-wheel drive vehicles.

"The Land-Rover Pick-Up is a long wheelbase four-wheel drive vehicle designed for use where load space is of major importance. It has a much longer wheelbase than the basic Land-Rover – 107" compared with 86" – and the spacious rear compartment thus provided is ideally suited for carrying bulky loads. The Fire Engine and Welding Unit versions of the Land-Rover are to be continued, and also the various extras – including a detachable metal Hard Top and a detachable metal Cab."

As for the new Station Wagon, which replaced the original wooden-Framed vehicle on the 80-inch chassis after a period of two years in which no Station Wagon body was available for the Land-Rover, Wilks noted that it would "make an interesting addition to our passenger car range."

Development

Surviving records from Rover suggest that the first Land-Rover with a lengthened wheelbase was in fact built in August 1950. This experimental vehicle, recorded in the photographic archives as a "Long Buss" *(sic)*, was clearly the forerunner of the 107-inch model, and had an interesting truck cab which used the doors, bulkhead and one-piece windscreen from the 80-inch Station Wagon.

Right from the beginning, the long-wheel-

> *This illustration of the Land-Rover chassis shows its clean, workmanlike design and emphasises the immensely rigid box-section chassis frame - specially proofed against corrosion and built to stand up to the most merciless treatment. Extra-wide semi-elliptic springs and telescopic-type shock absorbers are fitted front and rear.*

Δ An 86 chassis. The side members of the 107 chassis were deeper in the centre. Where the 86's side members were made of single lengths of steel plate, those on the 107 consisted of several lengths welded together.

wheelbases

base Land-Rover seems to have been intended primarily as a load-carrier, and this experimental vehicle therefore had a pick-up body. Demand for the extra carrying capacity came mostly from overseas and, as the Rover Board was told on 23rd July 1953, when the 1954-season new model plans were formally presented, the long wheelbase Land Rover was being introduced "to meet demand in the Export market."

However, after this first vehicle had been built, things went very quiet for some time as far as the long-wheelbase model was concerned. Attention turned to stretching the existing 80-inch Land-Rover, and it is likely that the first experimental "stretched" chassis was built in June 1951 and fitted with the experimental Army Staff Car body (see *Dead Ends* in the December 1991 *LRO* and *Updates* below). However, the design was not settled until some time later. The 86-inch prototypes were built up between June and September that year. These bore

chassis number P86/1 to P86/6. There then followed three more, P86/7 to P86/9, before the end of December.

Whether any more 86-inch prototypes were built is unclear, but it seems unlikely because the first production model was built in mid-February 1953, and further examples followed in March. Development work had now focussed once again on the long-wheelbase Land-Rover, and the first 107-inch prototype was built in December 1952. Records of no more than three prototypes – P107/1 to P107/3 – exist and, once again, there might well have been no others. The first production specification vehicles were coming off the assembly lines by June 1953.

The 86-inch

The whole point of stretching the original 80-inch wheelbase out to 86 inches was, of course, to improve the basic Land-Rover's load-carrying capacity. But the pick-up bed on the new vehicles was in fact nearly nine

inches longer than on the 80-inch models because the rear overhang had also been extended. The result was an increase in carrying capacity, as Spencer Wilks told his distributors and dealers at that September 1953 meeting, of 25%. There was no increase in payload, however, and no doubt this had been deliberately arranged so that those customers who needed a vehicle with a greater payload would turn to the long-wheelbase model.

Inevitably, the longer wheelbase made the 86-inch Land-Rover slightly less agile over really rough terrain because the longer belly of the vehicle was more liable to ground than before. Not many customers really needed all the Land-Rover's excellent off-road ability, though, and Rover must have been confident that the majority of customers would not complain. Similarly, the larger chassis and body added weight – some 108lbs (49kg) of it – but losses in performance and fuel economy as a result were negligible.

△ *107 inch pick-up. This vehicle is almost certainly one of the first prototypes*

In fact, the increased wheelbase brought about some unexpected gains. In particular, the longer rear propshaft allowed the axle a little more vertical movement, which in turn brought about an improvement in the ride; and the longer wheelbase itself meant that the vehicle was less prone to fore-and-aft pitching than the 80-inch, which also contributed to a better ride.

The 107-inch

The points which applied to the 86-inch applied also to the 107-inch Land-Rover, only more so. The longer wheelbase did allow a much better ride than the 80-inch had ever provided, although the longer chassis was considerably less agile over rough terrain – and, indeed, it seemed as if Rover did not expect the 107-inch to see much off-road use because all the early publicity pictures of the vehicles show them with road tyres instead of the dual-purpose covers normally associated with Land-Rovers.

The increased weight of the vehicle – it was 437 lbs (198kg) heavier than an 80-inch – did hit the road performance, however, and the long-wheelbase Land-Rover was altogether more sluggish and more thirsty than its short-wheelbase counterpart.

These were disadvantages, however. The real advantages of the long-wheelbase pick-up were a vast increase in the load-bed length, which was a now a full six feet long, and an increase in the payload to 1,120lbs (508kg)." No doubt to emphasise this element of its specification, the 107-inch model was initially marketed as the Land-Rover Pick-Up with a fully-enclosed cab as standard wear, and in fact that was the only body configuration it

would have for its first season of production.

The Station Wagon

The third new Land-Rover for the 1954 season was the Station Wagon. Based on the new 86-inch chassis, this represented a complete reversal of the philosophy which had produced the 80-inch Station Wagon. The earlier vehicle had been coachbuilt, using traditional methods, with the result that it had been far too costly for its intended market.

By contrast, the body of the 1954 Station Wagon was built up largely from existing parts, and Rover intended later to use as many of its panels as possible in a new Station Wagon on the 107-inch chassis.

Like its 80-inch predecessor, the 86-inch Station Wagon was a seven-seater, with three-abreast seating in the front and four inward-facing seats in the rear of the body. As the eye-level of tall passengers in those rearmost seats was well above the top of the sliding side windows, curved glass panels (known as "Alpine lights") were let into the sides of the roof. In addition, to prevent the interior from becoming too stuffy in hot weather or hot climates (for none of the windows in the rear body opened), the so-called Safari roof was standardised. This was simply an alloy panel mounted an inch or so above the main roof and designed to reflect the sun's heat while fresh air circulating in the airspace below could be admitted to the body through vents in the main roof; the arrangement was also rain-and dust-proof.

As a finishing touch, the new Station Wagon was also provided with its own badge on grille and rear panel. This fitted

underneath the standard Land-Rover oval and read "Four Wheel Drive Station Wagon".

Improvements

All three of the new Land-Rover models had the inverted T-shaped grille which had been seen on the last of the 80-inch models (the grille with headlamp cutouts had disappeared early in 1953), but their redesigned front wings were an instant recognition feature.

On the 80-inch Land-Rovers, the wings had consisted of two panels, one at the side and one which ran along the top and curved smoothly down to form the front end. On the 86-inch and 107-inch models, the wings were made in three pieces; side, top, and front. The result was a very noticeable horizontal panel seam just above the sidelamp, which had also now lost its fluted surround.

From the side, the 107-inch Pick-Up was of course readily recognisable because of its greater length, but the 86-inch was less easy to distinguish from an 80-inch.

The easy way to tell the difference was from the panel ahead of the rear wheel arch, where the extra length was immediately obvious and three rivet-heads were clearly visible.

Both new Land-Rovers also had recessed door handles, which were less prone to catching on undergrowth than the protruding type introduced for the 2-litre 80-inch.

Rover made much of what it called the car-type front compartment introduced with the new models.

To suggest that it was very much like Rover's own luxury cars would have gone too far, but it was certainly an improvement

△ *Probably a 107 prototype, circa 1951-52*

on earlier Land Rovers! Most obvious of the changes were a new instrument panel with two large circular dials and pedals which emerged from the toe-board at a less acute angle.

Twin scuttle ventilators, only optional on earlier vehicles, were now standard.

"Note too the full width parcel shelf," urged the 1953 dealer souvenir booklet, "the new car-type gear control, and the deep cellular rubber sprung seating. Less visible, but greatly to be appreciated by the 1954 Land-Rover owner, is the improved sealing against dust and weather. All door edges on the new bodywork and all-weather equipment butt into soft rubber, giving new comfort and quietness to the driving compartment." Such comparisons were of course relative!

Optional extras continued to be available. Most notable, perhaps was that the 1954-model Land Rovers could be had in blue or grey paint in addition to the dark green which had formerly been the only colour option.

Also new was a Tropical roof panel for the metal cab, which was essentially a short version of the Station Wagon's Safari roof. For the 107-inch Pick-Up, DeLuxe cab trim was available (again, all things were relative . . .), as were a full tilt cover, a tonnneau cover and inward-facing seats with upholstered backrests for the load-bed. All models could be fitted with a cap-stan winch at the front, with PTOs at the rear or in the centre, and with a rather crude cab heater.

Thanks to John Smith for helpful advice, and to Rover Group/BMIHT for permission to quote from the Rover Board minutes.

A Controversy

In my *Dead Ends* article in the December 1991 issue of LRO, I told the story of the 1951 Army Staff Car. I suggested then that it had an 80-inch chassis, and managed to stir up a proper hornet's nest.

No-one knows for sure, but several people went to a lot of trouble to 'prove' that the wheelbase was actually 86 inches. I am happy to accept that verdict - provisionally - and am grateful to everyone who wrote in to argue the case.

The most convincing argument came from Roger Crathorne at Land Rover, who pointed out that the relative positions of the gearbox and centre cross-member showed that it was definitely not an 80-inch chassis.

The point of mentioning this here is that the Army Staff Car now becomes a strong candidate for the first experimental 86-inch Land Rover, and in this month's episode of The Land Rover Story, I have argued that it probably was the first. All arguments to the contrary will be welcome!

THE LAND ROVER STORY

△ *This 86-inch Land Rover was delivered to Sir Winston Churchill on Sunday, 5th December 1954, a few days after his 80th birthday. He was then still Prime Minister*

The 86 and 107

The 86-inch and 107-inch models were in production for just three years — although the 107-inch Station Wagon carried on for a further two after that. James Taylor looks at their story.

THE CHANGEOVER in August 1953 from 80-inch models to the 86-inch and 107-inch models on the Land Rover assembly lines caused a slight hiccup in production, but by the time of the Board meeting on 11th December, things were proceeding satisfactorily. Nevertheless, Rover did not catch up with its production schedule until the beginning of March 1954.

Other production problems seem to have arisen in these early days, too. It looks as if the larger brakes intended for the 107-inch models were not available in time for the launch in autumn 1953, with the result that Rover had to fit early examples with the 86's brakes. They were clearly unable to cope with the vehicle's planned 1,500lb payload, and so a lower figure of 1,120lbs — just 120lbs more than an 86 — was quoted for safety reasons. As soon as the larger brakes did become available, in spring 1954, Rover started quoting the intended 1,500lbs figure.

For the 1955 models, which started coming off the lines in August 1954, there were further changes. The simplest way of distinguishing one of these Land Rovers from its forebears was by its round tail lamps, which replaced the D-shaped lamps used since the very beginning of production. But the real innovation for 1955 was another new engine — the third engine to go into Land Rovers since production had started in 1948.

In fact, inspection of a sales catalogue would have revealed no change at all — and Rover did not advertise the change, either. What had happened was that the original "siamese-bore" 2-litre engine had been swapped for the newer "spread-bore" design with the same bore and stroke which had been introduced in the P4 60 saloon car in October 1953.

How Rover got into the curious predicament of having two different 2-litre engines in production alongside one another is an interesting story in itself. As related in an earlier episode of the *Land Rover Story* (see *LRO* for March 1992), when the Rover development engineers bored out the 1.6-litre four-cylinder and 2.1-litre six-cylinder engines to give 2 litres and 2.6 litres respectively, they found that the resulting "siamese-bore" blocks could suffer from cylinder bore scuffing when used for prolonged high-speed work. The six-cylinder engine, which was intended for saloon

cars and would be subjected to such work, was therefore not put into production. However, the four-cylinder engine, intended for the Land Rover, was not expected to be used for prolonged high-speed work. As the Land Rover needed a new engine urgently, the 2-litre siamese-bore engine therefore did go into production in 1951 for the 1952 models.

Meanwhile, the six-cylinder engine was re-designed with the same bore and stroke dimensions but with water between all the cylinder bores. Plans were made to put it into a high-performance version of the P4 75 saloon to be launched in October 1953 and to be called the 90. Then, someone at Solihull had the bright idea of introducing a four-cylinder P4 as well, to sell at a price below that of the 75.

The obvious engine to put into this was the 2-litre Land Rover type which was by then in production — but in the saloon car application, it was likely to be used for the sort of high-speed work which had caused problems on test! As a result, the 2-litre engine was re-designed to give water between all the bores, and in this form it went into production for the P4 60. To change the engine in the Land Rover at the same time would have caused additional disruption on the production lines and incurred

△ *A familiar vehicle to Land Rover enthusiasts is "Sybil", the 1954 86-inch Station Wagon owned by LRO contributor David Bowyer*

Land Rovers

additional costs. As a result, the adoption of the revised engine in the Land Rover was deferred until the following year, and Rover made both types of 2-litre engine for the 12-month period between August 1953 and August 1954!

The 1956 models announced in September 1955 brought only a fourth body colour - beige - and glass instead of perspex for the sidescreens. But Rover also previewed a forthcoming new model - a 10-seater Station Wagon on the 107-inch wheelbase chassis.

The 107-inch Station Wagon

It was probably the success of the 86-inch Station Wagon which had prompted Rover to develop this larger personnel carrier on the long-wheelbase chassis. The first prototype of the 107-inch Station Wagon was road-registered in August 1954, but production examples did not arrive until early 1956.' The delay, probably, had been caused by an alternative plan for a forward-control minibus on the long-wheelbase chassis, which occupied the engineers' time during 1955.

However, the simpler and cheaper Station Wagon was chosen for production. It was, said the sales catalogue, "an important addition to the Land Rover range," and "an ideal means of carrying personnel and equipment over difficult country. Its possibilities are numerous; oilfield, survey and safari duties providing exceptional scope for its outstanding versatility and powers of progress."

The design of the 107-inch Station Wagon was cunning, for it made maximum use of panels already found in other Land Rovers, Others, such as the rear side doors, were so arranged as to minimise the number of new pressings required. The result was a vehicle which looked rather like a patchwork quilt but, like many patchwork quilts, was also quite imposing in its own way. Beautiful, however, it was not.

"The seating arrangement," explained the sales catalogue, "provides accommodation for three people in front, three on the back seats and four, facing inwards, on additional seats fitted to the rear wheel boxes. If the wheel box seats are removed — a simple operation — and the back seat is folded forward, the whole body is available for load carrying, or alternatively, the back seat squab can be folded backward and the front seat cushions and squab redisposed to form a comfortable bed."

This versatile vehicle sold quite strongly in its first season of production, and in fact remained unchanged for a further two years. When the other 107-inch Land Rovers were replaced in autumn 1956 by 109-inch models, the Station Wagon retained its original chassis. Why this happened is not entirely clear, although it may have been done to help Rover use up supplies of the older chassis. The 107-inch Station Wagon went on to outlast even the Series I 109-inch models, and was not replaced by the Series II 109-inch Station Wagon until autumn 1958. Only 239 107-inch Station Wagons were built for the home market in three seasons of production (the first a partial one), with the result that examples are rarely found in Britain today.

Production and sales

Just over 19,000 Land Rovers had been built in the final year of the 80-inch model's production. The total for the first year of 86-inch and 107-inch Land Rover production was within a couple of hundred of that, but for 1955, sales escalated dramatically to nearly 29,000 — an increase of some 52%. This, of course, was exactly what Rover had hoped would happen when the Land Rover's appeal was broadened by the introduction of the wider model range.

△ *1958 107-inch Station Wagon at the Series One Club's 40th anniversary celebrations in Wales in 1988*

THE LAND ROVER STORY

However, demand began to fall away, particularly in the home market, over the summer of 1955. At the October Board meeting, the Directors were informed that production had been reduced to 575 Land Rovers a week. This was a major cutback; seventeen months earlier, in May 1954, Sales Director Alan Botwood had reported that demand then stood at a minimum of 750 a week, and Spencer Wilks had gained agreement for a proposal to increase production to 1,000 Land Rovers a week by operating double shifts in the Assembly Shop.

This was in fact the beginning of a bad period for the British car industry, and other manufacturers also began to feel the pinch as the 1956 model-year got underway. In February 1956, Land Rover production was cut back further to 540 units a week; and, indeed, production would continue to fall even after the 88-inch and 109-inch models had replaced the 86-inch and 109-inch types in autumn 1956. At the end of the 1956 model-year, the last one in which the full range of 86-inch and 107-inch Land Rovers was still available, production had fallen by some 19% to just over 23,000.

Mergers and diesels

Throughout most of 1954 and the early part of 1955, there had been much talk at Solihull of expansion, mainly to cope with booming Land Rover sales. When sales began to fall in the middle of 1955, the Rover Directors must have offered a silent prayer of thanks that they had not yet over-committed themselves.

Rover's problem, of course, was that it was actually a relatively small company which was now having to cope with vastly increased production. If sales continued to expand at the rate they had in the early 1950s, then Rover was going to have to expand with them. That would mean investing in new buildings, as well as plant and machinery, and that in turn would mean that Rover would have to make larger capital investments.

One way around this was to seek a trading partner which already had the spare capacity which Rover needed and, in the second quarter of 1954, there was considerable discussion about a merger with Standard-Triumph. In particular, this company had an attractive pair of products in the Vanguard petrol and diesel engines, which were used to power the Massey-Ferguson tractors which Standard built under licence and which were selling well both at home and abroad. Well aware that a diesel engine would improve Land Rover sales, and well aware that the 2-litre petrol engine would also need to be replaced in due course, the Rover management clearly had its eye on using either or both of the Standard engines in its own best-selling product.

So it was that Spencer Wilks reported to the Board on 6th March 1954 that he had been involved in preliminary discussions with Standard about a merger. Some engineering collaboration must also have been going on at this stage, although it led nowhere. On 12th May, Wilks told the Board that neither the petrol not the diesel Vanguard engine would be suitable for the Land Rover. Worse, Standard would in fact have no spare plant capacity which could relieve Rover of capital expenditure, except on the engine side of the business. A full financial merger between the two companies was therefore ruled out, although the possibility of limited co-operation remained under consideration.

As for the diesel engine, Rover decided to go its own way. The need for one had been raised by Spencer Wilks as early as the December 1953 board meeting, when he had hoped that Rover would be able to build it in the Acocks Green factory when space became available as the production of Meteor tank engines ran down. However, nothing more happened before January 1955 — no doubt largely because of the negotiations with Standard — when he formally proposed to the Board that Rover should commit itself to developing a diesel engine for the Land Rover. Other manufacturers entering the 4x4 market, he said, were already introducing diesel power. He did not name names, but the manufacturers he had in mind can only have been the likes of Toyota and Nissan, whose products were beginning to come up against the Land Rover in some overseas markets. Fortunately for the future of the Land Rover, the Board agreed to Wilks' proposals.

Thanks to John Smith for advice.

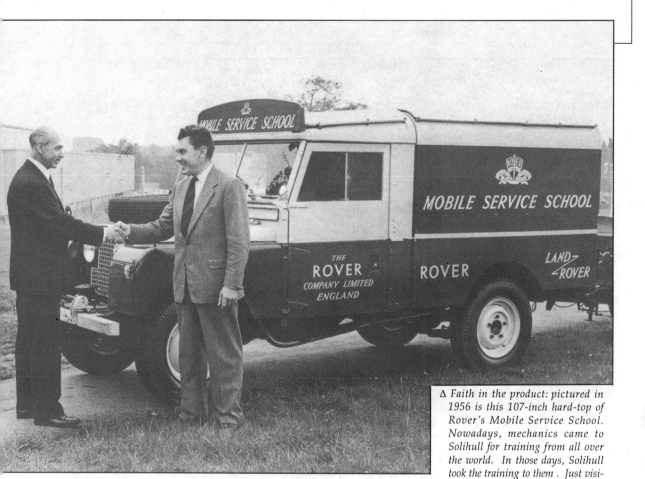

△ *Faith in the product: pictured in 1956 is this 107-inch hard-top of Rover's Mobile Service School. Nowadays, mechanics came to Solihull for training from all over the world. In those days, Solihull took the training to them. Just visible behind the vehicle is the Brockhouse trailer which completed the outfit.*

86-inch and 107-inch Land Rover production

1954 models
Chassis numbers beginning

4710/4713/4716/4763/4766 (86-inch)	15,080
4720/4723/4726/4773/4776 (107-inch)	3,820
	TOTAL 18,900

1955 models
Chassis numbers beginning

5710/5713/5716/5763/5766 (86-inch)	20,214
5720/5723/5726/5773/5776 (107-inch)	8,690
	TOTAL 28,904

1956 models
Chassis numbers beginning

1706/1736/1746/1766/1776 (86-inch)	14,048
2706/2736/2746/2766/2776 (107-inch)	7,835
8706/8736/8746/8766/8776 (107-inch Station Wagon)	1,266
	TOTAL 23,149

1957 models
Chassis numbers beginning

1317/1327/1337/1347/1357 (107-inch Station Wagon)	2,420

1958 models
Chassis numbers beginning

1318/1328/1338/1348/1358 (107-inch Station Wagon)	3,315

GRAND TOTALS

86-inch	49,342
107-inch	27,346

These figures are taken from the Rover Company despatch records currently held by BMIHT and are used by kind permission.

An important turning-point

Before 1956, Land-Rovers were limited by law to a maximum speed of 30mph on Britain's roads because they were classified as commercial vehicles. However, in that year a Mr Kidson from Wareham in Dorset appealed against a fine imposed for speeding in his Land-Rover. The Lord Chief Justice of the day ruled that a Land-Rover could be reclassified as a dual-purpose vehicle. Hardtop models, however, were still classified as commercial vehicles, and remained limited to 30mph.

△ *The Land Rover was first used as a review vehicle in October 1948, when King George VI and Field Marshal Alexander reviewed the Territorial Army from the back of a specially adapted example. However, the first custom-built State Review Land Rover was this one, built on a very early 86" chassis. It entered service in 1953 and was withdrawn in 1975. The vehicle now belongs to the Heritage Collection*

Beyond the

James Taylor takes a look at some of the special vehicles built on the 86 and 107-inch Land-Rover chassis.

BY THE time the 86-inch and 107-inch models were introduced in autumn 1953, Land-Rovers were already well established as fire engines and as military vehicles. In these two roles, they continued to find plenty of customers over the next few years, aided by the efforts of the new Sales Division which Rover created in 1954. And, during the lifetime of the 86-inch and 107-inch models, the Land-Rover also became established as a Royal vehicle.

Fire Engines

The 86-inch Land-Rover Fire Engine differed little in overall concept from the Fire Engine which had been available on the 80-inch chassis. It was, claimed the sales brochure, "a highly mobile, self-contained appliance particularly useful for towns and villages with narrow streets, rural areas, forestry service, factories, large estates ... anywhere in fact where speed, good ground clearance and general handiness are first essentials. Its powerful four wheel drive and compactness enable it to go practically anywhere and to get right up to

trouble spots inaccessible to larger vehicles."

The Land-Rover Fire Engines were offered with a basic specification which consisted of a 40 gallon tank in the load bed, a 120ft first-aid hose reel mounted above it, and a twin-outlet pump bolted to the rear chassis cross-member and the drawbar and driven from the centre PTO. The pump - manufactured by KSB - was rated at 210 gallons per minute and, like the rest of the bought-in equipment, was fitted to the vehicle at Solihull. Standard equipment included an engine oil cooler, hose mounting brackets (but not the hose itself) on the front wings and on a stand bolted to the front bumper, hose lockers above the rear wheels, a spare wheel carrier on the bonnet and 7.00 x 16 tyres instead of the 6.00 x 16s which were standard issue for the 86-inch. The truck cab was an extra-cost option.

Several hundred of these vehicles were built during the three years of 86-inch production, a figure which undoubtedly reflects the fact that the Land-Rover Fire Engine had no rivals at all in its home market, or in many of the Commonwealth markets to which it was sold. However, the model

never really made money for Solihull. The problem was that individual Chief Fire Officers all had their own preferred specification, and that it therefore proved impossible to produce a vehicle which suited every customer. Rover had to spend so much time modifying its Fire Engines to meet different customer requirements that the whole exercise was of doubtful benefit to the company. When the opportunity arose in 1957 to farm out fire engine conversion work on standard Land-Rovers to the fire equipment specialists, Rover grabbed it with both hands.

State Review Vehicles

King George VI normally rode in a Daimler on State Occasions, but such a grand car was not at all suitable for functions such as that of reviewing military regiments of which he was the titular head. As early as October 1948, a Land-Rover was pressed into service as a review vehicle, and the King inspected troops of the Territorial Army while standing in the back of a very early 80-inch. Rails around the back gave him something to hang on to as the vehicle drove around the parade ground, and this vehicle - registered LYR 437 - set the pattern

△ *This early 1957 88" fire tender conversion was sold to a Kent-based paper manufacturing company*

options list

for a whole line of State Review Land-Rovers.

However, the first State Review Land-Rover was not actually built until 1953, on a very early 86-inch chassis (number 4710008). The occasion was the first Royal Tour by the recently-crowned Queen and her husband, which lasted from November 1953 to May 1954 and took in almost every country of the Commonwealth and Empire. For many of the ceremonial visits, the Royal couple needed an open vehicle in which they could stand up to be seen by the huge crowds which attended. To meet this requirement, a very special Land-Rover was therefore built at Solihull; whether Rover had offered it or had been asked to build it is not clear.

The lessons learned from LYR 437 were incorporated into this vehicle in much-refined form. Instead of a simple rail around the load bed, Rover fitted a purpose-built, high-sided rear body with transparent screens around the upper part. The rear also contained two seats (which were of course considerably more comfortable than any standard Land-Rover type!), and the driving compartment had a specially-upholstered bench seat in place of the

usual individual seats. Other special features were hub-caps taken from the contemporary Rover saloon cars, and "modesty skirts" to hide the fuel tank and chassis rails, very similar to those which would be introduced on the Series II models five years later. The whole vehicle was painted in Royal Claret - the Sovereign's colour - and was generally seen in public with a large Royal crest on a board ahead of the radiator. It was, of course, never road-registered.

So useful did this first vehicle prove that the Royal Family took three more like it. Two of them were shipped abroad for use on various Royal Tours, and these remain in the hands of British High Commissions today, still in pristine condition. However, the original vehicle and one other remained in this country. That very first vehicle remained in service until 1975, and is now in the Heritage Collection. The other UK-based vehicle (built in 1954 or early 1955 on 86-inch chassis number 57102615) is still in service today-and is painted in the blue associated with lesser members of the Sovereign's family. As has always been the case with the State Review Land-Rovers, it is kept and maintained at Solihull.

Military models

Land-Rovers acquitted themselves well in British military service during the early 1950s; so well, in fact, that the Army announced in 1956 that it intended to standardise on the Land-Rover as its primary "forward area vehicle". Mostly, the Land-Rovers in service by that stage were 86-inch models, and so it would be fair to say that it was the 86-inch which really secured the Land-Rover's future with the British Army.

In Army parlance, the 1.6-litre 80-inch Land-Rover had been a Rover Mk.1, and the 2-litre model had been a Rover Mk.2. The 86-inch therefore automatically became a Rover Mk.3, while 107-inch models became Rover Mk.4s. The basic 86-inch vehicle shared the FV 18001 designation with the 2-litre 80-inch, but a special version developed for use in the desert by the Special Air Service was known as an FV 18006. The designations FV 18004 and FV 18005 were applied to 107-inch models, the first being a Station Wagon (or Heavy Utility, as the Army called it) of which probably only one was built, while the second was a special ambulance-bodied version.

It is not clear exactly how many 86-inch models entered service with the British

For 'Royal' or 'State' Occasion

By appointment to Her Majesty Queen Elizabeth II
Manufacturers of Land-Rovers
The Rover Company Limited

THE LAND ROVER STORY

Army in the mid-1950s, but records kept at the Museum of Army Transport in Beverley suggest that Solihull was favoured with regular orders for large batches. The first of these orders was probably made in 1954, and a typical example is order number 6/Veh/18599, placed in January 1955, which called for 1,050 vehicles, a figure which was increased during July by a further 450.

Although the Rover Mk 3. was classified as a 1/4-ton cargo vehicle, it was in practice used as a general purpose load-carrier and personnel carrier for anything the Army wanted! Its versatility of course had enormous appeal to the military, and no doubt all kinds of one-off specials were created in military unit workshops to perform special tasks. The FV 18006 - the SAS desert patrol vehicle based on a

standard 86-inch - was just such a vehicle.

The primary aim of the FV 18006 was to enable a patrol to operate in the desert for several days without support. It was therefore fitted with uprated springs, long-range fuel tanks, sand tyres, and a variety of cargo and jerry-can racks. The vehicle was also stripped of its canvas top and door tops, and was equipped with a radio transmitter/receiver and machine

△ The 1953 86" State review Land Rover at the Stoneleigh Royal Show in 1971

◁ There were several State Review Series I Land-Rovers. Second from top on the left in this picture, however, is a later Series II version.

gun swivel mount. An early example was shown at the SMMT/FVRDE annual exhibition at Chertsey in 1956, and the vehicle probably entered service at around the same time.

It is not clear how many of these vehicles were built. Most were probably converted from standard military-issue Rover Mk3s, and many were undoubtedly destroyed or abandoned in some of the world's remoter regions in ensuing years. However, educated guesswork suggests that there may have been 30 or more of these interesting vehicles. Very few indeed still survive.

In contrast to the versatility of the 86-inch, the 107-inch Land-Rover was of limited use to the British military. Rover displayed a prototype 107-inch Station Wagon (with interesting rubber-glazed side windows) at the 1954 SMMT/FVRDE military vehicles exhibition, but in spite of its catalogue designation as an FV 18004, it was not and did not become a British Army vehicle. One 107-inch Station Wagon did acquire a military registration - 42BR33 - and was shown at the 1956 SMMT/FVRDE exhibition, but surviving order details suggest that this was the only one of its kind.

However, the British Army did find in the 107-inch Land-Rover chassis an ideal basis for a forward-area ambulance. The first examples of the FV 18005 appear to have been ordered in 1955 and there were repeat orders in 1956 and 1957. Precise details are lacking, but perhaps no more than 20 of these vehicles were made, all on Station Wagon chassis.

The 107-inch military ambulance was not a pure Land Rover design, but had a body by a specialist manufacturer mounted on a 107-inch chassis. This body was made by Bonallack of Basildon, better know today a Freight Bonallack and a well-known builder of commercial vehicles bodies. It was a high-roof design - very much taller than any factory-produced body on the 107-inch chassis - and was designed to accommodate up to four stretchers in racks in the sides. As Bob Morrison commented in *LRO* for July 1988, the FV 18005 was actually better in one respect than later military ambulance designs on Series II and Series III chassis because its tall body enabled a medical attendant to stand almost erect. However, the long rear overhang greatly reduced the departure angle, which in turn limited the vehicle's usefulness.

Thanks to George Hassall at Land Rover for information on the State Review vehicles.

THE LAND ROVER STORY

Part fifteen by James Taylor

△ *This Minerva Land-Rover, restored to original condition in the Netherlands, demonstrates the grille and front wing shape characteristic of these Belgian-built vehicles*

THE LAND ROVER STORY

The Minerva

James Taylor takes a look at the curious 80-inch Land-Rovers built in Belgium.

IN THE early 1950s, the Rover Company was keen to preserve the momentum of its Land Rover exports, and was constantly seeking new opportunities to sell the vehicle abroad. However, protectionist import policies denied it access to several markets, while in others it could only operate by supplying CKD (Completely Knocked Down) vehicles from Solihull for local assembly. In some cases, these vehicles had to contain a high proportion of locally-sourced materials, and in others, the Rover Company had to allow the assembler/importer to redesign some elements of the vehicle to meet local market requirements.

In all such cases, Rover retained full technical oversight of the product; but a small number of companies turned out Land-Rovers which were very different indeed from the vehicles built at Solihull. Among these was the Belgian Minerva company, which produced some very special Land Rovers between 1952 and 1956.

The company

Minerva could trace its origins back to the very end of the 19th century. Between then and the beginning of the 1930s, it had become Belgium's most important car manufacturer, but poor sales in the first half of the 1930s forced it into a merger with Imperia, the other major Belgian manufacturer. Neither marque did well in the years which followed. The Minerva name all but disappeared, while the Imperia name was applied mainly to German Adlers built under licence.

After the 1939-1945 war, neither company was in a position to produce an entirely new car. However, the experience of licence-building Adlers had convinced the company's head, Monsieur Van Roggan, of the value of this form of manufacture. As British manufacturers were under pressure to export vehicles, it was to them that he turned for ideas and, from Standard, he obtained a licence for Imperia to assemble Vanguards in Belgium.

Casting around for opportunities to revive the Minerva name, Van Roggen was not slow to recognise the possibilities raised by the Belgian Army's quest for a new lightweight 4x4 vehicle. He immediately turned to the Rover Company to ask whether it would be prepared to allow Minerva to build Land-Rovers in Belgium under licence for the Belgian Army, provided that he was able to secure the contract.

The deal

Van Roggen made his approach to Rover in the late spring of 1951. To the British company, the deal sounded promising, and so negotiations went ahead. On 21st June, the Rover Board learned that a total of 2,500 vehicles would be required and that the major competitor for the contract was Willys. Van Roggen pursued the Belgian authorities and Rover doggedly over that summer, and in early October, he was able to sew up the deal. The Rover Compa-

In this rear view, note the distinctive hood, the jerry-can holder, the spare wheel location and the cross-member without a PTO aperture ▷

The bulkhead area also differed in several respects from British-built Land-Rovers. The chassis number ◁ *plate, however, was the standard Solihull type*

Land Rovers

ny would supply CKD chassis and other parts to Minerva's factory at Mortsel, near Antwerp, and Minerva would build its own adaptation of the Land-Rover to suit Belgian military requirements. An agreement was signed between Rover and Minerva on 7th May 1952.

Production of Land-Rovers appears to have started at Mortsel more or less immediately afterwards. In June 1952, Rover received a letter of appreciation from the Belgian Army, praising the high quality of the Land-Rovers supplied through Minerva; and in September, the original order for 2,500 vehicles was increased by 3,400. By the time the formal contract for these extra vehicles was signed in march 1953, that figure had become 3,421.

This appears to have been the last order Minerva received from the Belgian Army, but there could well have been more Minerva Land-Rovers than the 5,921 which was the combined total of the Belgian Army orders. There were probably no other military Minervas, even though the terms of the

agreement with Rover did permit the Belgian company to supply Land-Rovers on a non-exclusive basis to military customers in the continental European countries of the Atlantic Pact (i.e. NATO). However, the terms of the agreement did change in 1954, and it looks as if Minerva was then permitted to sell its Land-Rovers on the civilian market in some countries. By April 1955, for example, Rover was involved in approving a distributorship for Minerva Land-Rovers in the Belgian Congo. How many civilian Minervas there were and where they were sold remain uncertain at present, although it seems clear that they were available only in the standard Solihull colours of Dark Green and Light Grey.

Problems

The relationship between Minerva and the Rover Company was not always a happy one and, in September 1954, Minerva commenced legal proceedings against Rover for the recovery of £125,000 alleged to be due and for damages arising out of

alleged breach of contract. Exactly what the problem was is not revealed in the Rover Board Minutes of the time, but it is clear that the Rover directors wanted to settle out of court, and quickly.

It is not difficult to guess what the problem might have been, though. All the vehicles supplied to Minerva were 2-litre 80-inch models, to 1952/1953 specification, and, in fact, Rover appears to have built the whole lot during the 1952 and 1953 model-years and stockpiled them, releasing them in batches to Minerva over the next three years. This in itself cannot have been the cause of friction between the two companies; but the fact was that the 80-inch had been superseded by the 86-inch in autumn 1953, and the original 2-litre engine had been superseded by the "spreadbore" 2-litre in autumn 1954.

By the autumn of 1954, the CKD Land-Rovers being supplied to Minerva were well and truly outmoded. Add to that the fact that Rover had agreed to supply Tempo in Germany with 86-inch CKD chas-

△ *This Minerva assault vehicle, now preserved in a museum, lacks the grilles normally fitted in front of the headlamps*

Minerva for para-dropping, standing on the trolley from which it would be loaded into an aircraft. The vehicle stands on a wooden frame, and there are sandbags between chassis/axles and frame to absorb the impact of landing. All glass is taped up. The "load" in the rear is the parachute pack ▷

sis after first supplying 80-inch versions, and it is clear that Minerva must have felt insulted as well as injured.

The dispute was settled quickly. Van Roggen visited London at the end of November, when he met Rover's managing director, Spencer Wilks, and its commercial director, George Farmer. The outcome was that Minerva agreed to withdraw its two writs on condition that Rover supplied a further 900 CKD 'sets' at a reduced price, paid the £125,000 in full and released the Belgian company from the restrictions of the May 1952 agreement. To these conditions, Rover agreed.

Whether those 900 'sets' were part of the 5,921 vehicles ordered by the military is not clear. One way or another, Rover was still supplying CKD vehicles to fulfil that order for 900 as late as January 1956. By this stage, Minerva had almost certainly begun to develop its own lightweight 4x4 – the C-20 – and the Rover Board had quite clearly had enough.

In the event, agreement was reached that

Minerva's contract with Rover should terminate with effect from 30th June 1956. Minerva announced its C-20 later that year, but the vehicle was not a success and proved to be the last ever to bear the Minerva name.

The Rover Company engaged the old-established Brussels firm of Beherman Demoen as its new importers and, under the more relaxed trading conditions of the mid-1950s, began to export standard Solihull-built Land-Rovers to Belgium.

The vehicles

The vehicles supplied by Rover to Minerva were, of course, not complete CKD packs. Part of the agreement was that Minerva should fit a body of its own design and manufacture, with the effect that Rover needed only to supply rolling chassis. These were on the 80-inch wheelbase, and had left-hand-drive and 2-litre 'siamese-bore' engines, and all were numbered as 1952 or (mostly) 1953-season CKD vehicles, identified with an initial 2663 or 3663

in the chassis number.

There were some oddities, however: at least one vehicle was built on a right-hand-drive chassis in January 1953, and at least one was built on a left-hand-drive 86-inch chassis towards the end of that year. Where these two fit into the Minerva story remains a mystery, and it would be intriguing to know the history of the 86-inch, in particular. Was it, perhaps, built to demonstrate to Solihull that an 86-inch Minerva was a viable vehicle?

Minerva's body, designed of course to meet Belgian Army requirements, was very different from the standard 80-inch body built at Solihull. For a start, it was made of steel instead of Birmabright aluminium alloy. The front wings were angular and had sloping fronts instead of the neatly-curved shape of Solihull's product, and the grille was unique, recalling the pre-War Minerva grille and carrying a large Minerva badge. The small apertures on either side of the main grille opening in the front panel were covered by slatted oval panels, and

△ *A mystery: this is an 86-inch steel-bodied Minerva, built in 1953 and apparently a prototype. Note the unique door handles*

the front bumper was fitted with a single "pigtail" open towing eye on the driver's side.

The doors were made of steel as well, of course, and they lacked the external handles fitted to Solihull's Land-Rovers since the introduction of the 2-litre models in August 1951. There was a single ventilator panel running all the way across the bottom of the windscreen, and the windscreen, windscreen clips and bulkhead were all different from their Solihull equivalents. Instruments and controls, however, were the same as on standard 1953-model Land-Rovers.

Moving further back, the rear body lacked the galvanised cappings of the Solihull vehicles. Instead of a drop-down tailgate, it also had a fixed rear panel. Mounted to this were a jerry-can holder on the left-hand (driver's) side and the spare wheel on the other side. The rear crossmember was also plain, lacking the PTO aperture. Lastly, the canvas top fitted to all Minerva Land-Rovers was also completely different from the contemporary Rover item.

One source claims that only the first deliveries of Minerva Land-Rovers were put into service straight off the production lines, and that large numbers were stockpiled for future use. These were then gradually introduced into service to replace the older vehicles as these wore out. If this is true, it does help to explain why many of the Minerva Land-Rovers now appearing on the civilian market have remarkably low mileages, in spite of an age in excess of 35 years.

In service

The military Minervas were used by the Belgian Ground Forces, Air Force and Navy, as well as by the Gendarmerie. Most became General Service vehicles, although there were also several adaptations to suit special requirements.

Some Minervas were converted to field ambulances, carrying two stretchers supported by an outrigged section behind the tail panel. Some were used as review and parade vehicles (when the VIP stood alongside the passenger and held on to the windscreen frame for support).

Yet others were converted to "assault vehicles", with the spare wheel mounted ahead of the grille panel and parallel to the sloping wing fronts, on which the headlights had been relocated. No doubt there were other variations, too.

Today, these ex-military Minervas are readily available from specialist dealerships in the Low Countries. Some have been re-equipped and modified in much the same way as British enthusiasts modify the ex-military Lightweight Land Rover; and some have been rebuilt with "standard" Land Rover front wings and other items.

I am grateful to Henk Bruers, Robin Craig, Huub Houben and Brian Norman for help with this episode of the Land Rover Story. References to the minutes of the Rover Board meetings are made with the kind permission of BMIHT/Rover Group.

Anyone in the UK who is interested in obtaining a Minerva should contact Brian Norman through James Taylor.

Update

Further information has come to light since this feature was written. The Rover Board Minutes for 3rd March 1955 refer to the cessation of Minerva deliveries some time early in the then-current financial year - presumably about the time when Minerva issued its writs, which was in September 1954. From the same source, we learn on 28th February 1956 that Minerva had established a credit to cover 72 CKD "sets", thus leaving 180 to be supplied out of the 900 ordered.

Civilian Minervas may also have been available in colours which were not offered by Solihull. Owner Richard Hughes reports that his example is finished in a maroon paint which was certainly not available on British-built vehicles.

THE LAND ROVER STORY

STAND
PARA.CDO

86" WHEELBASE

WEATHER-PROOF COVER AND DOOR WINDOWS
ARE PROVIDED AS STANDARD EQUIPMENT

LAND ROVER

The 86-in. wheelbase, four-wheel drive Land-Rover is the general workhorse of the range, providing the sort of go-anywhere transport that is needed on farms, ranches, estates and indeed in any situation where versatility and cross-country mobility are required. It can operate as a completely open vehicle or be fully enclosed by the weather-proof canvas hood. In either event the body provides excellent accommodation for three people and loads of up to 1,000 lb. 454 kg.

All body panels are of non-rusting aluminium; steel portions, such as hinges, handles and reinforcements being galvanised to resist corrosion. The vehicle is thus not affected by weather or climate and can work incessantly under the most appalling conditions.

To add to its almost unlimited field of operation, the Land-Rover is provided with centre and rear power take-off points enabling many varied types of machinery to be driven.

All in all the Land-Rover can justly claim to be the world's most versatile vehicle.

Contempory sales material for the 86-inch models. Postcard-sized colour copies of these items are available from LRO Mail Order

Making light work of heavy duty . . .

- FOUR-WHEEL DRIVE
- EIGHT SPEEDS FORWARD AND TWO REVERSE
- FIXED WEATHERPROOF CAB
- OUTSTANDING PERFORMANCE ON AND OFF THE ROAD

ALL OVER THE WORLD, the 4-wheel drive Land-Rover is proving itself the toughest and most versatile vehicle ever designed. With a powerful 52 b.h.p. engine incorporating new long-life features, the 107" wheelbase model shown above has a payload space 57" wide and a full 6' long. In industry or on the land, as a load or passenger carrier, wherever the work is hard and the going tough, the long wheelbase Land-Rover is giving magnificent service. A de-luxe model is available with numerous refinements for the extra comfort of driver and passengers.

The Standard long wheelbase model (107") Land-Rover with comfortable, weatherproof cab. The canvas hood is available as an optional extra.

THE LONG WHEELBASE (107") *LAND ROVER*

MADE BY THE ROVER COMPANY LTD · SOLIHULL · BIRMINGHAM AND DEVONSHIRE HOUSE · LONDON

In this interior view of an unrestored 86-inch Tempo, the extra switch panel can be seen between he steering wheel and the standard two-dial panel in the centre

The Tempo Land Rovers

THIS MONTH, James Taylor looks into the history of some more curious Land-Rovers which were built abroad.

DURING THE first half of the 1950s, the Rover Company was constantly involved in discussions and negotiations about producing Land-Rovers abroad. Many of these discussions did not bear fruit; but others did, such as those with Minerva in Belgium, at whose products we looked last month.

The first approach to Rover about building Land-Rovers abroad under licence came from Automobiles Talbot in France as early as 1949. As recorded in an earlier episode of the Land Rover Story (see *LRO* February 1992), the Land-Talbot did not even get as far as the drawing-board; but at least two other French manufacturers also showed an interest in building Land-Rovers in France.

Few details of the negotiations with these two other manufacturers survive, but it is clear from the minutes of Rover Board meetings that the French military authorities were seeking a lightweight 4x4 and had put the contract out to tender in the customary fashion. Both Decauville – presumably not related to the original French company which had been wound up in 1910 – and Renault were in the running, and both must have approached Rover some time in 1955.

Decauville dropped out first, probably during April 1956, but Renault continued to negotiate over that summer and into the

autumn. Then, on 20th November 1956, the Rover Board was told that the deal with Renault was off. No reason had been given, but the Board was aware that the French military contract had gone to Hotchkiss, who were to produce Willys Jeeps under licence, and assumed that was the reason why Renault had lost interest.

Rover followed up swiftly, however, and Managing Director Spencer Wilks reported to the Board on 18th December that he had put a new proposal to Renault. This was that the Rover Company should build Land-Rovers in France, and that Renault should supply the engines to go into them. The French company did not agree to this, however, and nothing more was heard about the production or assembly of Land Rovers in France.

As noted last month, negotiations with Minerva had meanwhile begun in 1951. In September or October 1952, Rover also entered discussions with Premier Motors in India about CKD assembly of Land-Rovers in that country; but nothing seems to have come of the idea. The next approach came from Brazil in May or June 1953, where the local importer had already set up a company to assemble Land-Rovers in anticipation of reaching agreement with Rover. Negotiations were protracted, however, and finally fizzled out in September 1958.

Equally protracted were negotiations with Santana in Spain, where production of Land-Rovers did not begin until Novem-

ber 1958, even though discussions with Rover had begun in May or June 1953. There were also discussions with the Pressed Metal Corporation in Australia, which began in June 1955 and did eventually lead to CKD manufacture in that country. Lastly, there were also sucessful discussions with Tempo in Germany.

In the beginning

The first the Rover Board heard about negotiations with Tempo was on 22nd January 1953, when Spencer Wilks and Commerical Director George Farmer reported on their recent visit to Germany to meet Oscar Vidal, Managing Director of Vidal und Sohn (who used the Tempo trade mark). The subject of this meeting had been the partial manufacture of Land Rovers by Vidal's company.

Just as in the case of Talbot, Decauville, Renault and Minerva, the catalyst for these discussions had been a military contract which had been put out to tender. In this case, the military authority concerned was the West German Bundesgrenzchutz (BGS, or Border Patrol Guard), which was responsible for patrolling the border with East Germany. The BGS wanted 250 rugged six-seater vehicles which would be suitable for these patrol duties, and Oscar Vidal saw in this requirement an opportunity to provide work for his company.

By the early 1950s, Vidal und Sohn were well established as manufacturers of light

△ *This front view of an 86-inch Tempo shows the unique lighting arrangement in the wing fronts, the external horn, the capstan winch and the extra indicator lamps on the wing sides. The folding hoodsticks can just be seen at the rear*

commercial and light military vehicles. The commercials had begun in the 1930s with three-wheelers and, in 1949, had been supplemented by the four-wheeled, forward-control Matador. Matadors were used by a number of European military authorities as general haulage vehicles, but Tempo's real reputation in military circles rested with its astonishing G1200 Field Car, a 4x4 first seen in the late 1930s.

This reputation was undoubtedly a factor in Vidal's ability to convince the BGS that it could meet the requirement for a border patrol vehicle. As the Tempo factory in Hamburg was then in the British Occupation Zone, it was also axiomatic that Vidal should turn to a British company for his partner in this new venture. Negotiations with Rover went ahead with all speed, and the first Tempo-built Land-Rovers appear to have come off the assembly lines in Hamburg early in 1953.

The Tempo 80-inch

The BGS requirement for its new border patrol vehicles must have been fairly urgent, for it would have made better sense for Tempo not to start production until the summer of 1953, when the new 86-inch chassis would be available. As it was, the first Tempo Land-Rovers were built on left-hand-drive 80-inch chassis with the 2-litre engine, all sent out to Hamburg from Solihull in CKD form. Exactly how many were made is not clear, but perhaps fewer than 100 Tempo Land-Rovers had the 80-inch chassis.

Vidal und Sohn's contribution to the vehicles was the bodywork, which was made of steel instead of Birmabright aluminium alloy. It also differed considerably from the bodywork offered on the standard vehicles from Solihull. The most obvious difference was in the height of the body sides; where the Solihull doors and rear body sides lined up with the wing tops, the Tempo items lined up with the top of the front scuttle. the recess around the external door handles was also different from the simple cut-out on Solihull-built vehicles, and the folding framework for the canvas top was attached to the rear body sides. Lifting handles were provided under the rear body sides, behind the wheels.

The rear load-bed was taken up by two inward-facing bench seats, each capable of seating two border guards, and there were only two seats in the front of the vehicle. There was, however, plenty of storage space; there were lockers built into the tops of the front wings, and a large flat locker on top of the bonnet. The spare wheel was mounted on the rear panel. Most vehicles appear to have been fitted with a heater, a front-mounted capstan winch driven from the crankshaft, and a pair of sirens on the front dumb-irons below the headlamps.

Lastly, there were additional electrical items, backed-up by a negative-earth system with a high-capacity Bosch dynamo. All but the two-way radio (not fitted to every vehicle) were controlled from an additional panel mounted above the standard instrument panel in the centre of the dash; this incorporated a direction indicator switch, a switch for the sirens, a siren tuner, and a switch for a flashing blue light. The position of this light on the vehicle is not clear, but it might have been on the driver's side of the bonnet, where pictures show an additional lamp.

The Tempo 86-inch

When Solihull switched from the 80-inch wheelbase to the 86-inch wheelbase over the summer of 1953, the CKD chassis sent out to Hamburg also switched to the 86-inch wheelbase. Very little redesign work was necessary, but Vidal did take the opportunity to improve the vehicles in a number of areas. All the remaining BGS vehicles had the 86-inch wheelbase; again, exact figures are not available, but it would be reasonable to suppose that around 150 were built. The 86-inch Tempo was also offered on the civilian market in Germany, but not many were sold. Production of both the BGS and civilian Tempo Land-Rovers probably stopped in 1955, when Oscar Vidal sold a half-share in his company to Hanomag.

On the 86-inch models, Tempo extended the rear body sides to incorporate the extra length in the chassis. The spare wheel was repositioned, Solihull-fashion, on the bonnet, and the large bonnet locker disappeared. The hinged lockers in the front

△ *This rear view of a restored 86-inch Tempo Land Rover now in Holland shows the unique rear lights and jerrycan stowage arrangement*

wings remained, however. Lighting arrangements changed, and the front wings now incorporated an indicator lamp as well as a side light. Parking lamps, showing white to the front and red to the rear, were fitted to the wing sides to meet current German regulations, and there were additional lights mounted on stalks on the front wings, presumably intended as some kind of marker or convoy lamps. An additional feature was a loud hailer, mounted on the passenger side front wing..

Seating arrangements remained as before, with inward-facing benches in the load bed and just two seats up front. The dashboard, however, now had the two larger dials associated with Solihull-built 86-inch models and the additional switches had been displaced to a panel between the steering wheel and the main instrument board. They now included a dial gauge which was presumably either a volt meter or an ammeter.

Afterlife

The BGS replaced most of its Tempo Land Rovers in the late 1960s. By this time, Tempo no longer existed as a separate company (it had been fully absorbed by Hanomag in 1963), and so the Rover Company provided versions of the Series IIA 88-inch Land-Rover. Many BGS Tempos were sold off on the to the civilian market, although about 100 were transferred to the Budeswehr (West German Army), where they had a further lease of life. As far as it is possible to tell, none remains in service today.

I am grateful to Stan Wouters for help with this episode of the Land Rover Story, and acknowledge my debt to a feature on Tempo products which appeared in Wheels and Tracks magazine, issue 35, during 1991. References to the minutes of the Rover Board meetings are made with the kind permission of BMIHT/Rover Group.

THE LAND ROVER STORY

△ *1957 Series One 88 inch diesel*

Series One 88s

James Taylor tells the story of the final Series Is – stretched by two inches and then given a diesel engine option as well.

IT WAS not until 1954 that the Rover Company devoted any serious thought to the development of a diesel engine for the Land-Rover. Sales of the vehicle had already exceeded the company's original expectations by a huge margin, and it was no doubt with some reluctance that the company committed the resources necessary to widen the range's appeal through the enlarged 86-inch and 107-inch models during 1953. But it was probably their arrival, more than anything else, which started the company thinking that it should develop its world-beating product even further.

Two things happened in 1954 to focus Rover's thinking on diesel power for the Land-Rover. The first was the appointment of a sales director to oversee and strengthen the company's sales side. The second was the proposed merger with Standard, who had already developed a small diesel engine of 2.1-litres for use in saloon cars and tractors. The new sales director, Allan Botwood, was well aware that diesel power was almost universal in the commercial vehicle world and that most Land-Rovers were being bought for commercial use. It was he, then, who urged Rover to consider a diesel option for the Land-Rover as a high priority.

For a time during the first half of 1954, it looked as if the Standard engine might answer Rover's need for a Land-Rover diesel. However, it was a short-lived hope. The merger did not work out and, during the negotiation phase, the Rover engineers had in any case established that the Standard engine would not fit into the existing production Land-Rover. This left the company no real option but to build its own diesel engine; but there were many obstacles to be overcome before a Rover diesel could go into production.

Rover had of course already had some brushes with large diesel engines, in the shape of the 18-litre, 250bhp, Meteorite V8 which it manufactured for the Thornycroft Mighty Antar heavy haulage tractor. Downscaling this technology, however, was less than straightforward.

There was an even bigger obstacle in that there was simply nowhere for the company to make a new engine: all the available factory space had already been gobbled up by the constant expansion of Land-Rover production. And finally, there was also the problem that setting up new plant and machinery was going to demand considerable financial outlay.

Fortunately, the Rover Board did find a way forward. Space in the Acocks Green engine plant was expected to become free some time around 1955 or 1956 when Ministry of Supply orders for the Meteor V12 tank engine which Rover was building were fulfilled. So it was that, on 27th January 1955, the Rover Board approved managing director Spencer Wilks' formal proposal that diesel engine production should be established at Acocks Green as soon as capacity became available. It must have been shortly afterwards that technical Director Maurice Wilks asked his chief engine designer, Jack Swaine, to start work on a new Rover diesel engine for the Land-Rover.

In order to minimise the expenditure on design work and on new tooling, Wilks in fact asked Swaine to draw up a basic design which could also be adapted as a petrol engine: that way, if the expected demand for a diesel Land-Rover did not materialise, Rover would at least be able to put the petrol version of the new design into production as a replacement for the existing 2-litre IOE engine. Whether the plan was this clear-cut from the beginning of the project is not certain, but the two engines were certainly designed in parallel once serious work had got under way.

Designing the diesel

The design of the diesel engine seems to have been completed with considerable speed. The first prototypes were probably ready by the end of 1955, and the first prototype vehicles took to the roads as early as March and April 1956. The petrol versions of the engine, which of course had a larger bore and were intended for introduction some time after the diesels, were probably not far behind.

During the design phase of the new

△ *Series One 109 with truck cab and tilt*

and 109s

engine, it had become clear that a capacity of at lease 2 litres would be necessary in order to provide adequate performance. As diesel engines had to be more robust than petrol engines in order to cope with the greater stresses of the compression-ignition cycle, Rover's new 2-litre diesel would have to be physically larger than its existing 2-litre petrol engine. It was only prudent to allow during the design stage for capacity and power increases in the engine's later production life, with the result that the planned new diesel engine became too large to fit comfortably within the engine bay of the 86-inch and 107-inch Land-Rovers then in production.

The problem was soon solved. The Rover Board granted £240,100 on 28th February 1956 to cover tooling changes which would allow the Land-Rover's engine bay to be stretched by two inches; by this time the engineers had presumably already done the necessary design work. However, it obviously made good sense to spread the investment in new tooling over as long a period as possible, and the diesel engine itself would not go into production until the following financial year was well under way.

Contemporary press references to the extra two inches in the Land-Rover's wheelbases are hard to find, which reflects the success of the publicity strategy Rover adopted. This was to refer to the new models as "Regular" and "Long" Land-Rovers, so that their actual wheelbase lengths did

not have to be mentioned, and to focus press interest on the 107-inch Station Wagon, which was in fact several months old by the time the 88-inch and 109-inch models went on sale in September 1956.

Many customers probably did not even realise that there was any difference between these longer Land-Rovers and the superseded 86-inch and 107-inch types: it was (and still is) hard to spot the difference. The most reliable indications, however, are the position of the front wing lower retaining bolt (further behind the wheel on 88s and 109s), and the presence of only one aperture (instead of three) in the grille panel on 88s and 109s.

The diesel engine

The Rover engineers can have found very few examples of successful small-capacity diesel engines to study, but no doubt they had taken a close look at those built by Mercedes-Benz (a 1.7-litre OHV four-cylinder) and by Standard (a 2.1-litre OHV four-cylinder). Also clear is that they consulted Ricardo Engineering, whose involvement with small-capacity diesel engine design dated back to the mid-1930s.

As all modern designs, whether petrol or diesel, were now using overhead valves, Jack Swaine's choice of this layout for the new Rover engine was predictable. For strength, he decided on all-iron construction and, to make rebuilding cheap and simple when bore wear became excessive, he chose to use a wet-lined block.

Particularly noteworthy in the Rover design were the roller tappets in the engine's valve train, which were less prone to wear than the pad-type of the IOE petrol engines. Aluminium-alloy pistons were fitted on conrods shaped so as to be easily withdrawn up the bores when a major overhaul was needed, and the involvement of Ricardo Engineering was revealed in the engine's adoption of the Ricardo Comet V combustion chamber design. Pintaux-type injection nozzles were specified, and the CAV injection pump had a mechanical governor.

With 51bhp at 3,500rpm and 87lb/ft of torque at 2,000rpm, the 2052cc production diesel engine compared quite favourably with the 1997cc petrol unit, which then boasted 52bhp at 3,500rpm and 101lb/ft at 1,500rpm. One important result was that Rover found no need to change other elements in the Land-Rover's power train; and the diesel engine was, in theory, directly interchangeable with the petrol engine in 88-inch and 109-inch models.

The diesel engine did have one big failing, however, and that was combustion noise. As anyone who has ever driven an early example will agree, the 2-litre diesel was a raucous, unrefined-sounding engine which made long journeys a real trial. The very first engines were also prone to cylinder head cracking, although Rover attended to this as a running modification during the 1958 model-year.

Add to that the fact that the diesel Land -

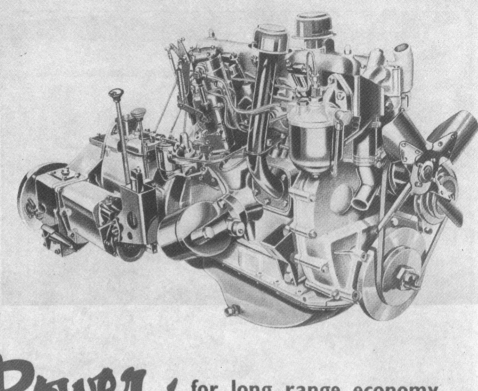

The 2-litre diesel engine of Rover design and construction gives further versatility to the Land-Rover by increasing its efficiency and economy in conditions favouring diesel operation. A truly rugged, four-cylinder unit, the Rover diesel engine develops 51 b.h.p. at 3,500 r.p.m. Its speed range is sufficiently close to that of the Land-Rover petrol engine that the same transmission units may be used for both.

DIESEL *Power* for long range economy

△ *2-litre diesel engine from a sales brochure of the day*

Rover – especially in long-wheelbase form – accelerated much more slowly than its petrol-engined equivalent, and it is clear that its appeal lay in other qualities. No doubt many customers hoped for the diesel engine's traditional reliability and longevity, and there can be little doubt that they got both of these; but probably the diesel's biggest attraction was its fuel economy.

According to an early publicity handout, "under normal operating conditions a 50percent saving in fuel consumption can be achieved as compared with petrol engined vehicles". And, in many of Land-Rover's overseas markets, diesel fuel was considerably less expensive than petrol to buy.

On sale

The 88-inch and 109-inch Land-Rovers arrived on the market at a bad time for Rover's sales. Demand was low; Land-Rover production had been reduced to 540 units a week, and the Car Assembly Shop started working a three-day week during September 1956. Production of the 1956-season 86-inch and 107-inch models was halted early, and the new 88-inch and 109-inch models went into production immediately after the annual works summer holiday. To protect their dealers, who still had stocks of the old models, however, Rover agreed not to make any deliveries of the new vehicles until after the end of August.

Sales continued at a low level when the 88-inch and 109-inch Land-Rovers reached the showrooms. With the motor industry already suffering hard times, the Suez Canal crisis erupted in autumn 1956 to make matters worse. With the introduction of petrol rationing after Nasser closed the

Canal to oil tankers, home market demand dropped off sharply.

Car sales were hit very badly indeed, and the Car Assembly Shop began working a three-day week in September. By January 1957, things were also looking gloomy on the Land-Rover front, as the Ministry of Supply was also expected to reduce its orders, and Land-Rover production was accordingly cut back to 520 units a week.

By February, the situation was worse. The Ministry of Supply had still not renewed its contract, and Land-Rover production was cut back yet again to 470 units per week. No doubt the Rover directors had their fingers firmly crossed behind their backs when they learned, on 26th February, that the new diesel engine would enter production in May or June and that Land-Rover production was to be increased to 520 units a week to cope with the expected demand.

Fortunately, the sales situation did improve. The Suez Canal was re-opened in April, and petrol rationing was ended. That month, the Rover directors agreed to increase Land-Rover production to 545 units a week by the end of July in order to allow for demand for the new diesel models. Even so, when demand did recover in earnest, during June and July, the company found itself unable to keep up with orders because its component suppliers were unable to increase their production to cope.

From then on, the situation got better and better. By the end of October 1957, Land-Rover production stood at 630 units a week; in January 1958 it went up to 660; and from April, it was increased again to 700 a week. Nevertheless, the problems of the 1957 model-year did persuade the

Rover directors to hold back the introduction of the Series II models until it was clear that sales had stabilised again: at the Board meeting on 24th October 1957, they agreed to put back the Series II launch by two months.

As the extra two inches in the wheelbases of the 88-inch and 109-inch Land-Rovers had been inserted forward of the front bulkhead, the bodywork fitted by Rover to the 86-inch and 107-inch vehicles needed no alteration. This was good news for the conversion specialists, too, for they did not need to alter their Land-Rover designs. As a result, the specialist conversions offered on 86-inch and 107-inch vehicles were also generally available on the 88-inch and 109-inch chassis.

Many 88-inch and 109-inch Series I Land-Rovers also went to military customers. The British Army used the same "Rover Mk.4" designation for the 109-inch model as it had for the 107-inch, but the 88-inch Land-Rover became a "Rover Mk.5". Interesting to note is that the War Department ordered a single 109-inch Land-Rover fitted with a Turner two-stroke, three-cylinder diesel engine. This order was placed in May/June 1957, by which time the British Army had probably already worked out that the 109-inch with Rover's own 2-litre diesel would be a gutless beast. The Turner engine, actually an Austrian Jenbach design built under licence in Britain, had been available as a conversion unit for Land-Rovers since 1954, but was never popular (see LRO, May 1991).

In the meantime, however, the Rover Company had been addressing the question of Land-Rover conversions, and had established a new organisation to deal with these.

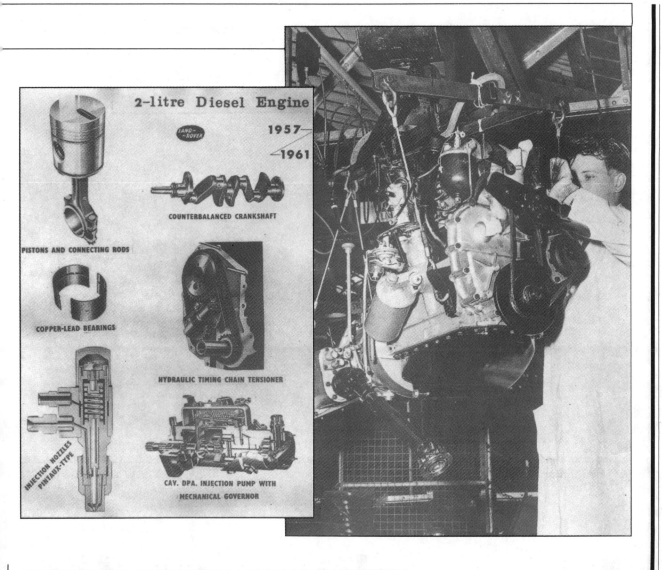

SERIES I 88-INCH AND 109-INCH LAND-ROVER PRODUCTION

1956 models (petrol only)
Chassis numbers beginning

1116/1126/1136/1146/1156 (88-inch)		2,270
1216/1226/1236/1246/1256 (109-inch)		1,152
	Total:	3,422

1956 diesel prototypes
Chassis numbers beginning

1166 (88-inch)		6
1266 (109-inch)		1
	Total:	7

1957 models
Chassis numbers beginning

1118/1128/1138/1148/1158 (88-inch petrol)		13,977
1167 (88-inch diesel)		298
1217/1227/1237/1247/1257 (109-inch petrol)		8,475
1267 (109-inch diesel)		153
	Total:	22,903

1958 models
Chassis numbers beginning

1118/1128/1138/1148/1158 (88-inch petrol)		7,338
1168/1178/1188/1198/1208 (88-inch diesel)		2,055
1218/1228/1238/1248/1258 (109-inch petrol)		5,405
1268/1278/1288/1298/1308 (109-inch diesel)		946
	Total:	15,744

GRAND TOTALS:		
	88-inch petrol	23,585
	88-inch diesel	2,359
	109-inch petrol	15,032
	109-inch diesel	1,100
	Overall, Ser.I 88/109	**42,076**

There were no 1956-model Station Wagons on the 88-inch chassis. The 88-inch Station Wagon arrived with the 1957 model-year vehicles, and all examples were numbered in sequence with other 88-inch types.

The 4x2 88s

Towards the end of Series I production, Rover built a special batch of 88-inch models with rear-wheel drive only. These 4x2 vehicles were produced specially for the War Department. There were 655 of them, ordered under contract 6/Veh/26222 on 1st November 1957, and all were described as "88-inch petrol, standard spec, 4x2, Mk.5". They were delivered in 1958 and were registered in the xxCExx series. As Robert Ivins explained in *LRO* for September 1991, they were withdrawn from active service after just five years. Some were used for driver training, but most went to the Ministry of Public Works in 1963 and were re-registered with reversed FUV civilian numbers.

It is not clear why the War Department wanted them in the first place, but it is clear that they also ordered some 4x2 Series IIs in August 1958, and that these met the same fate as the Series Is. Relatively few of these two-wheel-drive Land Rovers still survive with their original undriven front axles and modified transfer boxes.

△ *Welding equipment was still available, although Rover had long since stopped making Welder models at Solihull. This is a Lincoln LR150 welder, mounted on the tailboard of an early Series II Land-Rover*

Approved conversions

James Taylor explains how Rover tried to bring the conversion market under control during the late 1950s.

THE DEVELOPMENT of a conversions industry around the Land-Rover in the first half of the 1950s was inevitable. When Maurice Wilks had first conceived the vehicle, he had briefed has designers to make it as adaptable as possible, though it is unlikely that he ever imagined Rover would be able to manufacture all the add-ons which users were likely to want in order to make the vehicle suite their individual requirements.

One way or another, Rover could not and did not produce all the add-ons, and its own attempts to make adaptations in-house were never very successful. The Welder simply did not sell, and the Fire Engine probably caused the company more trouble than it was worth because it was impossible to manufacture the vehicle to a single specification which would suit every customer; as every Chief Fire Officer had his own views about equipment types, Rover spent an inordinate amount of time adapting the basic vehicle on what was often a one-off basis.

Meanwhile, those companies which already specialised in vehicle conversions for commercial users had seen the Land-Rover's potential and had started to exploit it. As early as 1948, Dorman Industries had adapted their crop-spraying equipment to fit the land-Rover, and this had been followed by Bullows with their compressor and by a number of others. However, it was the introduction of the 107-inch long-wheelbase Land-Rover which really made the commercial vehicle converters sit up and take notice. The 107-inch model was large enough to take bodies which had to carry a lot of equipment (such as the mobile cinemas built by British Films) and to take bodies which needed its extra length (such as the ambulances in which Pilchers specialised).

It was at this time, too, that Rover's Managing Director, Spencer Wilks, recognised the need to strengthen the company's sales side, and during 1954 he brought in Allan Botwood as its first Sales Director. Botwood established a new Sales Division, which set about earning its keep by reminding dealers and customers alike of the vast variety of uses to which the Land-Rover could be put. Among these users were of course many which depended on equipment or bodies available only from specialist manufacturers.

The inevitable and gratifying result was that orders started flowing in for specially-converted Land-Rovers. However, Rover had not foreseen the complications that this would cause. The conversion specialists and equipment suppliers of course needed to liaise with Land-Rover engineers in order to ensure that their conversions would not over-tax the vehicles to which they were applied, and in due course the Rover Company found itself handling a large volume of time-consuming enquiries and requests for help for which it had neither a budget nor the staff.

Rover struggled to cope. The responsibility for finding specialist equipment and other items needed to create a customer's adaptation was given to the Service Department, while the responsibility for ensuring that the adaptation worked without detriment to the basic vehicle was given to the

△ *Conversions gradually became more weird and wonderful. This is the Dixon-Bate articulated Land-Rover conversion. This picture was taken in 1961, but the conversion probably became available towards the end of 1960*

–the Technical Sales Department

Engineering Division. This was an arrangement which suited nobody. The Service Department lacked the specialist knowledge to do the job properly, and did not in any case have enough staff. In the Engineering Division, any work on special adaptations inevitably took staff away from development work on the company's mainstream products, with the result that important work was constantly being delayed. As cars and Land-Rovers were developed in the same department, the problems were far-reaching. It was clear that Rover needed a dedicated group of engineers to deal with Land-Rover conversions, and to this end, Technical Director Maurice Wilks decided to create a new Technical Sales Department.

The idea for such a department had actually been around since 1952, when Peter Wilks (Maurice Wilks' nephew) and George Mackie had discussed it. No doubt – though Mackie does not say so in his contribution to Ken and Julie Slavin's book, Land-Rover, the unbeatable 4x4 – they were hoping to create jobs for themselves back at Rover after the failure of the

Marauder sports car business for which they had left Rover some two years earlier. At the time, though, they agreed that there was probably insufficient demand for such a department at Rover, and took the idea no further.

What then appears to have happened is that, as soon as Maurice Wilks started thinking about creating a Technical Sales Department, George Mackie (who was now back at Rover) seized his opportunity to become involved. This must have been some time late in 1956, Wilks agreed with Mackie's proposals for the new department, but told him that he did not want it within his Engineering Division but rather within the Sales Division, which was now being run by his fellow Director Geoffrey Lloyd-Dixon, Mackie's first job, therefore, was to persuade Lloyd-Dixon and his colleagues of the wisdom of this arrangement!

It took time, Mackie has spoken of a year's determined lobbying before Lloyd-Dixon agree, and of a last-minute volte-face by the Sales Director, who was probably rather preoccupied with the company's tumbling sales at the end of 1956.. The sit-

uation was finally resolved by means of Maurice Wilks' direct intervention, however, and in January 1957 George Mackie became Manager of the new Technical Sales Department within Rover's Sales Division.

The Technical Sales Department took on those members of the Engineering Division who had become most involved in liaison with the Land-Rover converters, and started work. While liaison already established carried on, George Mackie made a study of how tractor manufacturers coped with specialist equipment and conversion manufacturers, and concluded that Rover should establish a system for "approving" land-Rover conversions.

What this meant in practice was that the Technical Sales Department would conduct trials of equipment and conversions proposed by the specialist manufacturers in order to determine whether they would interfere with the correct functioning of the vehicle. If the equipment or conversion proved not to compromise the Land-Rover's engineering integrity, and proved to be of a quality which would not bring

EAGLE

3 CUB. YD. REFUSE BODY

As approved by the Rover Co. Ltd. for use with the . . . . .

LAND-ROVER

AN ALL STEEL TIPPING BODY

OF LARGE CAPACITY

SPECIALLY DESIGNED

FOR

THE HYGIENIC COLLECTION OF REFUSE

THE EAGLE ENGINEERING CO. LTD.
P.O. BOX No. 43
EAGLE WORKS • WARWICK • ENGLAND
Telephone 42131
MANUFACTURERS OF ALL TYPES OF MUNICIPAL BODIES, INCLUDING REFUSE COLLECTORS, GULLEY AND CESSPIT EMPTIERS, TOWER WAGONS, ETC. ALSO MANUFACTURERS OF TRAILERS AND SEMI TRAILERS.

◁ *Another adaptation, and a typical sales leaflet to George Mackie's standardised pattern, The Eagle refuse cart body was fitted to the 109-inch chassis*

the Land-Rover name into disrepute, then "approval" was granted.

There were a number of advantages to this system. It clarified the warranty situation, where there had earlier been some confusion over responsibility for claims relating to converted vehicles. It improved the quality of the conversions, as Rover was now able to work closely with the converters during the development stages. And it gave Rover the opportunity to modify the design of the line-built vehicles to make them easier to convert. As far as the converters themselves were concerned, the Land-Rover approval gave their work a certain status, and also ensured that it would be brought to the attention of a greater number of potential customers through Land-Rover dealers.

From an early stage, the Technical Sales Department set about advertising its approved conversions, and George Mackie devised a system under which the advertising was largely funded by the converters themselves. Each converter arranged the production of a sales brochure or brochures for his own conversions, and

each brochure was produced to a standard format established by Technical Sales. These brochures – most of which were simply single sheets of paper – were then supplied by Rover to its dealers in a loose-leaf folder. All of them clearly stated that the conversion they described had the Land-Rover approval.

With the creation of the Technical Sales Department came two important changes. Firstly, as Macie's team began to get a clearer idea of what the Land-Rover really could do, the early notion that it could substitute for a tractor finally died. And secondly, the Solihull-built Land-Rover Fire Engine ceased production. From now on, chassis/cabs would come from the lines and go to the specialist converters who, with the assistance of Technical Sales, would custom-build fire engines to each customer's requirements.

Mackie had hoped to invite several fire appliance converters to submit designs to Technical Sales for approval, in order to give customers as wide a choice of options as possible. In this aim, however, he was initially thwarted by the Sales Division,

who went over his head and engaged Carmichael's of Worcester as exclusive converters of Land-rovers into fire engines for a period of three years. As a result, all the Land-Rover fire engines built between 1957 and 1959 were by Carmichael, and it was not until later that other specialists were able to obtain approval for their Land-Rover fire appliance conversions.

Even though demand for special equipment and conversions on Land-Rover was on the increase in the mid-1950s, it took some time for the Technical Sales Department to become properly established. Not the least of the reasons was that each new conversion took several months to develop and to put through the approval trials procedure. during 1957, therefore, as the final Series I Land-Rovers were coming off the production lines, things moved rather slowly. The situation was not helped by a slow start to sales overall in the 1957 calendar-year, and so it was that the Technical Sales Department did not really get into its stride until 1958.

Technical Sales' "coming-out party" was its display at the Commercial Motor Show

△ *Another early approved conversion used Wakefield Lubrequipment. It turned a long-wheelbase Land-Rover into a mobile servicing unit for vehicles in the field*

Carmichael of Worcester was the only approved fire engine converter between 1957 and 1959. These fire tenders all bore the Redwing name and were all based on long-wheelbase Land-Rovers; Rover's own fire tender
◁ *had always been built on the short-wheelbase chassis*

in September 1958. The idea of a special display had been mooted at the beginning of 1958, by which time the department had approved or was in the process of approving a wide variety of equipment and conversions. Mackie agreed that a major display at the Commercial Motor Show would be the best way of bringing the new Land-Rover approval system to as large a number of potential customers as possible, and so planning began in earnest.

At this stage, however, there was little Technical Sales could do except plan. By September, the new Series II Land-Rover would be on sale, and it would be important to us Series II models as the basis of demonstrator vehicles at the Commercial Motor Show. The problem was that Series II production was not due to begin until the early spring of 1958, with the result that there simply would not be any spare vehicles which Technical Sales could pass on to their approved specialist for conversion until very late on.

No doubt the summer of 1958 was therefore a busy time for Mackie's team. However, the event was a great success. As the display was going to be far too big for the Land-Rover stand within the Earls Court exhibition hall where the Show itself was to be held.

Technical Sales took over a portion of the nearby Rover Service Department in Seagrave Road, and displayed its wares there as an adjunct to the stand in the main exhibition hall. a picture of the event published in the Land-Rover Owners' Club

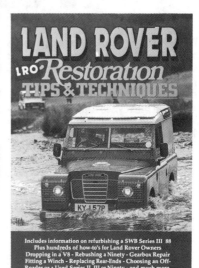

Review for December 1958 shows a packed display area, featuring Series II models fitted with approved equipment.

The Technical Sales Department continued to expand its work as the 1950s turned into the 1960s and, in the early years of that decade, it was taken out of the Sales Division and put into the Engineering Division under the new title of the Special Projects Department. In that guise it survived until 1985, when it was heavily reorganised as Special Vehicle Operations; and SVO in turn was re-established as Land Rover Special Vehicles in 1991.

THE LAND ROVER STORY

△ *This was the picture which introduced the 109-inch Series II to the press in April, 1958. The vehicle is fitted with the optional flashing direction indicators*

The Series II –

WITH THE Series II, Rover gave its best-seller both greater refinement and greater performance, says James Taylor.

THE VERY fact that the Rover Company described the revised Land-Rovers it introduced in April 1958 as Series II models tends to make them appear more different from their predecessors than they really are. In fact, the Series II models were just one more stage in the evolution of the Land-Rover in the mid-1950s.

Broadly speaking, Rover's plan for the Land-Rover's future in the later 1950s encompassed three major changes: the introduction of a diesel engine, the introduction of a new petrol engine, and the introduction of revised body styling. However, to introduce all of these at once would have been more than the company could afford, and the situation was further complicated when the development engineers found it necessary to stretch the wheelbase by two inches in order to accommodate the new diesel and petrol engines.

As a result, the introductions had to be made in order of priority. First came the stretched wheelbases in 1956; then came the diesel engine in 1957; and the new petrol engine and revised styling appeared together in 1958, the latter making the vehicle appear different enough to justify the "Series II" name. Not until the Series II had appeared in production were the earlier models collectively referred to as Series Is.

There seems little doubt that the key element in the Series II Land-Rover was always intended to be its new styling, and it is still this which helps to distinguish Series I from Series II at a glance today. "Styling" was not a concept which had really come into the design of the Series I models, and in fact Rover had no styling department as such before 1954, when David Bache was brought in to set one up. For his first two years at Rover, he was too busy with the forthcoming P5 saloon and with revisions to the existing P4s to turn his attention to the Land-Rover; but he began to look at ways of improving the vehicle's shape some time in 1956. It was probably at that point that the idea of a Series II Land-Rover took over from the philosophy of

continuous development which had been in force since 1948.

Bache has admitted that he had some difficulty thinking up improvements to the Land-Rover's styling: it was already so ideally suited to the vehicle's role that any self-conscious cosmetic work might have seriously detracted from the 4x4's utility appeal. The changes eventually approved are perhaps best described as refinements of the Series I shape, and in fact the modesty skirts on both sides which covered the exhaust pipe and chassis frame had already been seen on a Series I – albeit the rather special vehicle built on an 86-inch chassis as a State Review vehicle for the Queen in 1953.

Changes to the chassis, on which the Land-Rover designers had specified wider tracks, were the inspiration for the barrel-sides of the Series IIs; but it is to Bache's credit that he used this need for increased width to styling advantage, instead of simply widening the whole body and retaining flat side panels. The barrel-sides actually looked much neater and were, so Rover literature insisted, easier to keep clean.

△ Neat, but still rugged-looking: this is a Series II 88-inch, fitted with the optional truck cab. The spare wheel is also in its optional fitting on the bonnet. Note the barrel sides, "modesty skirt" sill panels, and improved hinges

an evolutionary step

Bache had paid attention to the shaping of the bonnet panel, too, which on long-wheelbase models and 88-inch Station Wagons had a neatly finished curved leading edge. Neater door hinges made the vehicle look less as if it had been built from a Meccano set.

Other visual changes, prompted by the engineering department rather than by the stylists, were new front indicator and tail lights, and new catches for the bonnet and tailboard. These latter were of a quick-action design and were both easy to use and (unlike those on Series I models) attached to the vehicle so that they could not be accidentally lost.

Sales literature at the time of the Series II launch made much of the improved visibility out of the revised cab, which was mainly attributable to the small, curved, windows in the rear quarter-panels. In addition, though, the use of glass for the side windows was an improvement over the perspex found in Series Is, which was easy to scratch and could rapidly become opaque.

The revised cab also had a neatly round-ed roof panel in place of the sloping type seen on Series Is but, as with these earlier models, the "standard" Land-Rover came without a metal cab at all. On such vehicles, the windscreeen came with a rubber top strip on which it rested when folded forward onto the bonnet – a great improvement over the windscreen prop arrangement of the Series Is.

All these were valuable changes, but there is little doubt that the strongest impact of David Bache's revised styling was seen on the 109-inch Station Wagon. Not the least of the reasons why was that the Series I long-wheelbase Station Wagon which it superseded was a rather untidy-looking creation. It looked as if it had been built up piecemeal from the Land-Rover parts bins and, to a large extent, that was exactly what had happened.

Bache's 109-inch Station Wagon succeeded in looking like an integrated piece of design while retaining all the rugged appeal of its predecessor. The proportions of the body were just right, and it is no surprise that these basic proportions are still found on the Defender 110 Station Wagon today. Where the 107-inch Station Wagon had looked like an uncomfortable vehicle, the 109-inch Series II had a certain sophistication about it which suggested it might even be enjoyable to ride in.

It must also have been the most expensive Series II model to introduce because of the large amount of new tooling which was necessary. No doubt Rover took care to spread the cost, which would explain why the 109-inch Station Wagon did not appear until the Motor Show in autumn 1958, some six months after the other Series II models went on sale.

The story of the diesel engine's development was told in LRO for October 1992, and it appears that the petrol engine was not far behind. The earliest known development vehicle was an 86-inch Series I, with chassis number 116600001, which ran a prototype 2.25-litre petrol engine and was road-registered as TWD 722 in March 1956. The engine itself was numbered 2.25/10, however, which suggests that the first of its nine predecessors dated from some time earlier.

The 2.25-litre petrol engine shared the

The 2¼-litre overhead valve petrol engine develops 77 b.h.p. at 4,250 r.p.m. and has a torque of 124 lb. ft. at 2,500 r.p.m. Thus, there is abundant power available for vehicle operation, hauling trailers or driving machinery. Power that is smooth and willing for normal work ; slogging, determined power for tough assignments. This is an outstandingly reliable engine, its robust construction giving it a long and trouble-free life.

PETROL *Power* to go anywhere

△ *The Series II came with the existing 2-litre diesel engine or with the new 2.25-litre OHV petrol engine, which was based on the diesel design. This illustration is taken from a contemporary sales catalogue*

The timeless shape of the Series II 109-inch Station Wagon is still in evidence on today's Defender 110. The very first examples had one-piece front doors, but later vehicles reverted to the two-piece type ▷

THE LAND ROVER STORY

diesel's overhead-valve layout, robust cast-iron block, and three-bearing crankshaft. However, whereas the diesel was a wet-liner design, the petrol engine used what was essentially the same block (though with detail changes) without the liners. Thus, while the two engines shared a common stroke, the larger bore size of the petrol engine made its capacity up to 2286cc while that of the diesel was only 2052cc. The cylinder heads were obviously different, too, and the petrol engine had a much lower compression ratio and breathed through a Solex carburettor.

The new 2.25-litre petrol engine offered 77bhp in place of the miserly 52bhp of the old 2-litre unit, and this extra 25bhp – an increase of very nearly 50 per cent – made the Series II Land-Rovers distinctly better performers on the road than their predecessors had been. 65mph was a real possibility, it took around 8 seconds less to reach 50mph from standstill, and cruising speeds of 55-60mph were the order of the day. In practice, however, only the 109-inch models had the new engine for the first few months of Series II production;

supplies took some time to build up, and all the 1958-model petrol-engined 88-inch Series IIs had to make do with the old 2-litre IOE petrol engine.

The improved performance which the 2.25-litre engine offered would undoubtedly have shown up the ruggedness of the original Land-Rover chassis in the worst possible light if it had not been accompanied by a package of other improvements. These improvements were aimed at adding to the Land-Rover's comfort levels without diminishing its ability to stand up to hard use.

According to an early Series II sales brochure, the rear suspension had been redesigned "with the springs now mounted on sturdy outrigger brackets to give greater overall stability. The springs themselves are of lower rate and, operating in conjunction with new shock absorbers, provide a well balanced ride for driver, passengers, and load." What the sales catalogue did not spell out was that much of the greater stability was actually due to the wider track, up by 1.5inches as compared to Series I models.

There were even improvements inside the Series IIs. The basic instrument and control layout remained unchanged, but the seat cushions were deeper than before and there was the option of a "De Luxe Cab", which added trimmed door casings and carpets to the basic specification. These items came as standard on both 88-inch and 109-inch Station Wagons, which also had the optional door locks and indicator flasher lamps as standard equipment.

Although the Series IIs were introduced during 1958, it is quite clear from surviving records that Rover had originally intended to launch the Series IIs during 1957 – probably at Motor Show time in the autumn. Poor sales during 1957 were probably the main reason for the delay, as it was important to clear dealer stocks of the old vehicles before the new ones became available, and the Rover Board learned on 24th October 1957 that the Series II launch had been put back by two months.

With the launch now scheduled for December or thereabouts, Rover decided on a further postponement. News had reached the company of BMC's plan to

Like all Land-Rovers the Long
Station Wagon has four-wheel drive, and
affords an ideal means of carrying personnel
or equipment over difficult country. Its possibilities are numerous; airport, oilfield, survey and
safari duties providing exceptional scope for its versatility and powers of progress.

launch the Gipsy - the first domestic rival the Land-Rover had ever had - and Rover probably decided that it would be prudent to wait and see what this offered before putting the Series II in production. If the Gipsy offered something unique, then there would still be time to redevelop the Series II to better the BMC Vehicle.

The Gipsy arrived in February 1958. In many ways, it offered a lot less than the Land Rover, although its most significant difference was an all-independant suspension system. No doubt the Rover engineers got their hands on one as soon as they could; but they were also unimpressed with the alleged advantages of the Gipsy's suspension. Convinced that beam axles were best for off-road vehicles - a view which still holds good at Land Rover Ltd. nearly 35 years later - they saw no need to make any changes to the Series II. (Nevertheless, they did go on to develop an independent front suspension for the Land-Rover, mainly as a safeguard in case the Gipsy was successful and

Rover was forced to offer such a system - see LRO, November 1991).

So it was that production of the Series II Land-Rover began in March

1958 and the vehicle was announced in April, exactly ten years after the original 80-inch Series I had been announced at the Amsterdam Show.

Series II Prototypes

NOT MUCH information is available about the Series II prototypes, and I would be very pleased to hear from anyone who can supply details additional to those I have set out below.

I have details of just one Series II 88-inch prototype: 88/7/S2 ("88-inch, number 7, Series 2"), which was not put on the road as XNX 541 until 1st January 1958. Presumably the six prototypes which preceded it were built up during 1957 - some perhaps as early as 1956. XNX 541 ran a prototype 2-litre diesel engine, though the diesel had actually entered production many months before this prototype was road-registered.

Details are similarly scant for the 109-inch prototypes. The first one (109/1/S2) must have run on trade plates for some time before being registered as 2593AC on 10th November 1958 - well after the basic Series II 109s had entered production. The fifth one (109/5/52) had meanwhile already become YNX 903 on 2nd June 1958.

It would be helpful to know whether details of any other Series II prototypes survive, and to have further information on build dates.

△ *Six Land Rovers were supplied to Donald Campbell as back-up vehicles for his 1960 attempt on the World Land Speed Record. The 109-inch seen with the record car 'Bluebird' is a 1960 right-hand-drive export model. Note the spare jerrycans on the wing fronts and the non-standard indicator and sidelamp housings on the wing tops*

The Series II

THE LAND ROVER STORY

THE PERIOD of the Series II's introduction coincided with the opening of the new Technical Sales Department, as explained in the November 1992 LRO, and all kinds of interesting special vehicles were built on Series II chassis. The British Army also took large quantities of Series IIs, putting in substantial orders for Rover Mk.7s (109-inch) and Rover Mk.8s (88-inch), and the Australian Army also took Series IIs as its first Land-Rovers, beginning with an order for 1,150 in November 1958. In addition, Series IIs were the first Land-Rovers to be assembled by Santana in Spain under licence from the Rover Company.

Yet in spite of all these new sales opportunities, the Series II took time to reach the sales volumes attained by the Series Is at their peak. Primarily, the problem seems to have been Solihull's inability to produce enough vehicles: the changeover of Land-Rover production from Series I to Series II models which began in March 1958 did not run smoothly, and as early as 10th April the Rover Board heard of the Sales Department's embarrassment at the shortfall in production. Orders, it appeared, were coming in, and there were insufficient vehicles to meet them.

Just how bad the problems must have been are suggested by the production figures for the 1958 model-year. Leaving out of account the 3,315 107-inch Station Wagons built (which spanned both Series I and Series II production), production dropped by around 25 per cent after the Series IIs came on-stream. In the first six months, when the Series I models were in production and demand was just beginning to pick up again after the Suez Crisis, nearly 16,000 vehicles had been produced. In the second six months, after the transition to Series II production, only just over 12,000 vehicles were built.

Demand seems not to have been affected significantly, however, and there is no indication from the Rover Board minutes of the time that the newly-introduced Austin Gipsy was having any real effect on Land-Rover sales. Customer reaction to the Series II models in fact seems to have been very positive, and the press of the time reflected this. The Scotsman "found it not only a better-looking, more comfortable and better-equpped vehicle, but more powerful with its new 2-1/4-litre engine, while its carrying capacity has been increased." Farmer's Weekly considered that "Land-Rover are going to be even easier to drive over rough country and they

will not need as much space in which to manoeuvre."

Country Life took a surreptitious sideswipe at the Gipsy, commenting that "Rover have remained faithful to the beam axle ... in preference to using some form of independent suspension. This is, no doubt, because of the simplicity and strength of the beam axle, which is best suited to the constant pounding of cross country motoring, often far from any Service facilities." Perhaps the most fulsome praise, however, came from Scottish Field magazine, which tried the Series II in the rough and "found general comfort to be much improved. The seating is soft without being too springy and the suspension system works wonderfully well on the worst of surfaces. ..... The central gear change is superbly easy to use. Every gear can be found and engaged with split second accuracy, and even relatively inexperienced drivers will find this mechanism really nice to use. The 24-litre engine is very smooth and quiet. It delivers power willingly at low speeds. With 4 wheel drive engaged the 109 model will climb almost fantastic gradients in first gear with the engine just ticking over."

Nevertheles, sales did not improve during the 1959 model-year, and in fact the fig-

△ *As this picture of a Series II 109-inch chassis shows, the layout of a Series II Land Rover was no different to that of a Series I*

on sale

ures for the 1958-1959 Financial Year show a drop of some 300 in worldwide sales as compared to the previous year. Production figures for the two years show an even greater discrepancy, with more than 31,000 Land-Rovers being built during 1958 but only 26,427 during 1959. As vehicles were being built to fulfil orders, it is therefore clear that orders must have been down.

There were several reasons for this, and none of them actually reflected badly on the Series II Land-Rover as a product. First of all, Gipsy sales were beginning to pick up, and almost every Gipsy sold represented the direct loss of a Land-Rover sale. Then there were problems in some overseas markets, such as Australia, where difficult economic conditions had left many Series I models unsold by the time the Series IIs were launched in the home market. As a result, no orders for Series II models from Australia were accepted until the old-stock Series Is had been sold.

Lastly, some production was undoubtedly lost to strikes at the Rover factory during the summer of 1959. The trouble seems to have begun in the autumn of 1958, when serious difficulties in the production of the new P5 3-litre saloon cars came to light. Rover, mercifully free of labour troubles

until this point, did its best to get the production problems rectified and the workforce pacified, but the discontent rumbled on into 1959 and eventually spilled over on to the Land-Rover assembly lines as well. Fortunately, it seems not to have affected them for long.

The 1960 figures were much more encouraging. Nearly 36,000 Land-Rovers left the lines, and this figure was closely shadowed in 1961, which was the last season of Series II production. Sales figures for these two years confirm the upturn in demand, and actually show a steady increase. From 28,371 sales in the 1958-1959 Financial Year, the figure climbed to 34,168 for 1959-1960, and then again to 35,148 for 1960-1961. One reason must surely have been that some of the Austin Gipsy's customers were returning to Land-Rover ownership; even BMC recognised the shortcomings of the Gipsy's all-independent suspension, and the long-wheelbase model introduced at the Geneva Show in March 1960 incorporated a leaf-sprung beam axle at the rear .....

During the period of the Series II's production, there was constant and steady expansion at Solihull. The car ranges were increased from one to two with the intro-

duction of the P5 3-litre in autumn 1958, and the first prototypes of the new P6 saloon, which was to be built in much higher volumes than the P4s it would replace, were built in 1959. The Land-Rover engineers were meanwhile looking at ways of making vehicles with higher payloads, and it was in this period that the project which eventually became the 109-inch Forward Control model was initiated. Alternative ways of coping with high payloads were also investigated, and among them was a 129-inch normal control model on which work started in 1960. As the Dead Ends feature in LRO for March 1992 explained, however, this massive vehicle did not go into productin.

Meanwhile, Harold Macmillan's Government was busily promoting a set of new labour policies which came into conflict with Rover's expansion plans. Intent on creating jobs in depressed areas, the Government refused planning permission for expansion on the Solihull site on the grounds that this would only create jobs in the already properous Midlands. Instead, it encouraged the company to build a satellite factory in one of its designated areas, where the creation of jobs would bring prosperity.

△ *Irrefutable evidence that scaled-down American styling did not work! This is a Series II Road-Rover prototype. By this stage, the Road-Rover had become more car than Land Rover, and all Series II versions had two-wheel drive only*

THE LAND ROVER STORY

This scheme brought with it all kinds of problems. Not the least of them was that the cost of transporting materials and components between Solihull and the new satellite factory would have to be passed on to the customers. Then there was the problem of starting up at the new factory with an unskilled workforce. However, the Rover Board examined all the possibilities, and during 1960 accepted that it would have to build its new satellite plant at Pengam, near Cardiff. For a time, there was a very real possibility that Land-Rover production would be moved lock, stock and barrel to the new factory in order to concentrate car production at Solihull. In the end, however, a rearrangement of existing facilities allowed the Cardiff site to be used primarily for parts storage, and both car and Land-Rover production remained at Solihull.

When Maurice Wilks had asked Jack Swaine to draw up the OHV four-cylinder engine for the Series II Land-Rover, he had always intended that it should have other applications as well. One of those was the Road-Rover, that curious utility car which Rover had drawn up in the first half of the 1950s to take over from the original 80-inch Land-Rover Station Wagon. In its original guise, the Road-Rover borrowed design concepts from both the car and Land-Rover sides of the Rover business (see LRO, April 1992), but its original purpose was usurped by the 86-inch Series I Station Wagon, and the project ran into the sand in the mid-1950s.

However, 1956 saw a major reorganisation of the Engineering Division at Rover, which for the first time was separated into Rover saloon and Land Rover sections. The Road-Rover was allocated to Dick Oxley, as the newly-appointed Chief Engineer (Cars), and he was instructed to revitalise it and get it ready for production. The so-called Series II Road-Rovers were much more car-like than the original versions, but they did take on the 2-1/4-litre Land-Rover petrol engine, and several of the prototype engines were fitted to prototype Road-Rovers between 1956 and 1959. However, the Road-Rover did not prosper. It never looked really convincing as a utility two-wheel-drive vehicle and, when Rover found in 1959 that it had more important things to spend money on, the project was scrapped.

By this stage, the 24-litre engine had already been accepted by the car side of the company as a viable saloon power plant, and it was introduced in the P4 80 saloon in October 1959. This car replaced the P4 60 which had used the spread-bore 2-litre IOE Land-Rover engine ever since its introduction in 1953. Like the 60, the 80 was always viewed as a sort of poor relation of the saloon car range, but in fact the OHV engine proved to be remarkably refined as well as robust, and remained available in the saloons until it was replaced by the 2.6-litre six-cylinder engine in 1962. That engine, in its turn, would also eventually appear in Land-Rovers.

Lastly, the period of the Series II's production saw Rover negotiating with two other companies about the manufacture of 4x4s. The first of these was Willys Motors, Inc, the American makers of the Jeep, who were seeking manufacturing facilities in Britain. Discussions about a joint venture were initiated in April 1958 and foundered early in1959, but not before Rover had built an intriguing 83-inch hybrid by mounting a Jeep CJ-5 body on to a cut-down Series II Land-Rover chassis.

The second company to be involved was David Brown Industries, who manufactured tractors and agricultural equipment, and who had started work on a light utility competitor for the Land-Rover in 1954. Among those working on this project was John Cullen, one of the original Land-Rover development engineers whom David Brown Industries had poached; but in spite of this pedigree, the new 4x4 never did get off the ground. Late in 1960, David Brown industries approached Rover with a view to disposing of their 4x4 interests, but Rover declined the offer.

All references to the minutes of the Rover Board are made by kind permission of Rover Group/BMIHT.

△ *The Liverpool City Police put this 88-inch hard-top into service during 1960*

SERIES II LAND-ROVER PRODUCTION

1958 models	Chassis nos beginning	1418/1428/1438/1448/1458 (88 petrol)	7,150
		1468/1478/1488/1498/1508 (88 diesel)	1,261
		1518/1528/1538/1548/1558 (109 petrol)	2,944
		1568/1578/1588/1598/1608 (109 diesel)	791
		Total	**12,146**
1959 models	Chassis nos beginning	1419/1429/1439/1449/1459 (88 petrol)	12,936
		1469/1479/1489/1499/1509 (88 diesel)	2,685
		1519/1529/1539/1549/ * (109 petrol, basic)	6,987
		1569/1579/1589/1599/1609 (109 diesel, basic)	2,127
		1619/1629/1639/1649/ * (109 petrol, S.W.)	1,660
		* /1679/ * /1699/ * (109 diesel, S.W.)	32
		Total	**26,427**
1960 models	Chassis nos beginning	1410/1420/1430/1440/1450 (88 petrol)	15,909
		1460/1470/1480/1490/1500 (88 diesel)	3,143
		1510/1520/1530/1540/1550 (109 petrol, basic)	11,438
		1560/1570/1580/1590/1600 (109 diesel, basic)	2,740
		1610/1620/1630/1640/1650 (109 petrol, S.W.)	2,643
		* /1670/ * /1690/ * (109 diesel, S.W.)	93
		Total	**35,966**
1961 models	Chassis nos beginning	1411/1421/1431/1441/1451 (88 petrol)	14,922
		1461/1471/1481/1491/1501 (88 diesel)	2,450
		1511/1521/1531/1541/1551 (109 petrol, basic)	12,364
		1561/1571/1581/1591/ * (109 diesel, basic)	2,641
		1611/1621/1631/1641/1651 (109 petrol, S.W.)	3,000
		1661/1671/ * /1691/ * (109 diesel, S.w.)	151
		Total	**35,528**
	GRAND TOTALS:	88 petrol	50,917
		88 diesel	9,539
		109 petrol, basic	3,733
		109 diesel, basic	8,299
		109 diesel, S.W.	7,303
		109 diesel, S.W.	276
			110,067

Notes:
1. The 88-inch Station Wagons did not have their own chassis number sequences but were numbered within the main petrol and diesel sequences.
2. An asterisk (*) indicates a sequence not used.
3. In 1960, the last five LHD CKD 88-inch diesel models (1500 series), and all five LHD CKD 109-inch diesel models (1600 series) had Perkins diesel engines.

Santana –

James Taylor tells the story of the Series II Land-Rovers built under licence in Spain.

DURING THE early 1950s, the Rover Company was constantly seeking new markets for the Land Rover. It received a number of enquiries from companies interested in building the vehicle under licence abroad, and the Belgian Minerva and German Tempo variants which were covered in parts 15 and 16 of the Land Rover Story (see *LRO,* August and September 1992) were two of the results.

Spain looked like another good bet as a market for the Land-Rover in the early 1950s, not least because it had no significant car or light commercial vehicle industry of its own. However, the Spanish Government was attempting to establish more heavy industry at the time, and in order not to destroy the potential for motor manufacture in Spain, it created a number of

trade barriers to control imports. So it was that, when Rover explored the possibility of introducing the Land-Rover into Spain to complement the saloon cars it was already selling there, it found that it would be unable to bring the vehicle into the country in worthwhile quantities.

Nevertheless, the Spanish Government was receptive to the idea of foreign motor manufacturers establishing satellite assembly plants in Spain. It believed that these could provide work for Spanish nationals and would help to build up a foundation of motor manufacturing skills on which a proper indigenous Spanish motor industry might be established. However, it kept a tight control over proposals, and subjected any satellite plant to certain conditions. Among these were that all vehicles built there must contain a proportion of locally-manufactured components from the beginning and that this proportion should increase to 100% within a given time-frame.

Rover decided it was prepared to investigate further on that basis, and in the spring of 1953, Commercial Director George Farmer went out to Madrid to discuss the possibilities with Tabanera Romagosa, S.A., Rover's Spanish importers. The exact details of these discussions are unclear, but it seems that Tabanera Romagosa wanted to become closely involved with the new venture which, if successful, was likely to be a money-spinner. Negotiations were protracted, however. Once again, the details are lacking, but it seems likely that the Spanish Government was stonewalling on the issue. Nothing of any substance happened for the best part of two years.

In the meantime, the Spanish Government's attempts to create new heavy industries had borne fruit in the southern province of Jaén. Here, the Government issued a public tender for a plan to set up a factory which would manufacture agricultural equipment. The successful bidders

△ Many Santana Land-Rovers were "window hard-tops", like this Series II 88-inch model. From a distance, it looks very much like the Solihull variety, but there are actually many detail differences

the early days

THE LAND ROVER STORY

were a group of Spanish businessmen, and they established their new company formally under Spanish law on 24th February 1955, It was to be called Metalurgica de Santa Ana, S.A. (which translates roughly as "St. Anne's Metalworks"), and its new factory was to be built near the town of Linares.

The new company was understandably ambitious, Not content with building agricultural machinery, it secured a contract to build gearboxes and supply them to the Citroën satellite factory which was being established in Vigo, and it was soon in discussions with Tabanera Romagosa about the assembly and progressive local manufacture of Land-Rovers. During 1956, Rover and Tabanera Romagosa reached agreement with Metalurgica de Santa Ana (MSA), and the wheels were set in motion for Rover to establish a satellite Land Rover assembly plant in the MSA factories at Linares.

Once again, however, progress was slow. The reason, as the Rover Board learned at its meeting on 10th September 1957, was the economic situation in Spain. Once again, the Spanish Government appeared to have been dragging its feet: "there had been difficulty in obtaining import licences for tooling and Land-Rover components", as the Board meeting minutes drily recorded the position. However, shortly after that September 1957 meeting, George Farmer intended to go out to the Linares factory, presumably to report on progress. It looked as if something was happening at last.

There could probably not have been a worse time to start tooling-up for the manufacture of Land-Rovers at a new overseas plant, as the Series II models were just about to come on-stream and would incorporate a number of new and relatively untried components which would also have to go into the Spanish-built vehicles.

Nevertheless, plans went ahead, and the new Land-Rover line went into the Linares factory during 1958. Exact dates are not available, but it looks as if everything was timed so that the production start-up would be around six months behind Series II production at Solihull. That way, Rover stood a chance of ironing out any in-service problems close to home before MSA came up against them.

At its meeting on 10th April 1958, the Rover Board learned that the Spanish Government had agreed to the importation of a small number of CKD or SKD (Semi-Knocked Down) Land-Rovers in advance of the scheduled start to production. These vehicles must have been shipped to spain in the summer or autumn of 1958, for production actually began that November. No doubt Solihull followed its usual practice of providing a team of technical advisers, and no doubt some of these stayed behind with MSA for some considerable time.

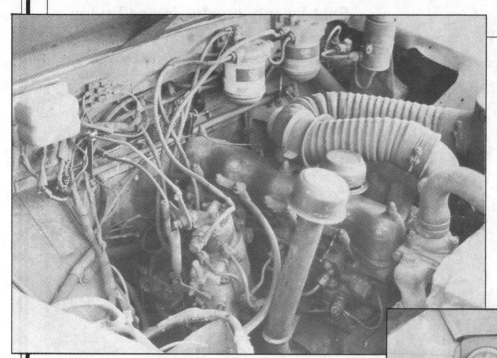

△ Under the bonnet of an early Santana-built diesel model. Once again, things look pretty standard, but there were detail differences from the British-built product

Characteristic of the early Santana Land-Rovers were these headlamps, which were manufactured locally. Also visible here is the unique badge applied to Spanish-built vehicles ▷

In all important respects, the first Santana Land-Rovers were identical to Solihull's own Series IIs. Indeed, they were Solihull Series IIs except for the fact that they were assembled in Spain and incorporated a small number of locally-produced items. The CKD kits sent out from Solihull had only minimal deletions, in areas such as instruments, trim and glass; and these items were sourced in Spain to meet the Spanish Government's requirements. The only way of telling an MSA-assembled Series II Land-Rover at a glance was by its special badging, which incorporated the Santana name (an obvious abbreviation of Santa Ana) below the Land-Rover nameplate. In due course, Santana introduced unique locally-manufactured options, such as chromed hub-caps and body edge trim; but these were probably not available from the beginning.

As far as it is possible to tell, the first Santana Land-Rovers were all 88-inch models, and 109-inch Series IIs followed rather later. The very first vehicle was presented to Generalissimo Franco in a gesture which attracted some welcome publicity for the new venture. Nevertheless, no Santana Land-Rovers went on public sale until the beginning of 1959, and production seems to have been slow and laborious.

Rover was no doubt hugely delighted to have got production under way at all, however, and it expressed its delight by passing an attractive styling prototype car on to Senor Tabanera of Tabanera Romagosa during November 1958. The car was in fact some four years old by this time, and had been rejected as a production option. Tony Poole of the Styling Department remembers that the Spanish driver sent to collect it returned sheepishly a few

minutes after sweeping proudly out of the Lode Lane works, having been involved in a collision at the traffic lights at the end of the road!

That accident was in some ways prophetic of the way the Santana project would run for its first few years. Certainly, there were problems in the early days. The original licensing arrangement from Rover had cited Tabanera Romogaso as an intermediary, and this soon proved a source of trouble. After friction between this company and MSA, Rover renegotiated the agreement, and in March 1959 the Rover Board learned that MSA would now hold its manufacturing direct from the Rover Company.

Production was abysmally slow to build up. It was June 1960 before the Rover Board learned that production at MSA had reached the dizzy heights of 10 Land-Rovers a day, and later figures suggest that the theoretical capacity of 50 a week or the 2,000-2,500 a year which this implies, can never have been achieved. Figures from MSA itself show than only 5,400 Land-Rovers had been built by 1968/ an average of some 600 a year! As far as the Series IIs in that total were concerned, all of them had been sold on the Spanish market; MSA did not begin to export its Land-Rovers until the Series IIA models come on-stream in 1962. As before, their introduction was a few months behind the introduction of the Solihull-assembled variety.

The local-content clauses in the agreement between Rover and MSA also became a source of difficulty quite early on. As the agreement provided for the eventual increase of local content in the MSA vehicles to 100%, it was not long

before MSA started to ask Solihull if it could produce its own special Land-Rover variants – which would, after all, fall within the letter of the agreement. There is an unspoken reluctance in the minutes of the Rover Board meeting held on 9th February 1961, when the Directors agreed to let MSA build a 109-inch Forward-Control Land-Rover on condition that it was sold only to the Spanish Government. That reluctance is understandable in view of the fact that Rover had not yet committed its own 109-inch Forward-Control model to production, even though the vehicle existed in prototype form! In fact, the Santana version did not appear until 1967, but that 1961 decision set an important precedent. As time went on, Santana Land-Rovers began to differ more and more from the Solihull product.

Many thanks to Peter Hobson and David Cullingford for their help with this episode of the Land Rover Story. All quotations from the Rover Board minutes are used with the kind permission of Rover Group/BMIHT.

We would be more than pleased to hear any further information which readers may have about the early days of the Santana Land-Rovers.

All trace of the styling prototype which went to Senor Tabanera in 1958 has now been lost. Can any readers help? It was Rover 90 with unique fixed-head coupé bodywork by Pininfarina. Originally built with right-hand-drive, it was later uprated to twin-carburettor 105S specification and converted to left-hand-drive, possibly by Rover at Solihull.

MOY
ALL-HYDRAULIC MOUNTED
CONVEYORS
LAND-ROVER CONVERSION
APPROVED BY THE ROVER COMPANY LTD.

These Conveyors have been designed to meet the ever-increasing demand for reduction in time and manual effort in the loading and unloading of packaged goods or loose (bulk) materials in applications where mobility of the equipment is of primary importance. They are available in two models, Standard and Low-Level.

THE STANDARD CONVEYOR, mounted on the 109″ wheelbase LAND-ROVER Truck, can be supplied fitted either with an endless belt suitable for packaged goods only, or with one suitable for loose materials or small packages. The equipment can be quickly dismounted from the LAND-ROVER, thus freeing the vehicle for other duties.

THE LOW-LEVEL CONVEYOR, which has been designed specifically as an **AIRCRAFT LOADER,** * is mounted on the 88″ wheelbase Regular LAND-ROVER with modified bodywork and offset steering. It is fitted with an endless belt suitable for packaged goods only. The low overall height and exceptionally low discharge or feed-on heights available at both ends make it particularly suitable for under-belly work with aircraft, and for gaining access to low or awkwardly situated freight compartments to which access by larger vehicles would be impossible.
* Code Name: SPALE (Self-Propelled Aircraft Loading Equipment).

TODAY'S PRICE AND FURTHER PARTICULARS AVAILABLE ON REQUEST FROM:—

PRECISION ENGINEERING PRODUCTS (SUFFOLK) LTD.,
BURY ST. EDMUNDS, ENGLAND. Tel. 2603

Detailed Specification of
THE STANDARD CONVEYOR

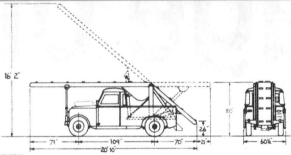

GENERAL
This equipment can be mounted on any 109″ wheelbase Series II LAND-ROVER Truck, provided that the extras listed below are first fitted: these do not restrict normal use of the vehicle when the Conveyor is removed. Dismounting can be effected in less than ten minutes by disconnecting two self-sealing couplings, removing four holding-down bolts and the control valve lever cover.

CONSTRUCTION
The conveyor booms are fabricated from light MS plate and channel sections, and the mounting frame from 10swg MS boxed channel and rectangular hollow sections.

MOUNTING
The conveyor boom is in two sections which articulate independently about a common horizontal axis at the apex of a robustly constructed mounting frame, within which is housed the complete hydraulic system, with the exception of the pump. The whole assembly is lowered on to the Land-Rover body and bolted through the floor to a special sub-frame secured directly to the chassis by U-bolts. This sub-frame consists of four members and may be fitted to the vehicle without removal of, or alteration to the body.

CONTROLS
The Conveyor controls consist of four levers, conveniently grouped in the LAND-ROVER cab: (a) P.T.-O. Selector for Pump Drive. (b) Belt stop start and direction control. (c) Front Boom elevation control and (d) Rear Boom elevation control. The four levers are guarded by a cover designed to fit in place of the centre seat squab panel, which, together with the seat cushion, back-rest and tailboard, must first be removed.

CONVEYOR BELT
For Packaged Goods
24″ wide endless flat, 2-ply, "grip-face" rubber belt, with rubber cleats vulcanised in pairs at 36″ pitch to permit operation at up to 40° elevation.

For Loose Materials
24″ wide, endless, flat, NUMEC 2-ply rubber-covered, cleated belt with fluted rubber sides 3″ high.

OPTIONAL EXTRA EQUIPMENT
Exhaust Flametrap, Fire Extinguisher(s). Two adjustable Floodlamps.

A LARGE FEED HOPPER can also be supplied for conveyors fitted with "bulk" belts, while special hook-on attachments for standard width (15½″) Gravity Roller Conveyor are available at extra cost for packaged goods Conveyors.

SHIPPING DETAILS. (Conveyor only, crated fully assembled).

Length	Width	Height	Volume	Gross Weight
23 ft.	3 ft. 6 ins.	5 ft. 3 ins.	422·625 cu. ft.	3,100 lbs.
7m.	1·06m.	1·6m.	11·88 cu. m.	1406 kgs.

LAND-ROVER extras required:
1. Front Springs: 276034 (both sides).
 Rear Springs: 272967 (both sides).
 Shock Absorbers: 508033 (Front). 508034 (Rear).
2. Engine Governor (petrol engines only): E.1219.
3. P.T.-O. Drive Unit, less Hydraulic Pump: 580026
4. Selector Unit Assembly Mechanical: 509076.
5. (Tropical climates only)
 Engine Oil Cooler—Diesel: E.1197. Petrol: E.1204.

OPTIONAL LAND-ROVER Extras:
Bonnet with Spare Wheel Dish: E.1059.
Flasher Equipment: E.1211.
Mudflaps, rear: 332963.
Socket and Plug, for Trailer: 502501.

Detailed Specification of
THE LOW-LEVEL CONVEYOR

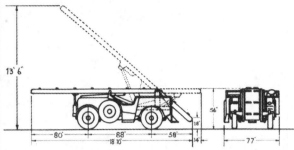

GENERAL
The 88″ wheelbase Series II Regular LAND-ROVER used as the prime-mover for this low-level conveyor has specially modified bodywork and offset steering to accommodate the front boom section of the conveyor, which is mounted centrally on the vehicle.

CONSTRUCTION
The conveyor booms are fabricated from light MS plate and channel sections, and the mounting frame from 10swg MS boxed channel and rectangular hollow sections.

MOUNTING
The conveyor boom is in two sections which articulate independently about a common horizontal axis at the apex of a robustly constructed mounting frame, within which is housed the complete hydraulic system, with the exception of the pump. The whole assembly is lowered on to the floor of the Land-Rover body, and bolted through the floor to a special sub-frame secured directly to the chassis by U-bolts.

CONTROLS
The conveyor controls consist of four levers, conveniently grouped near the driving seat: (a) P.T.-O. Selector for Pump Drive, (b) Belt stop/start and direction control. (c) Front Boom elevation control, add (d) Rear Boom elevation control.

CONVEYOR BELT
A belt suitable for handling packaged goods only is fitted to this Conveyor. It is a 24″ wide, endless, flat, 2-ply. "grip-face" Rubber belt, with rubber cleats vulcanised in pairs at 36″ pitch to permit operation at up to 40° elevation.

SPECIAL EQUIPMENT
An Exhaust Flametrap, a fire extinguisher, two adjustable floodlamps and an airfield "marker" light are all fitted as standard equipment.

OPTIONAL EXTRAS ALTERNATIVES
Two easily-detachable Hard-Tops for Operator and Crew Compartments.
Hook-on attachments for gravity roller conveyor.
Larger or smaller wheel tyre equipment.

SHIPPING DETAILS. (LAND-ROVER with Conveyor mounted, complete).

Length	Width	Height	Volume	Gross Weight
18 ft. 9 ins.	6 ft. 6 ins.	5 ft.	610 cu. ft.	4910 lbs.
5·72m.	1·98m.	1·52m.	17·12 cu. m.	2227 kgs.

LAND-ROVER extras required:
1. (Tropical climates only) Engine Oil Cooler: Diesel: E.1197. Petrol: E.1204.
All other necessary extra or non-standard components are included in the Specification to which LAND-ROVERS for MOY Aircraft Loading Equipment are assembled.

Printed in England by the Lavenham Press Ltd., Lavenham, Suffolk

---

Aftermarket conversions approved by Rover for The Series II and IIA models were advertised by brochures like these.

GENERAL DETAILS of STANDARD and LOW-LEVEL CONVEYORS

The combination of single endless belt and articulated conveyor boom, (British Patent No. 880149: Overseas Patents Pending) is common to both models. This is an essential feature, (not previously applied to vehicle-mounted conveyors), since it enables the heights of both feed and discharge ends to be varied independently of each other, and also ensures that the main boom of the conveyor is supported in a horizontal position during movement of the vehicle. Note also these other important features of both models:

* On-or-off the road mobility is assured by mounting on the LAND-ROVER, the World's most versatile vehicle. It is, however, recommended that a maximum speed of 30 m.p.h. is not exceeded.

* All-hydraulic operation, powered by the Land-Rover's engine through a hydraulic pump directly coupled to the centre power take-off. All hydraulic units are standard D O W T Y products, as already approved for use with the Land-Rover for other equipment.

* Hydraulic Locks fitted to main boom rams to ensure safety in operation.

* Simple controls grouped in the driving compartment. Belt and Boom elevation controls are also duplicated remotely at both ends of the Conveyor.

* Single endless 24″ wide, flat, rubber-covered Belt operates in both directions. Belt speed is variable, normally between 15 and 90 ft. (4.5 and 28.5 metres) per minute for packaged goods conveyors, or between 150 and 450 feet (45.7 and 137.2 metres) per minute for "bulk" conveyors. Alternative reduction gear ratios can be supplied to give faster or slower belt speed ranges as required. An engine governor ensures constant belt speed and economy in operation.

* Capacity: 976 lbs. (406 kg.) distributed, or unit loads of 224 lbs. (101 kg.).

* No guard rails or side boards to restrict width of packages which may be conveyed.

* Provision for towing at both front and rear of vehicle.

* Maintenance of the conveyor equipment, (apart from periodic changing of filter elements and hydraulic fluid), is negligible since all bearings and bushes are either self-lubricating or pre-packed-for-life with a special lubricant on assembly. Maintenance and Operating Instructions are supplied with each machine.

The Rover Company are not responsible for the manufacture of approved equipment and/or bodywork, although they have closely examined specification and design.

Matters concerning Sales (including Shipping, Delivery, etc.), Service or Warranty Claims, are the responsibility of the Manufacturer (whose name and address is given on this leaflet) or his Agent.

In cases of difficulty concerning approved equipment, the Special Projects Section of the Land-Rover Engineering Department is available to offer advice.

THE LAND ROVER STORY

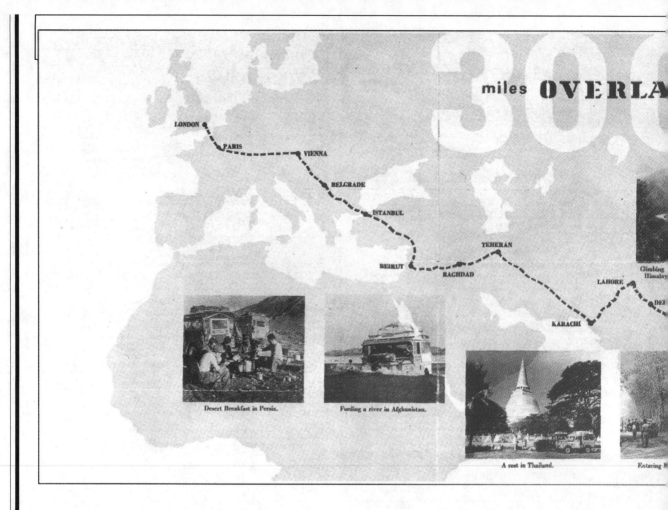

miles OVERLA

Desert Breakfast in Persia.

Fording a river in Afghanistan.

A rest in Thailand.

Entering

The age of

During the 1950s, explorers and adventurers pioneered the use of the Land-Rover in long-distance expedition work. James Taylor reviews the period.

IN DRAWING up the original Land-Rover during 1947, there can be little doubt that Maurice Wilks and his design team had been thinking of a vehicle which would not be called upon to undertake long journeys. Dual-purpose though the vehicle was expected to be, its whole design was biased heavily towards rough-terrain use, with rudimentary seats, instrumentation and weather-proofing. The absence of creature comforts was a deterrent to using a Land-Rover for long-distance work, although there was never any doubt that the vehicle was structurally and mechanically capable of such use.

This combination of qualities was not lost on professional explorers who, in earlier years, had relied on the packhorse and the mule for overland transportation. Quite prepared to accept discomfort as part of the long-distance travelling, they were

more than happy to use Land-Rovers as expedition vehicles. After all, as long as adequate supplies of petrol and oil were carried, a Land-Rover could go anywhere a horse had done and - even better – it would not get tired after a hard day's travelling. Moreover, one Land Rover could do the work of several horses, which minimised expedition logistics problems.

It is not clear who was the first of the professional explorers to make use of Land-Rovers for expedition work, but a strong contender for that title must be Colonel Leblanc, who drove one from Britain to Abyssinia in 1949. He was followed in the 1950s by others, such as Laurens Van der Post, who helped to establish Land-Rovers as ideal expedition vehicles. Before long, amateur explorers and adventurers also began to mount overland expeditions using Land-Rovers and – as often as not – securing some kind of support from Solihull, which was not slow to recognise the publicity value of such activities.

The news that Solihull was prepared to support expeditions in return for some free publicity soon got round, and the requests

for support began to multiply. It was quite clear that the publicity budget could not cope with every request and, as time went on, there was also nothing more than any expedition could prove about the Land-Rover's qualities, so that the publicity benefit of expeditions had dwindled to nothing by the end of the 1950s. As a result, the Rover Company changed its policy. It continued to support certain expeditions (notably those of the Royal Geographical Society, for example), but to other enquirers it merely dispatched a helpful booklet entitled *A Guide to Land-Rover Expeditions*.

It is fascinating to trace the story of the Rover Company's pursuit of publicity through its sponsorship of Land-Rover expeditions in the 1950s, and it is interesting to reflect how much this publicity contributed to the worldwide image which Solihull's four-wheel-drives have today. Although Rover's public relations efforts in the 1950s were amateurish by comparison with their modern counterparts, they were characterised by a sometimes surprising amount of clear thinking and flair.

Rover's first direct link with the world of

by LAND-ROVER

An improvised "bridge" on the derelict remains of the Ledo Road in Burma.

LEDO

MANDALAY

BANGKOK

SINGAPORE

△ *Three of the four Land-Rovers used by Colonel Laurens Van der Post on his expedition to find the Kalahari Bushmen. The vehicles were owned by the factory*

◁ *This spread from a Land-Rover publicity leaflet shows the route taken by the first Oxford and Cambridge Expedition*

expeditions

expeditions came in 1951, when the company decided to team up with Colonel Leblanc, the explorer who had taken a Land-Rover overland to Abyssinia in 1949. The link-up with Leblanc was not primarily to improve the Land-Rover's image in the developed countries, however, but rather to gain sales for it in those which were undeveloped and where Solihull saw that it could have most appeal.

The strategy was simple. Rover found it hard to attract the attention of potential customers – mainly Government agencies like the police and military authorities – in the undeveloped countries, because their representatives did not attend the major Motor Shows and other events at which Land-Rovers were displayed to potential buyers in the developed world. Short of taking Land-Rovers out to inhospitable regions at vast expense, there was little which Rover could do. But somebody like Leblanc was ideal. His whole life revolved around travel in those very inhospitable regions which were inaccessible to the Rover Company, and so if he could be persuaded to do his travelling in Land-Rovers

and to demonstrate their abilities *en route…*

A deal was struck. Leblanc turned down Rover's original offer of a retainer fee, settling instead for an arrangement under which he would receive half a percent of all future Land-Rover sales in the Middle East. Rover also agreed to provide him with the Land-Rovers he needed for his expeditions. Leblanc set out on his first sales expedition at the end of February 1952, taking not only Land-Rovers but also (at Rover's request) a P4 75 saloon, some Rover salesmen and service engineers. This expedition went south from Algiers to Nairobi, and then returned north through the countries of West Africa. It was to be the first of many such expeditions made during the 1950s with Leblanc at the helm.

Roger McCahey, later manager of UK Sales Operations for Land Rover Ltd, went with Leblanc on some of those sales expeditions. He recalled for Ken Slavin's book, *Land Rover, the unbeatable 4x4*, how the system worked. "We would stop outside the towns to wash the vehicles down," he remembered, "put on clean shorts and

clean shirts and polish our shoes, before going in to see the local police chief, army, oil companies or whoever might be interested."

When Leblanc succeeded in persuading a customer to place an order for a batch of Land-Rovers, he went on to help Solihull establish a dealership in the region which would support those vehicles and promote further sales. His sales commission of half a percent, which had looked like peanuts in 1951, become a very worthwhile source of income which continued long after old age had forced him to give up his expedition activities.

Leblanc's activities undoubtedly inspired a number of others to undertake Land-Rover expeditions abroad, and the mid-1950s saw a great increase in the number of amateur explorers and adventurers who set out into uncharted territory with a helping hand from Solihull. They did not, of course, have long-term agreements with Rover like Leblanc's; but many of them did manage to secure some support from the company, in the shape of vehicles, expedition equipment, or even financial sponsor-

△ *Barbara Toy took her 80-inch Land-Rover around the world. capitalising on this achievement, the factory presented her in 1958 with a brand-new Series II. She has since re-acquired her original vehicle and driven it around the world again. Miss Toy is Vice Chairman of the Land-Rover Register*

Two of the Land-Rovers which went on the third Oxford and Cambridge expedition at a Solihull photocall in 1957. Once again, the vehicles were factory-owned ▷

THE LAND ROVER STORY

ship.

Reports of their exploits filtered back to the UK and were used to make publicity capital whenever Rover saw the opportunity. It was inevitable that, after a time, the press should lose interest in publishing these stories as they were becoming too commonplace!

Some expeditions were undertaken without any support from Solihull, however. In 1954-1955, for example, a group of Australians drove a short-wheelbase Land-Rover from Hobart to London, a trip of some 32,000 miles which lasted 12 months. What sort of a reception they received from Rover on arrival in Britain is not recorded, but it is reasonable to assume that the publicity department had a hand in persuading *Motor* to publish an account of the journey in August 1955.

Two years later, the French owner of a rubber plantation in Vietnam drove the 12,000 miles from Saigon to Solihull for recreation. So confident had he been of the abilities of his short-wheelbase Land-Rover that he had not even troubled to fit a winch before setting out. Again, it is not clear what the Solihull publicity staff said to him when he arrived on their doorstep, but it would be hard to imagine that they made him pay for the new brake linings which they claimed were the only work necessary on his vehicle; there was good

publicity to be made out of the story of his exploit.

By the mid-1950s, Solihull had enough knowledge of expeditions and adventures undertaken in Land-Rovers to offer assistance to explorers and adventurers on a paying basis. From the beginning of 1957, the repository of that knowledge was George Mackie's Technical Sales Department, and the staff there were no doubt responsible for equipping a special vehicle which was delivered to Canadian biologist Paul foster in June 1957.

Foster and his companion Paul Bateman had planned an 18-month round-the-world expedition on behalf of some Canadian natural history institutions, and their objectives were to study and photograph wildlife and to collect specimens of some of the smaller species for shipment back to Canada. Their requirement was for a two-berth caravan with plenty of storage space, and Solihull came up with a custom-built one-off vehicle in the shape of a 107-inch Station Wagon chassis with a Pilchers high-roof ambulance body which had been specially equipped internally.

There was limited publicity capital to be made out of the preparation of such vehicles, however. Much more important to John Tracey's publicity team at Solihull was Rover's sponsorship of the Oxford and Cambridge Expeditions in the mid-1950s.

There were three of these, the first setting out in 1955 and the last returning in 1958.

In each case, rover supplied and equipped the vehicles; and in each case, the expeditions were intended to achieve scientific objectives as well as to demonstrate the Land-Rover's abilities over inhospitable terrain.

The first of these expeditions was known as the Oxford and Cambridge Far Eastern Expedition, and consisted of six graduates from the two Universities, who set out from London in two Land-Rovers on 1st September 1955. "Their main aim," according to Land-Rover publicity of the time, "was to drive overland to Singapore, a journey, which though often attempted, had never been completed because of the difficulty of forcing a route through the jungles of Burma and Southern Thailand. Other objects of the Expedition were programmes of research into irrigation developments in Pakistan and India, and into the mineral resources of Upper Burma.

"The Expedition was made financially possible by the support of many firms which supplied their products, and by the revenue from filming for television, the sale of articles and photographs to the press, the publication of a book, and from public lectures. The Royal Geographical Society and other foundations contributed towards the cost of research,"

Much of the flavour of these expeditions can still be captured today in the books and other accounts which were published at the time, although some of these are not easy to find. Several films were made, too, but these seem to have disappeared altogether.

As for the vehicles which were used on these expeditions, most have also disappeared. Some were undoubtedly sold off abroad, and those which Rover itself owned were sold off through the trade when they returned to Britain.

One historic expedition Land-Rover does survive. "Pollyanna", the 1950 80-inch model in which the Australian adventurer and writer Barbara Toy circumnavigated the globe single-handed in the 1950s was bought back by its original owner in 1988 and completed its second drive around the world in her hands during 1990.

In the late 1950s, LROC affiliated clubs could hire items 5, 6 and 8 from the Rover Publicity Department (see list of films). By the end of the 1960s, items 5, 7 an d 8 could be hired from the British Leyland Specialist Car Division Film Library (which was based at Triumph's Canley headquarters), and these films probably still existed in the early 1980s. All of them appear now to have disappeared from circulation. All were originally available on 16mm stock, in colour and with sound.

Early Expedition Books

1. Tim Slessor - First Overland. The story of the Oxford and Cambridge Far Eastern Expeditionin 1955-1956.

2. Barbara Toy - Columbus was right. The story of the first circumnavigation of the globe in "Polyanna".

3. Col. Laurens Van der Post - The Lost World of the Kalahari. A 3,000 mile expedition to find the elusive tribes of the Kalahari Desert.

4. Eric Williams - Dragoman Pass. The tale of a 1950s Land-Rover expediton.

5. Group Captain Peter Townsend - Earth My Friend. A 57,000 - mile circumnavigation of the globe by Land Rover in 1956.

Early Expedition Films

1. In search of the Kalahari Bushmen (25 mins). Laurens Van der Post's expedition.

2. Overland to Singapore (13 mins). The first Oxford and Cambridge Expedition.

3. Overland to the Lost World (25 mins). The third Oxford and Cambridge Expedition, to the Amazon Basin.

4. Safari to London (30 mins). From Cape Town to London by Land-Rover.

THE LAND ROVER STORY

△ *This publicity shot from 1966 shows a Series IIA 88-inch model rather artistically posed with some fishermen.*

The early

James Taylor looks at the life and times of the first Series IIA models.

IN THE first half of the 1960s, Land-Rover production at Solihull expanded enormously. The quarter-millionth Land-Rover had come off the lines in November 1959, just over 11 years after the first one; but the next 250,000 Land-Rovers took under seven years to build, and the half-millionth vehicle was made in april 1966. The 1965–1966 financial year broke all home and export sales records for Land-Rovers, in spite of signs of a downturn in sales towards the end of the year as the world entered an economic recession.

Order-books were full and customers were being quoted lengthy waiting-times for new Land-Rovers. Rover was simply unable to build vehicles fast enough to keep up with demand, and even the proliferation of overseas assembly plants during the early 1960s was not enough to solve the problem. By the end of 1966, more than 30 per cent of export vehicles leaving Solihull were kits destined for assembly in one of no fewer than 29 overseas plants.

New projects also proliferated in the early 1960s, although only a small proportion of them became production models. the Land-Rover engineers were heavily involved in developing vehicles specifically to meet military requirements, and there were no fewer than three new model introductions: the Series IIA in September 1961, the 109-inch Forward-Control in 1962, and the special 12-seater version of the Station Wagon for the home market.

On the saloon side of the business, Rover was also expanding. The P6 2000 model was introduced in October 1963, and by the end of 1965 this was being built in twice the number attained by its P4 predecessors at their peak. Rover's financial position was healthier than ever, and during 1965 it took over the old-established Alvis company, thus adding military vehicles and traditionally-crafted luxury sporting cars to its range of products.

Yet the first half of the 1960s were the final years of the Rover Company's independence. Despite its healthy financial position, it could not protect itself from the effects of mergers elsewhere in the British

motor industry.

In the same year that Rover bought out Alvis, BMC bought out Pressed Steel, who supplied all of Rover's saloon bodies. this left the company in a dangerously vulnerable position, as its body supplier was now owned by a potential rival. Talks with Leyland Motors (which already owned Standard-Triumph and had its own body pressing plant) began in 1966 and, early in 1967, Rover agreed to join the Leyland empire.

It was the end of an era in more ways than one. The rapid expansion of the early 1960s could not but destroy the "family" amosphere so characteristic of the Solihull plant, and indeed the Wilks family which had run Rover since the 1930s and had created that atmosphere was slowly losing its grip on the company.

In 1962, Spencer Wilks stepped down from the Chairmanship, retaining his seat on the Rover Board but taking a less active role than before. He was succeeded by his brother Maurice, the brilliant engineer who had originated the Land-Rover; but Maurice Wilks died just over a year later, on 8th September 1963. The Wilks broth-

△ *This 109-inch Series IIA was posed on a construction site for the Publicity Department. How long would it have stayed this clean in real life?*

sixties

ers' nephews Peter Wilks and Spen King were already in senior positions at Rover, but the merger with Leyland (and, later, the creation of British Leyland) inevitably created a new and different culture at Solihull.

A new diesel

As the 1960s opened, Rover was building Land-Rovers in just two basic forms. These were the 88-inch and 109-inch wheelbase models, each one available with either a 51bhp, 2-litre, diesel engine or a 77bhp 2.25-litre petrol type. The last major changes had taken place in 1958, when the original 88-inch and 109-inch models had been substantially revised to create the Series II versions.

Customers continued to demand custom-built vehicles for special jobs, and the Land-Rover engineers were continuing to look at ways of building variants with bigger payloads. On the whole, though, the customers were satisfied with what was on offer. There was just one exception to this general satisfaction – and that was the diesel engine.

Right from the beginning of diesel engine production, Solihull had know that the engine did not give the Land-Rover a good enough road performance. High torque at low engine revolutions was all very well when towing or labouring across rough terrain, but on the road the engine was a liability. the customers thought so, too, and a look at the production figures for Series II Land-Rovers given in the January 1993 issue of Land Rover Owner shows that only around one in every five vehicles built was diesel-powered.

The 2-litre engine had been designed with capacity increases in mind, however, and as early as May 1958, an internal Solihull memorandum shows that a 2.25-litre version was under consideration. The basic capacity increase was simple enough: the engine was a wet-liner design, and the engineers had already obtained a 2.25-litre capacity for the related petrol engine by fitting different cylinder liners to give a larger bore.

However, there were doubts whether the three-bearing crankshaft would be tough enough for the stresses of a 2.25-litre diesel

engine, and some consideration appears to have been given to redesigning the engine with a five-bearing crankshaft. In the event, improved combustion chamber design reduced the stresses and Solihull did not change to a five-bearing crankshaft for another 20 years!

Experimental prototypes of the enlarged engine first ran during 1958, and the 2.25-litre diesel was signed off for production in July 1960, with an anticipated on-sale date of September 1961. Ten pre-production prototypes had been completed by the end of 1960, and some of these were probably built into a special batch of pre-production 88-inch models between about April and June 1961. Production proper began on schedule, and the 2.25-litre diesel engine replaced the old 2-litre type for the 1962 model-year which began in September 1961.

The 2.25-litre diesel certainly made a difference. It offered 62bhp at 4,000rpm instead of the 51bhp at 3,500rpm of its predecessor, and maximum torque went up from 87lb/ft at 2,000rpm to 103lb/ft at just 1,800rpm. Thus, both higher road speeds

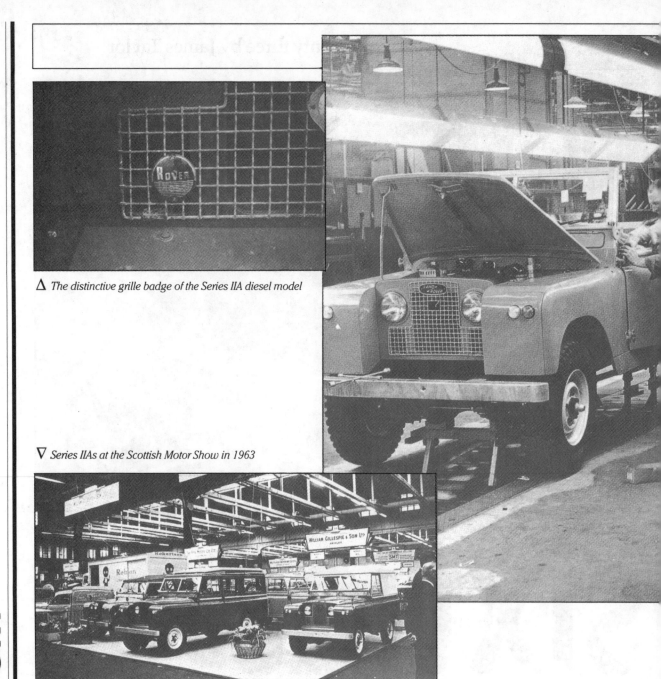

△ *The distinctive grille badge of the Series IIA diesel model*

▽ *Series IIAs at the Scottish Motor Show in 1963*

and greater lugging power were available.

Sales literature attributed the improved bottom-end torque to a new inlet manifold design, and referred to the special combustion chamber design which helped to cut down noise. This, it said, was a Ricardo Comet V type, modified with "pimples which improve the heat transfer between the chamber surface and the gas and assist the mixing of air and fuel."

According to Jack Swaine, then Chief Engine Designer, the combustion chamber had actually been developed for the multi-fuel Land-Rover engine which the military wanted (but eventually did not take); it also appears possible that a version of this combustion chamber was incorporated into the 2-litre diesel engine from about 1958 with the aim of cutting down combustion noise.

The Series IIA

The Series II Land-Rover needed no modification to take the 2.25-litre diesel engine,

and the production vehicles fitted with it could not be distinguished from their 2-litre forebears in any way. It was probably for this reason that Rover decided to fit them with a small grille badge which read, "Rover Diesel". The 1962 model-year vehicles, whether petrol- or diesel-powered, were also known as Series IIA models.

The reason for this change of designation was actually a change in the Rover chassis numbering system. For the 1962 model-year, Rover saloon and Land-Rover chassis numbers lost the digit which indicated model-year and acquired instead a suffix-letter which indicated major specification changes. As these did not always occur at the model-year changeover, the new system was considerably less confusing and more flexible than the old.

The first suffix letter to be used was, of course, "A"; and so the 1962 Land-Rovers became A-suffix models. It became commonplace to refer to the versions with the 2.25-litre diesel engine as Series IIA types;

subsequent suffixes, however, were not generally elevated to the status of model-names.

There were no major changes to the Series IIA models for the first half of the 1960s, although minor specification changes did occur. In October 1963, for example, new headlamps with flat lenses replaced the convex-lens type fitted since the beginning of Land-Rover production. A similarly minor change put the seating capacity of 109-inch Station Wagons for the home market up from 10 to a rather uncomfortable 12, early in 1962.

The change itself was minor – six inward-facing individual seats replaced the two benches in the rear – but it made a big difference to the purchase price and therefore also to sales. With 10 seats, a Station Wagon was a car under UK taxation law, and as such it was subject to Purchase Tax. With 12 seats, however, it became a bus and was therefore exempt from purchase Tax. The price difference was astonishing:

Δ *Pumping out Land-Rovers as fast as they could: This is the Solihull assembly line in 1964*

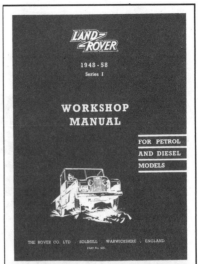

Available from
the
LRO BOOKSHOP

placed above.

where a petrol-engined 10-seater cost £1,293 early in 1962, its 12-seater equivalent cost just £950.

New models

Even though demand for the 88-inch and 109-inch Land-Rovers comfortably exceeded Solihull's ability to supply the vehicles during this period, the Rover Company did not rest on its laurels. In September 1962, it introduced yet another variant of the Land-Rover, this time a Forward-Control model based on the 109-inch chassis; and the first half of the 1960s saw a great deal of experimental work on new models, particularly to meet military requirements.

It was an incredibly busy period. The airportable 88-inch and 109-inch models, the 112-inch and 120-inch Forward-Controls, the 129-inch bonneted model, and the 110-inch gun tractor were all projects from these years; 2.25-litre turbocharged diesel engines and a 2.25-litre multi-fuel engine were also developed, and six-cylinder

engines of both 2.6-litre and 3-litre capacities were tried out in Land-Rovers.

Perkins diesels figured in a number of projects and, after 1965, the Land-Rover engineers started looking at the Buick V8 to which managing director William Martin-Hurst had bought manufacturing' rights. They even considered V6 versions of it.

There was more: vehicles like the OTAL (One-Ton amphibious Land-Rover), the six-cylinder 88-inch and the 2-litre OHC Land-Rover with its P6 saloon car engine all date from this period. However, the only ones which actually went into production were the six-cylinder 109-inch models, the 88-inch airportables and (after a delay of more than 12 years), the V8 Land-Rover.

All of these production models will be covered in later episodes of *LRO*'s Land Rover Story; the projects which did not prosper have already been or soon will be covered in our Dead Ends series.

The information on which this feature is based comes from various documents of the period and from a series of individuals who worked at Solihull during the early 1960s. I am grateful to all of them for their help. Regrettably, I am no longer able to quote from Rover Board meeting minutes: these are protected by a 30-year publication rule, which means that those from the beginning of 1963 onwards are currently out of bounds.

THE LAND ROVER STORY

95

ASSEMBLED BY
ROVER
(ZAMBIA) LIMITED

the toughest vehicle on 4 wheels!

SOLE DISTRIBUTORS IN ZAMBIA: CAMS Ltd

HEAD OFFICE: P.O. BOX 1053, KITWE. BRANCHES THROUGHOUT ZAMBIA

◁ *Overseas assembly became a very important element in Land Rover production in this period. This advertisement is indicative of what was happening.*

Facts, figures

James Taylor looks at the production and sales of the Series IIA models built before the Leyland merger of 1967.

THE FIRST half of the 1960s was a period of further expansion for the Land Rover side of the Rover Company. With the exception of a slight dip caused by poor trading conditions in 1962-1963, production figures increased steadily every year from 1961 to 1966; and in fact, the 1965-1966 Financial Year figures represented a record, with 47,941 Land-Rovers rolling off the production lines.

In 1966, the Rover C company was among the recipients of the newly-introduced Queen's Award for Industry, awarded for outstanding service to the economy; and in April 1966, the 500,000th Land Rover came off the production lines at Solihull. The August 1966 Annual Report to Shareholders proudly recorded that Land-Rovers had earned over £245 million in foreign revenue since their introduction in 1948.

There seemed no end to the demand for Land Rovers. Production was already at full capacity on the Solihull lines, and the only way to meet demand appeared to be by expanding the assembly facilities. Rover had already spent huge sums of money to get its new P6 (Rover 2000) saloon into production, and so was not best placed to spend more. As a result, Chairman George Farmer announced in Rover's 1963 Annual Report that the company planned to raise a further £2 million through a Rights Issue in order to finance the expansion of Land Rover manufacture.

These expansion plans were completed in late 1964 or early 1965, but by this stage the Rover Board was referring to them only as an interim measure. The 1964 Annual Report explains that Land-Rover production capacity would be increased even further as soon as the company could find somewhere to put the necessary new buildings!

Yet, by August 1966, these plans for additional expansion were on hold. One reason was the economic recession which was affecting all Rover's markets at the time; the other main one was that a major increase in overseas assembly of Land Rovers had reduced the need to expand assembly facilities at Solihull.

Rover had entered the period of the Series IIA's production with a total of 20 overseas assembly plants already up and running. In 1961-62, it opened new plants in Nigeria, Turkey, Ghana and Costa Rica. Others were opened in Southern Rhodesia (1962-63), Zambia, Ethiopia, Peru and Trinidad (all in 1966).

Some of these plants turned out relatively small numbers of vehicles, but there was no doubt of their importance to the Land Rover side of Solihull's business. Around 70% of all Land-Rovers went for export, and of these more than 30% were assembled abroad. In round figures, that meant that

△ *Production built up steadily during the early 1960s, and it was a Series IIA which became the 500,000th Land Rover to be built, in April 1966. Looking to the future, the celebrations centred on the 500,001st vehicle – on to the next half-million!*

and 'funnies'

almost 10,000 Land Rovers a year were being assembled outside Solihull in the mid-1960s.

At home, Rover had begun to suffer from the production stoppages which were the bane of British industry in the 1960s. The Chairman's Statement in Rover's 1964 Annual Report plaintively noted:

"Whilst we continue to enjoy the best of relations with the Trade Unions with whom we have to negotiate, we are all too frequently the subject of unofficial stoppages which take place before recourse is made to the procedure agreed between the Union and the Employers for the settlement of disputes. Disruption of production and rising costs are two of the most serious problems we are faced with, and the results of the current year will depend to a large extent on these two factors."

A similar comment appeared in the 1965 Annual Report, but the problem had presumably lessened by the following year, for

no comment was made in the 1966 Report.

Not every Land Rover made in the first half of the 1960s was a straightforward 88-inch or 109-inch model, of course. For a start, the range had been swelled after 1962 by the 109-inch Forward Control model, and some 2,500 of these had been included in the 500,000 Land Rovers production milestone which Rover announced in April 1966. On top of this, Solihull was still turning out military models and custom-built "specials" for civilian customers.

The military models

Military Land-Rover orders formed a large and important part of total sales during the early 1960s. The British Army had long since standardised on Land-Rovers as general-purpose light 4x4s, and was also beginning to look at their possibilities for other roles. Regular large orders for Rover Mk. 8s (88-inch Series IIAs) and Rover Mk. 9s (109-inch Series IIAs) reached Solihull,

and Series IIA models entered service in the EK (1962), EL, EM (1963), EN, EP (1964), ER, ES (1965), and ET (1966) registration series. Further batches would follow in the later 1960s.

Most British military Land Rovers had canvas cab roofs and tilts because these made them more versatile as load-carriers or troop carriers; however, some hardtop models and station wagons were bought to fill specialist roles, and of course the specially-built ambulance versions were also delivered in quantity.

In addition, small numbers of 109-inch models were equipped from the beginning with WOMBAT missile launchers in their load-beds. Many 109-inch models were called upon to tow the new 105mm Pack Howitzer (which they could do far more easily than the older Series I 88s), and many were seen in the 1960s towing English Electric trailers bearing Thunderbird missiles.

Military sales continued to be important in the first half of the 1960s. ▷

The Australian military also took quantities of long- and short-wheelbase Series IIA Land Rovers in the first half of the 1960s. These were all shipped out as KD packs to Australia, where they were both assembled and adapted to suit their intended roles. Characteristic of these vehicles were the angular front wheelarch cutouts and (in most cases) the large brushguard mounted on the front bumper.

Many were specifically equipped, for example to carry the US-made M-40 106mm rifle; and the adaptations were quite different from those seen in British military service.

Further afield, Land-Rovers served in the military or other Government agencies of dozens of countries, and in 1966 Rover proudly produced a full list of these.

It was an impressive list, consisting of some 120 entries which ran to four pages of an A5-sized sales catalogue, and it demonstrated quite clearly how successfully the Land Rover dominated the light 4x4 military market all over the world during the 1960s.

Special Projects

Many of the military versions of the Series IIA Land-Rover differed considerably from their civilian counterparts, and Solihull had a special Military Development Section which oversaw the development of military-specification vehicles. Today, it is the responsibility of Land Rover Special Vehicles to develop military variants to meet customer requirements.

In the 1960s, however, George Mackie's Special Projects Department steered well clear of such matters, and had nothing to do with the development of vehicles like the 109-inch Shorland Armoured Car, which was announced in 1965 and was initially based on a 109-inch Series IIA Land Rover.

The objectives of the Special Projects Department remained what they had been when the Department had been established in 1957. The Department's role was to assist or promote the development of bespoke Land Rovers by liaising with the manufacturers of specialist equipment, bodywork and other items. Rover was the only 4x4 manufacturer which offered such a service, and in this it scored heavily over its rivals from Willys (the Jeep), Austin (the Gipsy), Toyota (the Land Cruiser) and Nissan (the Patrol).

During the period of the Series II's production, a huge number of adaptations had been tested and given the much-prized Land Rover "approval" – and a number had also been rejected as unsuitable for use with Land Rovers. In the early days of its existence, the Special Projects Department had naturally concentrated on testing and granting approval for the more popular types of adaptation; but as the Series IIAs came on stream, so the Department began to look at ever more extraordinary adaptations of the Land Rover.

Among these were Carmichael's Red-

△ *This familiar publicity picture was issued during 1965, and showed no fewer than 38 different types of Land Rover which could be bought from the factory. That's not counting engine options, of course . . .*

wind FT/6 fire appliance, a purpose-built forward-control conversion which did not use Solihull's own Forward-Control chassis but rather an adapted 109-inch normal-control type. This intriguing vehicle did go into production, but attempts to produce a Land-Rover which would run on railway lines and could be used for light shunting duties were abandoned when the BR Chairman Dr Beeching embarked on a policy of closing down most of the small branch lines on which such a vehicle might have been useful. Nevertheless, one of the prototypes was used to demonstrate the new 2¼-litre diesel engine when the Series IIA models were launched in 1961, and hauled some wagons around on a siding at Dorridge and Knowle railway station for the benefit of the Press.

Not everything which Special Projects looked at was quite this extraordinary, of course. Among the Department's bread-and-butter approved conversions of the Land-Rover were the fire appliances, now made by several different manufacturers because the original exclusivity agreement with Carmichael's had expired; ambulances continued to be in demand; and there were all kinds of simpler adaptations, in which the vehicle's PTOs were harnessed to drills, saw benches, generators and so on.

"For every job," boasted one 1962 advertisement, "there's a made-to-measure Land Rover". And by the mid-1960s, Land Rover advertising could proudly boast that there were 27 body-styles, 80 catalogued options and no fewer than 120 approved items of specialised equipment. In addition, there were chassis/cab versions of every model for custom-built bodywork, as well as both petrol and diesel engines. It is hardly surprising, then, that no two Land Rovers from this period ever seem to be exactly alike!

Thanks to the Road Transport Fleet Data Society for information about military Series IIAs.

Was this the 500,001st Land Rover?

Unfortunately, the fate of the 500,001st Land-Rover is not known for certain. However, *LRO* Technical Editor Robert Ivins did come across an unusual Land-Rover which might have been this commemorative vehicle.

The one he knew of was a 2.25-litre petrol-engined 88, registered at Solihull with a D-suffix (1966) number. It had been painted bright yellow from new, and had a red-painted chassis and axles - so it must have been some sort of special vehicle, even if not the 500,001st!

Sadly, the vehicle no longer exists. It was broken up about 15 years ago after an accident on its owner's Nottinghamshire farm. So far, no-one has been able to confirm that the 500,00st Land-Rover was specially painted in yellow and red, but surviving black-and-white pictures do not rule out the possibility.

△ *This picture of the first prototype Forward Control chassis, dated May 1960, was found in the archives of conversion specialists Pilcher-Gree Note the absence of the production-style girder-frame above the chassis*

The 109 Forw

James Taylor tells the story behind one of the rarest production Land-Rover models.

THROUGHOUT THE 1950s, the Rover Company was persistently badgered by both actual and potential customers to build Land-Rovers capable of carrying bigger and bigger payloads. The 86-inch and 107-inch models of 1953 were the first attempts to meet this need, but even they were not enough. So it was that, towards the end of the decade, the Land-Rover design engineers started to look at ways of making Land Rovers with very much larger carrying capacities than those which were already in production.

Exactly what it was that set them thinking about a Forward-Control vehicle as one way of meeting the high-payload requirement is no longer clear. As early as 1955, there had been an experimental forward-control 107-inch Land-Rover, but this seems to have been designed from the outset as a minibus rather than as a load-carrier, and was probably not the inspiration

behind the eventual production vehicle. Far more likely as the source of inspiration is the Forward-Control Jeep, which had been announced in two wheelbase lengths during 1957. By april 1958, a Forward-Control Land-Rover featured on the list of future projects at Solihull.

There were several theoretical advantages to the forward-control layout. As the cab was sited above the engine instead of behind it, a greater proportion of the vehicle's overall length could be devoted to the loadspace. This in turn meant that a relatively large load could be carried in a relatively short vehicle. But no doubt the primary appeal of the ideal to the Land-Rover designers was that it would be possible to modify the existing normal-control chassis to create a new forward-control model, which meant that there would be savings in development time and in manufacturing costs.

Work on the new forward-control Land-Rover probably began in 1959. As the main objective was to design a vehicle with a high payload capability, the largest exist-

ing chassis the 109-inch Series II type – was used as the starting-point. Whether there were plans from the beginning to build an 88-inch forward-control as well is not clear, although no doubt the theoretical advantages of a short vehicle capable of carrying a high payload would have been obvious at Solihull.

One way or another, the first running prototype had a 109-inch wheelbase, and it appears to have been ready by May 1960. It was only after this that the Land-Rover designers started looking at an 88-inch forward-control model, building a prototype over the summer of 1960 (see Dead Ends in LRO November 1992). A second 109-inch prototype was built before the end of the year, and work also started on a third.

Presumably, these 109-inch prototypes all had the ordinary Land-Rover axles and large 9.00x16 tyres which became standard on the production vehicles. however, the first two appear not to have had the heavy girder frame above the main chassis which was characteristic of the production vehicles. Without this, the floor of the load-bed

◁ *This is the second prototype, pictured in September 1960. The low chassis gave a low load-bed, but made for a very strange-looking vehicle!*

Perhaps the most original 109-inch Forward Control still around is this 1962 example, which belongs to the Dunsfold Land Rover Museum. The girder-frame above the chassis can be seen just below the bodywork ▷

ard Control

was of course much closer to the ground, and there is some evidence to suggest that this feature prompted the Land-Rover people to consider making a special low-loader variant of the 109-inch Forward-Control alongside the standard type: certainly, papers dated October 1960 from the Engineering Department refer to discussions about such a vehicle.

The girder frame appears to have been added to the third prototype, which was put on the road in January 1961. As it brought with it several disadvantages – a higher floor for the load-bed, extra weight, and extra cost – there must have been some very good reasons for incorporating it into the specification. A best guess is that the standard 109-inch chassis was not sufficiently rigid to take the stresses imposed by the 30cwt payload which was a design target, and that this extra frame welded above it was the simplest way of adding the necessary strength without completely redesigning the chassis.

Several more prototypes were built during 1961, and Rover started to demonstrate

their new vehicle to potential customers in the hope of attracting bulk orders. At this stage, of course, the 109-inch Forward-Control was still only a development project, and large advance orders would help persuade the Rover Board to sanction actual production of the vehicle. Prototypes were demonstrated to the Swiss Army, the Nigerian Police, the Spanish Army, the Spanish Guardia Civil and the Portuguese Army, among others. Advance information was also sent out to importers overseas in order to assess the likely sale potential. Some importers – Rover New Zealand among them – were also given advance details of the 88-inch Forward Control.

Whether Rover did secure the large advance orders they had been hoping for is unclear, but something must have tipped the balance in favour of the 109-inch Forward Control during the autumn of 1961. That November the other large load-carrier which was under development at Solihull (the 129-inch model, see LRO for March 1992) was put on temporary hold and the Rover Board agreed that the 109-inch For-

ward-Control should go into production.

It was probably also at around this time that development work ceased on the 88-inch Forward-Control model. Yet the idea was not completely lost. During this period, Rover was trying to find extra production capacity to cope with increasing Land-Rover orders and with the forthcoming high-volume P6 saloon car, and in April 1961 negotiations had begun about sub-contracting manufacture of the new 109-inch Forward Control to aircraft manufacturers Alfred Miles, Ltd. Those negotiations came to nothing, but it must have been while they were under way that Alfred Miles came across the 88-inch Forward-Control, learned that Rover would not be putting it into production, and secured agreement to develop their own version (see LRO for June 1992). Sadly, it remained very rare.

On Sale

The 109-inch Forward Control land-Rover was announced at the Commercial Motor Show in September 1962. This was

△ *Few Forward Controls saw this kind of work! This one was owned by farmer Stewart Hibberd, a founder of the Land Rover Owners' Club, who has recently bought it back and is now restoring it. The Land Rover development engineers used to test Forward Control models on Mr Hibberd's land in Dorset*

more of an achievement than it appeared, because a hiccup in development during August 1961 had led Rover's planners to expect an autumn 1963 launch. The problem was that the standard Land-Rover transfer box had proved inadequate for the job, and the designers gloomily predicted a two-year delay if they had to design a new one and get it into production. However, it proved possible to save time by adopting a simplified design for the new transfer box, with the result that the vehicle entered production a full year ahead of its original schedule.

As announced, the Forward-Control was available only with the four-cylinder 2.25 litre petrol engine. Diesel versions had been built, but they proved so embarrassingly underpowered that Rover decided against putting them on the market after just five had been made. Standard body configurations were a fixed-side lorry, a dropside lorry, and a flat-bed lorry. All came with a truck cab, and all were capable of carrying 30cwt on the road or 25cwt off it. Chassis/cab versions and chassis cowl versions, either with or without the girder frame above the chassis, were also available to the specialist converters. It was possible to order inward-facing seats for the load-bed, and a tilt for the rear of dropside or fixed-side bodies. The tilt could be

fitted optionally with perspex side windows. With the late, b-suffix chassis, heavy-duty ENV axles became an option.

It was apparent from the moment the Forward-Control Land Rover was announced that its most serious failing was a lack of performance. The vehicle was very much heavier than the normal-control 109-inch, and when fully laden (with a payload which was exactly double that of the normal-control 109), it struggled to reach 45 mph. Fuel economy was also pretty disastrous, with 10-12mpg being quite normal. Before long, the Land-Rover engineers were instructed to give the Forward-Control more power - and quickly.

production engines which offered more power than the 77bhp 2.25-litre petrol engine already in the Forward-Control. These were both six-cylinder 10E types, related to the 2-litre petrol engine of the Series One Land-Rovers. The smaller one was the 2.6-litre engine used in the P4 saloons, and developed 104 bhp and 138 lb/ft of torque at a usefully low 1,500rpm. The larger one was the 3-litre type used in the P5 saloons, and at this stage it had just been redeveloped to offer 134bhp and 169 lb/ft at 1,750rpm. Either would have cured the Forward-Controls performance problems, but the engineers settled on the 2.6-litre, probably because it would offer better fuel

economy than the larger engine.

The six-cylinder engine was quickly modified to suit its new Land-Rover application. Its compression ratio was lowered to the 7:1 which was compatible with the poor-quality fuel often used in Land-Rovers abroad, a different camshaft was fitted, and the result was an engine which had just 90bhp at 4,500rpm and 132 lb/ft of torque at 1,500rpm.

The 109-inch Forward-Control thus became the first production land-Rover to have a six-cylinder engine when it was announced in the autumn of 1963. Strangely, however, the six-cylinder model was never offered on the home market. Just one was built to home market specification, presumably as a trials vehicle, and the sale catalogues always stated quite categorically that the model was for export only. The situation remained the same until production of the 109-inch Forward-Control ceased in 1966.

The customers

The 109-inch Forward-Control was always a rare beast in its home country. In four years of production, just 353 examples with the four-cylinder petrol engine were made to home market specification. Even adding the five diesel models and one six-cylinder (all of which were probably re-

This caravan conversion was built in 1964 by Glover, Webb and Liversidge ▽

109 inch Forward Control Prototypes

109/FC/1 Completed by May 1960, Left-hand-drive, 24-litre petrol engine. No girder frame above chassis.

109/FC/2 Completed by September 1960. Right-hand-drive.

109/FC/3 Registered 6087 UE on 1st January 1961. Engine no. 2.25/46 (2-1/4-litre petrol). Left-hand-drive. Probably first vehicle with girder frame above chassis. Demonstrated to Spanish and Portuguese military and Spanish Guardia Civil in September-November 1961.

109/FC/4 No details known.

109/FC/5 Registered 4301 WD, probably on 1st September 1961. Engine no. 2.25/50 (2-1/4-litre petrol). Right-hand-drive.

109/FC/6 No details known.   **109/FC/7** No details known.

109/FC/8 Registered 8356 WD on 1st February 1962.

Further details would be welcome!

109 inch Forward Control Production

Chassis numbers beginning	286/287/288/289/290 (4-cyl petrol)	2,091
	30/301/302/303/304 (6-cyl petrol)	1,097
	305 (4-cyl diesel)	5
		3,193

These figures are taken from the Rover Company despatch records currently held by BMIHT and are used by kind permission

---

tained at Solihull anyway), the total is not great. Most numerous of all were the right-hand-drive export four-cylinder petrol types, of which 940 were built, and the left-hand-drive six-cylinder petrol types, of which 940 were built, and the left-hand-drive six-cylinder types, of which there were 633. Both four-cylinder and six-cylinder versions were also assembled overseas from CKD packs sent out from Solihull, and there were just 42 of these with left-hand-drive and 399 with right-hand-drive, with four-cylinder models predominating in each case.

The British Army examined a four-cylinder 109 Forward Control, probably some time around 1962-1963. An ambulance version is also said to have been under consideration, but no order was placed for either. The Indonesion Army did take a number of vehicles, but the armed services of most other nations seem to have declined. No doubt the main reason was that the Forward-Control was underpowered as a four-cylinder and too thirsty as a six-cylinder. But there were other failings: braking was marginal when the vehicle was fully laden, even though all models came with a vacuum servo as standard; off-road stability was sometimes questionable because of the vehicle's height; and hand-

ling at speed could sometimes be quite exciting.

Few special-bodied versions seem to have been built. Martin Walter of Folkestone built a bus-bodied version during 1963, but whether there were every any more than the one which appeared at a Special Projects demonstration at Packington Park (near Solihull) that September is unclear. Glover, Webb and Liversidge turned one into a caravan in 1964, but this was probably a one-off to special order.

Overall, Rover must have been rather disappointed with sales of the Forward-Control, yet the company continued to believe in it.

Over in the USA, Jeep gave up on their forward-control models in 1964 after just seven years of low-volume production, but Rover decided to give the Forward-Control Land-Rover another chance. In 1966, the company announced a revised version: the Series IIB 110-inch Forward-Control. The history of that vehicle will be covered in a later episode of the Land Rover Story.

Many thanks for information and/or pictures to Stewart Hibbard, David Millard, Roger Crathorne, Brian and Philip Bashall of dunsfold Land-Rovers, Nick Dimbleby and the British Motor Industry heritage Trust.

Update

Since this article was written, former Land-Rover engineer Norman Busby has confirmed that a Forward-Control Jeep was examined at Solihull during the development of the 109 Forward-Control Land-Rover. He recalls that he and his colleagues were most unimpressed by the ride quality, and that the Jeep had a huge weight incorporated in the rear of its chassis to counteract pitching!

The Land Rover logo was joined by British Leyland's on promotional material in the late 1960s.

A typical 1967 Series IIA Land Rover doing what such vehicles typically did on the farm. ▷

Leyland and

In this episode of our complete Land-Rover history, James Taylor explains what was happening in the second half of the 1960s.

THE 1960s were the age of the great mergers in the British motor industry. The movement started in 1960, when Jaguar bought our Daimler, an acquisition which it followed up in 1961 with the annexation of Guy Motors of Wolverhampton, builders of buses and trucks. Next on the scene was Leyland, another truck and bus manufacturing concern, which rescued an ailing Standard-Triumph in 1961 and then in 1962 merged with AEC, its own long-term rival in the heavy commercial vehicle field. Rover's contribution to this trend was its purchase of Alvis in 1965.

All these changes made the British motor industry stronger and fitter than it had been at the end of the 1950s, but things were soon to take a turn for the worse. During 1965, BMC (itself formed by the merger of Austin and the Nuffield Group in 1952) bought out Pressed Steel, the independent body manufacturer which supplied several of the car makers – Rover among them.

From BMC's point of view, the acquisition was a brilliant business move, because it put the company in a position from which it would be supplying bodies to its own competitors. It would thus learn of their new-model plans well in advance and (if it so chose) could use its position to manipulate its competitors as well.

Jaguar quickly recognised which way the wind was blowing, and during 1966 sought to guarantee its long-term body supplies through a merger with BMC. This resulted in a new grouping known as BMH (British Motor Holdings). The Rover directors recognised that they would have to act fast and, by the end of 1966, were in discussion with Leyland about a merger which would assure Rover of body supplies through various Leyland-owned plants. Early in 1967, Rover became part of the Leyland combine.

The British Government now took an interest in what was going on. Concerned that the two major groupings within the British motor industry – Leyland and BMH – would cut one another's throats in export markets and thus lose overseas trade for

the country, it encouraged them to discuss a merger. The precise details of those discussions have never been made public, but the evidence suggests that what the Government actually did was to arrange a shotgun marriage. Early in 1968, Leyland and BMH merged as the new British Leyland, a combine which probably did more damage than any other single body to the British motor industry.

At first, BL was content to let its constituent companies carry on in much the same way as they always had, and it was only later that BL management attempted the massive task of product rationalisation. As far as the Land-Rover marque was concerned, there was little change during the lifetime of the Series IIA models. Sales catalogues started to sport the BL logo during 1968 but that, as far as outside observers could see, was all. What was going on behind the scenes was quite a different matter, of course, and even the Land-Rover people were to some extent kept in the dark.

In April 1967, just a few weeks after joining forces with Leyland, Rover announced

△ *With the six-cylinder engine came more power and more refinement. This is an early example, with the SU carburettor.*

the later IIAs

a set of production changes for the Series IIA normal-control Land-Rovers. The first vehicles built to the new specification had D-suffix letters to their chassis numbers, although Rover continued to refer to them as Series IIA models, even if Series IID might have been more logical.

The only significant mechanical change was that a Zenith carburettor now replaced the long-serving Solex type; power and torque ratings remained unchanged, however. Following industry trends, a negative-earth electrical system replaced the positive-earth type, and this was accompanied by some minor changes to the electrical system. Most noticeable, perhaps, was that there was a key-starter in place of the old-fashioned push-button variety, while the two independent wiper motors had given way to a single motor which drove both wipers through a rack.

There were also some worthwhile improvements to the instruments and controls. The handbrake lever had been lengthened, and could now be reached comfortably by a driver wearing one of the static safety belts which were the only type

then available. The instrument panel was still centrally-mounted and still had two large dials, but the minor controls and warning lights had been rearranged within it. There were now three warning lights in the speedometer face, a charging circuit warning light instead of an ammeter, and a water temperature gauge.

These upgrades to the specification of the existing 88-inch and 109-inch Series IIA models were rather overshadowed by the arrival, also in April 1967, of a new six-cylinder 109-inch model. the original idea of putting the Rover six-cylinder engine into a normal-control Land-Rover may have surfaced as early as 1962-63, when the first six-cylinder Forward-Controls had been drawn up. Prototypes were probably running by 1964, and as early as 1965 one six-cylinder 109-inch Station Wagon was hand-built for the Queen Mother. During the mid-1960s, the six-cylinder engine was also tried out in 88-inch models, although no production examples were made.

The six-cylinder engine was the same 2.6-litre type as was already available in export models of the Forward-Control Land-

Rover, and was offered in the same state of tune. The exact reason why Rover decided to put it into production is not clear, but it seems possible that there was some concern about competition in export markets from the latest Toyota Land Cruiser, which came with a big and powerful six-cylinder petrol engine. In addition, there was no doubt that the extra smoothness and power of the six-cylinder engine would add to the appeal of the 109-inch Station Wagons in all markets and, in fact,half of all the six-cylinder Series IIAs built between 1967 and 1971 were Station Wagons.

The six-cylinder petrol engine made a very welcome difference to the performance of a 109-inch Land-Rover. There was much more torque available in top gear than with the four-cylinder petrol engine, and acceleration through the gears was noticeably improved. The six-cylinder Land-Rover was still laughably slow by saloon car standards, of course: 29 seconds for the 0-60mph standing-start might have been good by the standards of the four-cylinder models, but it compared poorly even with the 18 seconds of Rover's

△ *There cannot have been many One Ton Land Rovers built with the early headlamp arrangement, and YXC 320 F was probably a prototype or a very early production vehicle. Note the bulkier look given by the 9.00x16 tyres.*

slowest saloon, the 2000 Automatic.

There was rather more to the six-cylinder Land-Rovers than a simple engine transplant, however. As the vehicles were capable of around 77mph, the standard 70mph speedometer had to be replaced by one calibrated up to 90mph. These higher road speeds would have made the six-cylinder models harder to stop if Rover had not fitted wider front brakes (which gave a 12 per cent increase in lining area) and a vacuum servo as standard. The battery was relocated under the left-hand front seat (mainly because there was no room for it in the engine bay), the tool locker was thus displaced to the centre seat box, and for good measure there was a new dynamo with a higher charge rate than on four-cylinder models.

At home, the six-cylinder Series IIA Land-Rover sold steadily, but it was always a fairly rare beast by comparison with the four-cylinder petrol-engined 109s. Few changes were made during its production run, the most notable being that the original SU carburettor was replaced by a Zenith CD2S type late in 1967 after just under 500 vehicles had been made. In other respects, the six-cylinder models followed the development of the other normal-control Land-Rovers.

While it was undoubtedly true that the main reason for offering a six-cylinder engine in the 109-inch Land-Rover was to improve its performance, the Land-Rover engineers were well aware that its additional power and torque could also be used to improve the payload. So it was that the September 1968 Commercial Motor Show saw the introduction of a new version of the 109-inch normal-control Land-Rover, powered by the six-cylinder engine and called the One Ton.

The main attraction of the One Ton was that it could actually carry a payload of one ton (2,240lbs) across rough terrain, whereas the standard 109-inch models were limited to 1,800lbs off-road and 2,000lbs on the road. In order to achieve this increase, the Land-Rover engineers had backed up the six-cylinder engine with heavy-duty ENV axles (which were in fact already available as extra-cost options), heavy-duty suspension and 9.00x16 tyres instead of the 7.50x16 variety standard on other 109s. These tyres were already standard on the Forward-Control models, but extended spring shackles were needed to allow them to clear the wheel arches of the normal-control 109. As a result, the One Ton Land-Rover stood some two to three inches higher off the ground than its standard counterparts.

To maintain performance with its higher payloads, the One Ton model had lower gearing than the standard models, which was achieved simply through the use of the 110-inch Forward Control model's transfer box. Servo brakes were of course standard, as on the existing six-cylinder models, and an hydraulic steering damper was fitted to counter kickback from the large wheels and tyres.

As Rover's press release put it, the vehicle was intended to "fill a gap in a specialised sector of the market where there is a need for greater load carrying capacity than is provided by the basic 109-inch Land-Rover." The release went on to explain that the One Ton was expected "to appeal particularly to contractors, commercial fleet users, public authorities and manufacturers specialising in Land-Rover conversions, as well as farmers and other individuals who may need greater payload capacity, or who are using basic vehicles to their fullest extent."

The One Ton models were never strong sellers, but they were an essential addition to the range because they allowed the converters to develop a wider variety of special bodies for the long-wheelbase chassis. What proportion of Series IIA One Ton models were equipped with special bodywork is not clear, but an educated guess is that over half of the 308 built were deliv-

△ *Was this publicity picture taken at the same sawmill? Most production One Ten models had the revised headlamp/grille arrangement seen here. The late Series IIA wire mesh grille was actually shaped l;ike a cross rather than the inverted T seen on Land Rovers since the early 1950s.*

ered as chassis/cabs to the converters. Just 170 with the standard six-cylinder engine were sold on the home market, plus a further 22 with four-cylinder petrol engines, which appear to have been built to special order in 1970-71. These were given chassis numbers begining with 231, even though blocks of numbers begining 246 to 250 had already been allocated for four-cylinder One Ton models in case there were any orders. Perhaps this was symptomatic of the internal co-ordination problems which would afflict British Leyland more and more as time went on.

The mid-1960s saw the beginnings of a radical change in the automotive world. Largely as a result of Ralph Nader's book, *Unsafe at any speed*, the US car-buying public had become acutely conscious of safety-related issues. In addition, there was increasing concern at the smog problem in the

cities of the western seaboard, and the two issues were united when the US Government announced that every vehicle sold in the USA after 1968 would have to meet a set of safety criteria and a set of exhaust emissions criteria. As time went on, these regulations became stricter and were joined by others; and other countries began to follow the US lead.

One of the casualties of the new standards which were being set for automotive manufacturers was the Land-Rover's characteristic headlamp installation. The two lamps had been set into the grille panel ever since the 1948 centre-steer prototype had drawn its inspiration from a Willys Jeep, and their position there gave them a certain amount of protection in off-road conditions. However, the new regulations in some countries insisted that headlamps had to be closer to the outboard edges

of a vehicle, so that oncoming drivers could more easily see how wide the vehicle was. As a result, the Land-Rover engineers had to reposition their vehicle's headlamps in the wing fronts.

The first Land-Rovers with the redesigned front end carried a G-suffix on their chassis numbers, although they were still known as Series IIA models. For those markets which needed the repositioned lamps, the new front end became available in the spring of 1968, but the assembly lines did not go over completely to the new styling until several months later: it was February 1969 before they were available in Britain, for example. While it is true that the repositioned headlamps were rather forced upon the Land-Rover, those responsible for the restyle made such a good job of it that it was carried over in essence to the Series III models which replaced the IIA in 1971.

THE REDWING
FT/6
FIRE APPLIANCE

As approved by
The ROVER CO. LTD.

Threequarter Front View

- Based on the 109″ Land-Rover chassis converted to Forward Control by Carmichael & Sons (Worcester) Ltd.
- Seating for crew of four.
- Choice of Fire Pumps
- 140 gallon Water Tank.
- Fully enclosed Crew and Equipment Space.
- Fibreglass Roof, Waterproof, Rustproof.
- Four-door Cab for ease of entry and exit.
- Conversion makes the maximum use of Standard Land-Rover parts.

> *Demand for a Forward-Control fire tender prompted Carmichael's to design their own conversion before Land-Rover's vehicle was ready.*

APPLIANCE

BODYWORK. All aluminium body with full length fibreglass roof. Body sides fitted with drop down shutters. Rear enclosed by roller shutter.

PUMPS. Alternative pumps are mounted in the same position immediately behind the driving compartment.

PUMP A. K.S.B., 380 g.p.m. centrifugal two-stage with inbuilt water ring primer.

PUMP B. Coventry Climax 300/350 g.p.m. centrifugal with automatic water ring primer.

TANK. 140 gallon capacity, baffled and mounted at rear of appliance Hydrant filler provided also water level indicator adjacent to hydrant connection.

HOSE-REEL. Mounted above tank, containing 120′ × ¾″ hose, fitted with shut-off nozzle. Isolating valve fitted to shut-off reel from pump. 180′ of hose can be supplied if required.

STOWAGE. Two 8′ or 10′ lengths of 4″ suction hose and a light alloy ladder may be carried on the roof. Up to twelve 75′ lengths of 2½″ delivery hose may be carried in the rear hose racks. There is space for additional equipment behind the rear crew seats.

CREW ACCOMMODATION. Seating for 4 crew, 2 in front and 2 behind, with 4 door cab for ease of entry and exit.

FINISH. Painted red, all stucco aluminium left in natural finish. All external steel fittings heavily galvanised.

EXTRA EQUIPMENT. Twin flashing lights are fitted to the roof as standard. Siren, bell, etc., available at extra cost. Details and prices by request.

SHIPPING DETAILS

LENGTH	16′ 3″
WIDTH	5′ 4″
HEIGHT	7′ 4″
WEIGHT	4,557 lbs. approx.

CHASSIS

CHASSIS. Welded fabricated box section with box section cross members, providing great torsional and diagonal rigidity. The body is mounted on outriggers welded to side members. The front forward control extension is fabricated in the same manner as the main chassis. Special front and rear springs and shock absorbers are fitted. Four wheel drive is provided, automatically selected when transfer box low ratio is engaged. Drive to front axle optional with high ratio engaged ; this is selected by an independent lever.

POWER UNIT. Four cylinders. Overhead inlet and exhaust valves. Bore 90.49 mm. (3.562 in.), stroke 88.9 mm. (3.5 in.), capacity, 2,286 c.c. (139.5 cu. in.). Maximum B.H.P. 77 at 4,250 r.p.m. Maximum torque 124 lb. ft. (17 mKg.) at 2,500 r.p.m. Compression ratio 7 to 1. Cylinders cast integral with crankcase. Detachable cast iron cylinder head carrying all valve gear. Forged steel 3-bearing crankshaft fully balanced and counterweighted. Copper-lead main and big-end bearings. A distributor cut-out limits the engine speed to 4,200 r.p.m.

GEARS. Four forward speeds and reverse. Two-speed transfer box in conjunction with main gearbox gives eight forward speeds and two reverse.

CLUTCH. Single dry plate, 9″ diameter, hydraulically operated by pendant pedal.

BRAKES. Hydraulically operated foot brakes requiring light pressure on the pendant pedal. Two leading shoe brakes on front wheels. Mechanically actuated handbrake operates on transmission shaft to rear axle.

TYRE SIZE. 750 × 16. T29A Dunlop Trackgrip.

COOLING SYSTEM. By pump and fan, thermostatically controlled. Capacity 17½ pints (9.95 litres). Pressurised.

ADDITIONAL COOLING is provided by an oil cooler working in conjunction with the fire pump enabling long periods of pumping to be maintained.

ELECTRICAL SYSTEM. Lucas 12 volt. Coil ignition.

FUEL SYSTEM. 10-gallon (45 litres) tank with external filler at side of body. Solex down-draught carburettor with oil bath type air cleaner and silencer and integral centrifugal pre-cleaner. Mechanical pump and sediment bowl with gauze filter.

The Rover Company are not responsible for the manufacture of approved equipment and/or body work, although they have closely examined specification and design. Matters concerning Sales (including Shipping, Delivery, etc.), Service of Warranted Claims are the responsibility of the Manufacturer (whose name and address is given on this leaflet) or his Agent.
In cases of difficulty concerning approved equipment, the Special Project Section of the Land-Rover Engineering Department is available to offer advice.
The information contained in this leaflet is correct at the date of publication, but is subject to alteration without notice.

CARMICHAEL & SONS (Worcester) LIMITED

△ *Exports accounted for a claimed 80% of Land-Rover sales by the end of Series IIA production. This late Series IIA 109-inch model is being loaded aboard a cargo ship at a British port. Bumpers and other items were stowed under the wooden load-bed cover.*

Sales in the later sixties

Land-Rover sales held up very well in the first years of British Leyland, while over in Spain, Santana had started to do their own thing.

WHEN SERIES IIA production came to an end in the summer of 1971, Land-Rover sales were still booming. In fact, the annual figures had actually improved since the Leyland takeover in 1967. The 1967 financial year had seen a drop in production as compared to the 1966 record of 47,941, but 1968 saw a small improvement, 1969's figure was 50,561, and 1971 hit an all-time record of 56,663. It was a record which still stands today.

Also impressive were the total production figures for the Series IIA models. As the tables given at the end of this episode of the Land-Rover Story show, more than 343,000 normal-control Series IIA models had been built in 10 years of production. That figure actually exceeded the combined total of Series I and Series II models built during the 13 years from 1948 to 1961, and the Series IIA production total has still not been exceeded by any subsequent

Land-Rover variant.

In the meantime, the Land-Rover had passed yet another significant point in its career. The last occasion for celebrations had been in 1966, when the half-millionth vehicle had come off the production lines. This time, the occasion was the Land-Rover's 21st Anniversary, celebrated in April 1969 to publicise 21 years of continuous production. A centrepiece of the celebrations was R.01, the very first pilot-build Land-Rover, which had been bought back from its owner some years earlier and restored – albeit using some parts from later 80-inch models.

Throughout the 1960s, Land-Rovers had been assembled both at Solihull and in a whole series of plants overseas. The latter were supplied by Solihull with kits of parts, either CKD (Completely Knocked Down) or SKD (Semi-Knocked Down), which they then assembled into Land-Rovers. Many of these plants incorporated a limited number of locally-sourced components into the Land-Rovers they built, and these components were usually such things as tyres, glass, or (less commonly) electrical items.

However, by the end of Series IIA production, one overseas assembly plant was actually building its own Land-Rovers from the ground up, without any parts from Solihull.

Santana in the Sixties

That overseas plant was the MSA (Santana) factory at Linares in Spain. Established in the 1950s (see the February 1993 episode of the Land Rover Story), MSA was obliged by its agreement with the Spanish government to gradually increase the proportion of locally-manufactured components in its Land-Rovers over a ten-year period. At the end of that period, MSA had to be able to build Land-Rovers with 100% Spanish content; and the ten-year period was up in 1968.

MSA did not start building Series IIAs at exactly the same time as Solihull, because there was always a delay of some months between a KD pack leaving Solihull and that pack's emergence from the Linares plant as a completely built vehicle. Exactly when the first Series IIA KD packs left Solihull for Spain is not clear, but what is clear

The Land-Rover comes of age... this picture was taken at the 21st Birthday celebrations for the Land-Rover, in April 1969. The vehicle is R.01, the first pilot-build Land-Rover; the smiling gentleman is William Martin-Hurst, then Rover's Managing Director

is that the Santana Series IIAs did not go on sale until some time in 1962. In fact, 1962 was an important turning point for MSA. Until then, all the Land-Rovers it had built had been sold on the Spanish home market, and production had been very small. However, in 1962, it began to export Land-Rovers as well. Its first overseas market appears to have been Colombia, but in due course it expanded further and was able to sell vehicles in some markets which were denied to British-built Land-Rovers for political reasons. By 1968, MSA had built some 5,400 Land-Rovers in total, although it is not possible at present to say how many of these had been Series Ones and how many Series IIAs.

Most of the first Series IIA Santana models were window hardtop models, on both the 88-inch and 109-inch chassis. On the home market, only four-cylinder diesel engines could be had, although petrol engines were available for export and were specified for those Land-Rovers taken by the Spanish military in the late 1960s. Six-cylinder engines were not available in Santana-built Series IIAs.

The first indication that MSA was ready to stand alone was its 1967 announcement of the Santana 1300, an individual variant of the 109-inch Forward-Control Land-Rover (see LRO, April 1993). By the time a 109-inch normal-control Station Wagon appeared in 1968, MSA had probably become completely self-sufficient in manufacturing terms, and from now on its products began to differ more and more from Solihull's Land-Rovers.

The 1970 Santana 88-inch and 109-inch Especial models, for example, had no direct equivalent in Solihull's product range, although they were essentially Series IIA Station Wagons with upgraded seats and trim and De Luxe bonnets. They were also the first Santana Land-Rovers to have their headlamps in the wings (the change had taken place in 1968-69 at Solihull), and it would be 1972 before the wing-mounted lamps became standard on all Santana models.

From 1972, Station Wagons were fitted with single-piece rear lamp units while others retained the Solihull-style separate indicator and stop/tail lamps, and Santana

Series IIAs did not give way to Series IIIs until 1974. Exactly how many Santana Series IIAs were made is impossible to say, but the figure could be as high as 10,000. At a guess, 40% of these would have been totally manufactured in Spain.

Taking stock

A press release from Rover dated July 1969 summarised the Land-Rover's position during the final period of Series IIA production. "Over the years," it said, "the Land-Rover has become synonymous with the best in British Engineering and a universally known form of durable and reliable transport, and there is scarcely any country in the world – from China to Costa Rica – to which the vehicle has not been exported.

"In fact, since its introduction in 1948, over 630,000 have been produced for the world's markets, earning for this country well over £300 million in foreign exchange, and demand is currently greater than at any previous time in the vehicle's remarkable history.

"Assembly lines are running at peak pro-

A pair of late Series IIA Station Wagons pose with a Vickers Viscount airliner belonging to British European Airways (remember them?). The location is probably Birmingham's Elmdon Airport, the date probably 1969

Special Projects continued to approve a number of specialist bodies and other conversions. This is a 1970 Series IIA 109-inch equipped as a fire tender by H.C.B. Angus. (Photo by courtesy of Peter Lamb and the Series II Club)

SERIES IIA NORMAL-CONTROL LAND-ROVER PRODUCTION

N.B. No records of CKD production after 1965 exist, and no detailed records of vehicles manufactured (as distinct from assembled) by MSA are available. Actual totals are therefore in many cases higher than those given here. These figures also do not include Series IIA military lightweight models or Series IIA airportable 109-inch vehicles.

88-inch models, 1961-1971 (including Station Wagons to March 1965)

Chassis numbers beginning	241/242/243/244/245 (2-1/4-litre petrol)	112,061
	271/272/273/274/375 (2-1/4-litre diesel)	26,180
		Total: 138,241

88-inch Station Wagon, 1965-1971

Chassis numbers beginning	315/316/317/318/319 (2-1/4-litre petrol)	11,650
	320/321/322/323/324 (2-1/4-litre diesel)	1,922
		Total: 13,572

109-inch models, 1961-1971 (except Station Wagons)

Chassis numbers beginning	251/252/253/254/255 (2-1/4-litre petrol)	107,590
	276/277/278/279/280 (2-1/4-litre diesel)	31,168
		Total: 138,758

109-inch Station Wagon, 1961-1971

Chassis numbers beginning	261/262/263/264/265 (2-1/5-litre petrol)	33,627
	281/282/283/284/285 (2-1/4-litre diesel)	7,551
		Total: 41,178

109-inch six-cylinder models, 1967-1971

Chassis numbers beginning	345/346/347/348/349 (basic models)	5,481
	350/351/352/353/354 (Station Wagon)	4,949
	343 (NADA Station Wagon)*	811
		Total: 11,241

109-inch 1-ton, 1968-1971

Chassis numbers beginning	222/223/229 (2.6-litre petrol)	286
	231 (2-1/4-litre petrol)	22
		Total: 308

GRAND TOTALS: 88-inch 151,813
109-inch 191,485
343,298

*Production of the NADA (North American Dollar Area) six-cylinder Station Wagon ended in 1968.

The four-cylinder One-Ton models were built only in 1970-1971.

These figures are taken from the Rover Company despatch records currently held by BMIHT and are used by kind permission.

duction to meet demand both on the home market and from overseas . . . Land-Rovers are now sold in 182 markets throughout the world and exports currently represent 80% of total production."

To the buying public of the late 1960s and early 1970s, however, the Land-Rover also conjured up what another July 1969 press release called "thoughts of exciting overland journeys to previously unexplored areas . . . Hardly a week goes by without reports reaching the Rover Company's main headquarters at Solihull, of someone's Land-Rover exploits in remote areas of the world . . . Because of the number of private owners who set out on expeditions, the Rover Company has over the years geared itself to help and advise would-be travellers, and among literature available is a comprehensive *Guide to Land-Rover Expeditions* made up from reports on previous expeditions and on the Company's own technical experiences. There is also a thriving Land-Rover Owners' club which organises safaris, rallies and meetings for its 2,000 members."

As the final Series IIAs were being built in

1971, the best-sellers remained the 2.25-litre petrol-engined short-wheelbase models. Diesel engines were considerably less popular, but the slowest sellers among the normal-control models were the six-cylinder petrol types. Station Wagons of all types were far less numerous than the basic soft-top and hardtop models. Land-Rovers continued to appeal to the emergency services, and military orders continued to flow in – boosted, of course, by the arrival of the 88-inch Lightweight a few years earlier. The Special Projects Department remained busy, testing a wide variety of bolt-on extras, conversions and adaptations, and granting approval to those which would not tarnish the good name of Land-Rover. And the Forward-Control model, now in Series IIB 110-inch form,

remained a steady, low-volume, seller.

At this stage, the British Leyland merger of the late 1960s had still had very little effect on the Land-Rover. Yet BL's Chairman, Lord Stokes, did hint at the sort of problems which might arise when he made a statement to BL employees at the end of the 1971 financial year. It had been a better year than the previous one, he said, but "we must achieve substantially higher profit to support the major product and modernisation programmes which are essential if we are to remain viable as a major world motor manufacturer." It was already clear that budgets were going to be tight for some time to come and, out of the public eye, Solihull was discovering that it no longer had control over the profits which its own products made.

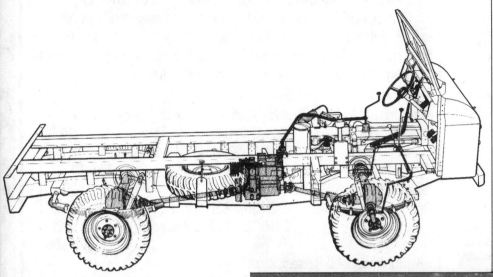

◁

Some of the major changes made for the 110 Forward Control are highlighted on this drawing. Note the gearchange linkage, handbrake and anti-roll bar

OXC 191 D was one of the earliest 110 Forward Controls. The low-mounted headlights and squared-off rear mud-flaps are instant recognition features of the Series IIB model ▷

The 110 Forward

Even rarer than the 109 Forward Control, the 110 Forward Control was nevertheless a much better vehicle. James Taylor tells its story.

THE ORIGINAL Forward Control Land-Rover, the 109-inch model introduced in 1962, was never wholly satisfactory. It was awkward to drive, mainly because the gearchange was very vague and the handbrake rather inaccessible, and it could be uncomfortable over rough surfaces because the cab-over-axle configuration caused the driver and passengers to take the worst of the bumps.

Unfortunately, its customers also expected too much of it. Solihull had designed the 109 Forward Control as a four-wheel-drive light lorry for the dirt roads of developing countries, and it had quite clearly stated in all the relevant literature that the vehicle should not be asked to carry a payload of more than 25cwt in off-road conditions. However, that did not deter owners from loading their vehicles up to the full

30cwt on-road capacity and then expecting them to perform properly off-road. Their argument was that every other Land-Rover they had owned could be overloaded like this and suffer nothing worse than the occasional spring breakage, so why should they not do the same with the Forward Control?

There were several good reasons why not, and one of them was that the Forward Control models were very close to the limit of their capabilities with a full payload. they were much heavier than the normal-control models, thanks mainly to the additional reinforcing frame above the chassis, and yet they were using components which for the most part had been borrowed from the normal-control models. Not surprisingly, Solihull soon started hearing complaints about axle failures.

Customers also complained – somewhat unreasonably – that the Forward Control models higher centre of gravity made it less stable off-road than the normal-control Land-Rovers. Then there were braking and

handling problems, which were rather less forgivable. Finally, customers complained that a fully-laden 109 Forward-Control lacked performance. The six-cylinder models (which were available only for export) were adequate, but the four-cylinder petrol types were seriously underpowered; as for diesels, Solihull had decided against putting them on the market at all! As all these criticisms began to multiply, so the 109 Forward Control acquired a rather questionable reputation. For a time, there must have been real worries that the Forward Control models would tarnish the good name of Land-Rover.

Development

So it was that word came down from Rover management to the Land-Rover engineers that the Forward Control model needed to be redeveloped. Tom Barton entrusted the project to Norman Busby, and work probably began around 1963 or 1964. As Norman Busby recalls it, the development programme was both thorough and

△ *This specially-equpped ambulance version was used in New Zealand. The headlamps have been relocated to clear the frame at the front of the vehicle*

Control

expensive.

Work focussed initially on the weak axles, and the changes made here affected the whole shape of the revised vehicle. ENV were persuaded to provide heavy-duty axles, with a track which was all of four extra inches wider than that of the 109-inch models. This took care of overloading problems and also contributed to lateral stability. At the rear, the axle was mounted below the spring (instead of above it, as on the 109 Forward-Control), and then the front axle had to be moved forwards slightly in order to prevent fouling under certain conditions. The axle ended up three-quarters of an inch further forward than on the 109 models; in spite of its 109-3/4-inch wheelbase, however, Rover chose to describe the revised Forward Control model as the 110-inch wheelbase model.

The next stage was to improve handling, and so Norman Busby's team fitted an anti-roll bar to the front axle. To improve the ride and handling of a fully-laden vehicle, they also fitted stiffer springs with uprated

dampers. To give better off-road performance, they gave the transfer box lower 'Low' gearing. They repositioned the handbrake and re-routed the gearchange linkage above the engine, so adding a degree of precision which the 109 Forward-Control's gearchange had sorely lacked. They reorganised the instrument panel layout and fitted the interlinked windscreen wipers like those in the latest normal-control models. Lastly, they replaced the 109's positive-earth electrical system with a negative-earth type, in accordance with the policy which Rover was applying to all its cars and Land-Rovers in the mid-1960s.

Naturally, the Rover sales division were keen to distinguish the 110 Forward-Control from its 109-inch predecessor as much as possible, so that sales of the new model should not be affected by the old one's poor reputation. This was probably one reason why the front panel was redesigned with the headlamps lower down – although regulations in some export territories might also have influenced this. Flat

rear mudguards might well have been added for practical rather than cosmetic reasons, but they too helped to distinguish a 110 Forward Control from a 109 model at a glance. Lastly, 109 models had been Series IIAs, but the 110s were Series IIBs – a distinction which Solihull probably thought would help to emphasise the point that there were considerable differences between this new model and the old one.

On sale

The 110-inch Forward-Control Land-Rover was announced at the Commercial Motor Show in September 1966. It was, said the sales catalogue, "a more powerful and robust development of the 109" wheelbase model which has been in operation for some years." And, the catalogue reassured potential customers, "the Forward-Control model includes a very high percentage of standard Land-Rover parts, a factor of great importance to fleet operators all over the world."

This time around, the model mix was different, too. The home market was offered either six-cylinder petrol or four-cylinder diesel versions; four-cylinder petrol versions were available only for export. The

△
This view of the cab shows the re-positioned gearchange lever (formerly alongside the transmission tunnel) and the lengthened hand-brake lever

A Firefly fire tender on the 110 Forward Control chassis, Q 579 OBP has been re-registered since demobilisation. In service, it would have carried a ladder on the roof
◁

110 Forward Control came as a flatbed lorry, a dropside lorry or a fixed-side lorry, although chassis/cab versions were also offered for special bodywork. all versions were painted in Land-Rover Mid-Grey unless to special order.

Although the 110 Forward Control was undeniably a better vehicle than the 109 model it replaced, it never really made the sort of impact on the market which its makers had hoped for. In fact, sales were even poorer than those of the 109-inch model. The 109-inch achieved a production total of 3,153 in four years; the 110 managed just 2,304 in six years. Of those, 529 were home-market models, a total made up of 360 six-cylinders, 168 diesels, and one four-cylinder petrol example which might well have been built specially for British Army trials.

Norman Busby believes that the best export sales were achieved in Malaya, where Rover's agents, Champion Motors, were doing a splendid job of keeping around four hundred 109 Forward controls going to the satisfaction of their owners. He be-

lieves that a similar number of 110 Forward controls were sold to the Malayans. Other large export orders are said to have included a quantity for South Africa.

Not surprisingly, it was poor sales which killed off the 110 Forward Control. By the early 1970s, British Leyland was trying to get its vast empire under control, and it was rationalising and cutting costs wherever possible. To this end, it set a minimum viability figure for models in current production. One source believes that this figure, at least as applied to the 110 Forward Control, was 28 vehicles a week. With an average weekly production of just eight vehicles, there was no way the big Land-Rover could qualify, and so production was shut down during 1972.

Military versions

The 110 Forward Control was tested by the British Army in 1966 as a potential one-ton load carrier. However, the vehicle tested was a four-cylinder petrol model, and so it was hardly surprising that the Army de-

cided not to place an order! Pictures show that the test vehicle was a dropside lorry version with a full canvas tilt, and that it was registered as 21 BT 29 or 21 ET 29. The ET series would match with the vehicle's 1966 build date, but the BT numbers were reserved for second-hand vehicles which were not acquired under a standard military contract. It would be interesting to know more about this vehicle and its eventual fate.

However, the 110 Forward Control did enter service in the late 1960s with the Army Fire Service. The vehicles were ordered from Solihull in chassis/cab form, and were then sent to fire engine specialists HCB-Angus to have custom-built bodywork fitted. The resulting vehicles, known as "Firefly" fire tenders, were extremely attractive. The earliest examples were probably a batch of six registered as 22 FG 67 to 22 FG 72 in 1969. Next came 31 FH 33. Later batches included 03 FK 04 to 03 FK 05 and 05 FK 85 to 05 FK 88 (all entering service in 1973), and 24 FK

△ *Michael Thorne's splendid late low-mileage example belonged until recently to the Dunsfold Land Rover Museum*

36 to 24FK 76 (some with left-hand drive and all entering service in 1971 despite the later registrations). There could well have been others. Further special-bodied vehicles appear to have been ordered by the RAF for airfield control duties, but it is not clear how many of these there were.

Thanks to Brian Bashall, Norman Busby, Geof Miller and Michael Thorne for information, guidance and pictures. Information about the Firefly fire tenders was provided by the Road Transport Fleet Data Society, of 18, Poplar Close, Biggleswade, Bedfordshire, SG18 0EW.

110-inch Forward Control Production

Chassis numbers begining	
325/326/328 (2.25-litre petrol)	527
330/331/333 (2.6-litre petrol)	1,254
335/336/338 (2.25-litre diesel)	524
Total	2,305

Note: These figures are taken from the Rover Company despatch records currently held by BMIHT and are used by kind permission. The despatch records contain no details of CKD vehicles (327/329/332/334 and 337/339 series), but it is possible that some vehicles were shipped from Solihull as CKD packages. Information would be welcome.

THE LAND ROVER STORY

△ The original vehicle was very stark indeed. This is a prototype, shown at the 1966 SMMT/FVRDE exhibition. Note the curious grille pattern.

The Half-

James Taylor investigates the origins of the Military Lightweight, more properly known as the Half-Ton or Rover 1.
AT THE end of the 1950s, the buzz-word in British military transport circles was airportability. The new Blackburn Beverley transport aircraft looked as if it would open exciting new possibilities for moving military vehicles by air, and the Army had begun to look for a lightweight airportable runabout which the Beverley could carry in quantity. The Royal Marines, meanwhile, already had a fleet of 65 lightweight Citroen 2CV pick-ups on board the commando carriers *HMS Albion* and *HMS Bulwark*, and were slinging these beneath the carriers' Whirlwind helicopters and flying them ashore in support of operations.

The 2CVs had been chosen because, stripped of non-essential body parts such as windowscreens and doors, they were just light enough to be carried by the helicopters then in service. They had disadvantages, though, not the least of them being that they were not very strong and that they did not have the four-wheel-drive needed for rough terrain work. The Army was not interested in following the Marines' example and buying such vehicles, and in due course the marines also began to look around for replacements.

Although the Army, Navy and Air Force bought their vehicles through separate procurement executives, only the Army had a proper vehicle proving ground and so it was the Army which carried out type approval testing for all three services, at FVRDE in Chobham. As the 1960s began, a variety of strange lightweight vehicles passed through the hands of the Chobham test staff. Most notable among these were the Steyr-Puch Haflinger, an Austrian-built four-wheel-drive first produced in 1959; the Mini-Moke, derived from the BMC Mini and available to Chobham as early as 1960; and the Standard Pony, which became available in 1964.

Unfortunately, none of these minimalist machines really fitted the bill and, by the end of 1964, the search for a lightweight airportable military runabout seems to have ground to a halt. By this time, a new factor had also entered the equation: the Argosy had started to replace the Beverley as the main transport aircraft in 1962, and its narrow fuselage placed new size restrictions on the vehicles which could be carried in it.

Rover, of course, had good links with the three procurement executives and with FVRDE, and were well aware of the military requirement from the beginning. How-

ever, a plan to build a very special lightweight Land-Rover, the L.4, had foundered in 1959 after a year or so of work when sales forecasts in the civilian sphere looked disappointing. In the early 1960s, they had developed a 109-inch derivative suitable for airloading in the Argosy, but the One-ton AOGP (see LRO, September 1993) was far too heavy to be carried under the Marines' helicopters, as indeed were all other Land-Rover models then in production.

Having a go

Nevertheless, when the military issued a new Statement of Requirement for a vehicle which was narrow enough to fit two-abreast into an Argosy transport and light enough to be lifted by one of the new Wessex helicopters which were then entering service, Rover decided to do what they could.

Land-Rover chief Tom Barton agreed to take the job on, and appointed his assistant, Mike Broadhead, as Project Engineer. Broadhead in turn took on Norman Busby as his assistant for the project. The two men were the ideal choices for the task: Broadhead had been Project Engineer on the ill-fated L.4 lightweight project, and Busby had already worked on the one-ton air-

Δ *VXC 702F was probably the first production vehicle, and was built in 1967.*

Ton, Rover 1

portable vehicle.

Broadhead and Busby put their heads together and started from basics. To design a completely new vehicle would be enormously expensive and would take several years of work and, in the meantime, the military might find what they wanted elsewhere. The answer would therefore have to lie in an adaptation of an existing Land-Rover, but even the lightest of those then in production, the petrol-engined 88-inch Series IIA, exceeded the 2,500 lb (1,135kg) payload of a Wessex helicopter by around 450 lb. It was also too wide to be carried two-abreast in an Argosy.

There was no chance of losing any weight in the chassis or drivetrain of an 88-inch Land-Rover, but there was a chance of losing weight from the body. By redesigning the body panels, Broadhead and Busby also reasoned that they could make the vehicle narrow enough to fit two-abreast in an Argosy. By designing a very simple body to clothe the essential mechanical element of an 88-inch Land-Rover, they could also save on time and tooling costs. In any case, the military authorities had always said that the existing Land-Rovers were really too civilised for what they wanted and that stripped-out versions would not go amiss. Here, then, was the beginning of an idea.

The new vehicle – known at this stage as the Lightweight – started to take shape on an 88-inch chassis in a workshop at Solihull. A narrower bulkhead was fabricated, body panels were cut and shaped (as little as possible) by hand, and before long a rudimentary body had been built.

"We were always very aware of width and size and weight," recalls Norman Busby. "We even tried out foam pads instead of seats, but we eventually remembered that somebody was going to have to drive this thing. There was a really determined effort to keep the weight down."

Twin fuel tanks under the seats (like the single tank on a Series One) avoided the need for complicated filler arrangements, and weight had even been saved by using thinner 6.00x15 tyres instead of the 6.50x15s on standard production vehicles.

Even so, it was difficult to get the Lightweight to be light enough. In the end the project team had to resort to the same trick which the Marines had used to keep their 2CV pick-ups within limits. They made the doors, tailgate, windscreen assembly and body top demountable, argued that the bumpers and spare wheel were not essential items in a battle zone, and got the weight of the stripped-out vehicle to within an ace of the 2,500 lb weight limit for the

Wessex helicopter.

Before the project entered its final stages, Norman Busby had moved on – to become Project Engineer of the 110 Forward Control. "I only worked on the Lightweight with Mike Broadhead for six or nine months," he explains, "and Mike stayed in charge when I was moved. But I don't think there were very many prototypes made before it went for military trials."

Military trials

Trials of the new lightweight Land-Rover began at FVRDE in Chobham during 1965, and the military immediately took to it. However, they did request some specification changes, such as an oil cooler and standard 6.50x16 tyres instead of the 6.00x16s on the prototypes. These modifications inevitably added weight, but fortunately the Army had also discovered that it could increase the external payload of a Wessex helicopter if it stripped out some of the internal fittings, and so the equation still balanced

When the new vehicle was shown in prototype form at the three-day SMMT/FVRDE military vehicles exhibition in October 1966, it was described as a "Truck, General Service, Lightweight (Rover Mk1 1/4-ton 4x4)". According to the Exhibition cata-

△
*A stripped-down
Half-Ton Land-
Rover is hooked up
to a Wessex heli-
copter before being
airlifted*

*Inside a left-hand-drive Half-
Ton, in this case a 24-volt
FFR vehicle. The two 12-volt
batteries are under the metal
cover between the seats; on
12-volt models, a third seat
was fitted in the centre*
◁

logue: "this vehicle has been developed to meet a General Staff requirement for a lightweight airportable, helicopter liftable vehicle, having a useful payload and capable of towing light support weapons".

It differed from the standard 88-inch GS Land-Rover "in regard to body construction, which has been designed to meet the same roles as the existing vehicle and offering (sic) a similar degree of weather protection . . . It is also capable of being reduced in weight and bulk to a greater extent for air transportation and helicopter lifting, resulting in a stark but useful vehicle as exhibited weighing approximately 2,500lb. This vehicle is capable of carrying a payload of 896lb plus driver and one passenger. This exhibit is fitted with 8.20x15 ribbed desert pattern tyres."

By this stage, the Army had also decided that it might like an FFR version of the Lightweight, and a 24-volt vehicle was already under assessment and was shown at the Chobham exhibition. Scarcely light in weight, although the catalogue still called it a Lightweight, this one weighed-in at 3,514lb in full trim without its radio sets.

As development continued, the Army soon abandoned the rather inappropriate description of Lightweight and settled instead on the title of Half-Ton GS for all

versions. Not that the vehicle's payload had actually been increased from the quarter-ton of the prototypes: it was simply that the Army had now decided to rate the "Rover 1" according to its overall payload rather than according to the weight it could carry in the back.

Acceptance

A substantial order followed the Chobham trials. As far as it is possible to tell, that order was for 1,000 right-hand-drive 12-volt vehicles, was placed on 31st August 1967, and became contract number WV/7478. At Solihull, the Half-Ton project was granted production status, and Bob Seager was made Project Engineer with the task of getting the vehicle into production.

Records show that just two "production" vehicles were built in 1967, both with left-hand-drive. One of them was road-registered as VXC 702F. The first right-hand-drive production vehicle was built in 1968, and became CXC 212G. Another early vehicle, either the second in one of the production series or the first 24-volt FFR production example, became EXC 809G. As their civilian registration numbers suggest, all these vehicles remain at Solihull for evaluation and development work, and were never delivered to the Army.

The Army placed further orders for the new Half-Ton before the first production vehicles had entered service, and both the Royal Navy and Royal Air Force followed suit. Rover's despatch records show that 512 vehicles (of which only three had left-hand-drive) were built during 1968. However, none of these appear to have entered service until 1969, when they began to replace older civilian pattern "Rover 10" 88-inch GS Land-Rovers. The first examples of the "Rover 1" to enter service had FG registrations, and it looks as if the very first batch was registered 33 FG 35 to 43 FG 34.

The Half-Ton had disappeared from the public eye after the 1966 SMMT/FVRDE Exhibition, but it re-emerged at the Commercial Motor Show in September 1968. Rover's accompanying press release stated that: "the Army has already placed orders for the new vehicle and it is expected that gradually it will succeed the normal 88" Land-Rover which is the standard light 4x4 in its load class in all British Forces. Several overseas armies have also shown keen interest in the new model . . . The Half-Ton Land-Rover can be dropped by parachute from an aircraft and a special air-dropping platform has been developed for the purpose. When the vehicle reaches the ground it can be immediately driven

△ *This picture from a 1970 sales catalogue shows how much could be taken off the vehicle for airlifting. It is just possible to see that this example has the later headlamp arrangement, with the lights in front of the wheels*

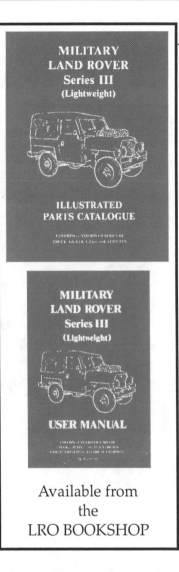

Available from
the
LRO BOOKSHOP

away."

Uses which the press release foresaw were "as a personnel or cargo carrier or in numerous other roles including mobile radio station, recovery vehicle, emergency two-stretcher carrier, mobile work shop and reconnaissance and fire service vehicle." And in practice, it would not be long before the Marines were using it to carry the WOMBAT 120mm gun.

In production

All the Series IIA Half-Tons which were not retained at Solihull as development and demonstration vehicles went to the British Armed Forces, which took both right-hand-drive and left-hand-drive examples, the latter for use in areas such as West Germany to suit local driving conditions. No Half-Tons were ever sold on the civilian market when new, and no overseas military orders were met by Series IIA models. Production continued into 1972 to meet outstanding orders, and the revised Series III Half-Ton models did not appear until that year, several months behind their civilian Series III counterparts.

In the meantime, however, there had been one change to the vehicle's specification. The original headlamp arrangement, with the lamps in the grille panel,

would not meet the lighting regulations in certain countries where the Army needed to operate, and so the front end had to be redesigned with the lamps placed further outboard. Exactly when the change was made in production is not clear, although development work was under way in 1968 or 1969 and the revised design seems to have been in production well before the middle of 1970. It therefore seems probable that no more than about 1,400 Half-Tons were built with the original lighting arrangements – which makes them relatively rare animals today. After that, just over 1,500 more Series IIA versions were made.

Most of the Series IIA Half-Ton Land-Rovers were withdrawn from military service in the mid-to-late 1970s, although a few lingered on until the early 1980s. Many civilian owners who bought these vehicles from military auctions or from specialist dealers ran them into the ground, with the result that relatively few still survive.

I have been unable to consult documents covering the early days of the Half-Ton, and have therefore based this part of the Land Rover Story on the recollections of people who were involved in the vehicle's development and testing. Many thanks go in particular to Norman Busby, Michael Pickering

CXC 212G

Further research since this article was written has shown that CXC 212G, the first right-hand drive production Lightweight, was used for early military trials. It then wore the registration number 20 BT 91. The vehicle has since found a home with the Dunsfold Land Rover Trust.

SERIES IIA MILITARY HALF-TON PRODUCTION	
Chassis numbers beginning	
236 (RHD, 2.25-litre petrol)	1,893
239 (LHD, 2.25-litre petrol)	1,096
	2,989

Note: These figures are taken from the Rover Company despatch records currently held by BMIHT and are used by kind permission.

and Bob Seager, all of whom did their best to remember what happened nearly 30 years ago, and all of whom warned me that their recollections might not be perfect! Further material came from BMIHT, Brian Bashall, Peter Cooke, Roger Crathorne, the Museum of Army Transport at Beverley and the Road Transport Fleet Data Society. Thank you to all of them.

THE LAND ROVER STORY

△ *Short Brothers and Harland introduced their Shorland armoured car in 1965. This is a very early example, not yet fitted with a weapon in the revolving turret*

Approved accesso

In this episode of our long-running series, James Taylor looks at some of the specialist Land-Rover conversions available for the Series IIA models.

THE CREATION of the Technical Sales Department – later the Special Projects Department – towards the end of the 1950s gave a new impetus to the Land-Rover conversion industry. Not only did it set standards which were their own guarantee of quality, but it also offered the converters (many of which were relatively small businesses) the ability to promote their products on a wide basis, wherever new Land-Rovers were for sale.

Land-Rover salesmen in the mid-1960s were expected to have more than a passing acquaintance with what was available, too. The properly trained salesman was expected to be able to respond promptly to any customer enquiry he might receive, and the Salesman's Manual on which he had to base himself contained a long list of the different categories of conversion available.

In addition, he was provided with a slim booklet, "Land-Rover approved imple-

ments, accessories and special vehicles", to carry around in his pocket so that he had information ready to hand. Finally, if a customer proved to be seriously interested in a converted vehicle, the salesman could refer to a green loose-leaf folder which contained details of every conversion or accessory which had Land-Rover approval. As new conversions and accessories were approved and their manufacturers provided explanatory sales leaflets to the approved Land-Rover pattern, so these leaflets were sent out to the dealers and inserted into the green folder. No doubt some customers were actually given copies of these leaflets to take away and ponder at leisure. However, this standardised leaflet system appears to have broken down in the late 1960s, shortly after the British Leyland takeover, and converters began to produce advertising material to their own pattern.

Some of the Approved Conversions sold in very small numbers, and some of the Approved Accessories must also have had a very limited appeal; others, however, were much more numerous. As is the way with specialist machinery, unfortunately,

many of the converted vehicles or unusual accessories were simply scrapped when they had outlived their useful working life, and so examples are relatively rare today.

AIR CONDITIONING could be fitted to any Land-Rover, and the approved suppliers were the Normalair division of Westland Aircraft Ltd., at Yeovil.

AGRICULTURAL IMPLEMENTS of several kinds could be fitted to Land-Rovers, and a hydraulically-operated three-point linkage could be added so that the Land-Rover could be used with farm machinery designed to be towed behind tractors. Specialist machinery came from Gascoignes of Reading, who offered a front-mounted milking machine; Hayters of Bishop's Stortford, who offered a PTO-powered grass cutter to be towed behind the vehicle; and F. W. M. McConnel Ltd., of Ludlow, who made a saw-bench which could be towed from site to site and was driven by the rear PTO. In addition, two companies made spraying equipment of various types: one was Evers and Wall of Newbury, and the other E. Allman and Company of Chichester.

AMBULANCES were usually on the long-

△ *One of a variety of fire tenders available from Carmichael's of Worcester during the lifetime of the Series IIA, this one sports the grille protection bar commonly fitted to vehicles destined for the RAF as crash tenders*

ries in the sixties

wheelbase chassis and were made by Pilchers of Burgess Hill, Herbert Lomas of Wilmslow and Invercarron of Stonehaven in Kincardineshire. The rarest version was the Invercarron.

ARMOURED CARS came from Short Brothers and Harland of Belfast. The "Shorland" had an armour-plated body on a 109-inch chassis (later a 109-inch One-Ton) and could be fitted with a rotating gun turret.

ARTICULATED SEMI-TRACTORS were offered by Dixon-Bate of Chester. The semi-tractor was an 88-inch Land-Rover fitted with a fifth wheel coupling and a vacuum brake system. A variety of semi-trailers could be had, and there was a demountable pick-up body available as an option.

BAGGAGE LOADERS could be mounted on both 88-inch and 109-inch Land-Rovers. They consisted of a three-section continuous conveyor belt, each section of which could be elevated by a hydraulic ram. They were made by the H.W. Edghill Equipment Company of Hook in Hampshire, and were sometimes known as Moy-Edghill loaders after their inventor, Peter Moy.

CARAVANS AND CAMPERS were available on both the 88-inch and 109-inch chassis. Martin Walter of Folkestone offered their Dormobile conversion with its famous elevating roof on the long-wheelbase Station Wagon. R. J. Searle of Sunbury-on-Thames (later trading as Carawagon International) offered a much wider choice: hardtop-based conversions called the Mini-Carawagon (88-inch) and Carawagon (109-inch); Safari Sleepers on the 88-inch Station Wagon; and Continental caravans and Ultimate folding-roof caravans on the 109-inch Station Wagon. Searle also offered de luxe conversions: the Royale on the 109-inch Station Wagon and the Super Estate Wagon, based on an 88-inch hardtop. However, some Land-Rover price lists did not include all the Searle conversions, and it may be that some of them were not Land-Rover-approved.

COMPRESSOR VEHICLES could be had from Lawrence Edwards and Company of Kidderminster or from Broom and Wade of High Wycombe. The Edwards type could be fitted to operate from either the centre or the rear PTO, and was a light-duty com-

pressor for spray guns, tyre inflation and the like. The Broom and Wade compressor was a rotary type which offered up to 100cfm and was installed under the floor of a 109-inch diesel Land-Rover.

DIFFICULT TERRAIN CONVERSIONS were available from Cuthbertson's of Biggar, who provided caterpillar tracks on a bogie to attach to each wheel of a long-wheelbase Land-Rover. In addition, Roadless Traction of Hounslow offered the Roadless 109, which had tractor wheels to minimise ground pressure and maximise traction in soft ground.

DRAIN CLEANERS were offered by Metering Pumps Ltd., of Ealing, London. Their conversion was known by the trade name of the Atumat.

DRILLING EQUIPMENT was available, but it is not clear who was the approved manufacturer.

ELECTRICAL POWER SOURCES could be built into the Land-Rover or fitted on demountable tailboard frames. The approved manufacturers were Tooley Electro-Mechanical of Earl Shilton, Leicester, and English Electric of Bradford.

FILM AND CINEMA VEHICLES were al-

This ambulance conversion was available from Herbert Lomas ▷

◁

A variety of special adaptations on Land Rovers at the 1964 Paris Motor Show. In the centre is a fire tender, while the 109 Forward Control on the right has an interesting-looking four-door cab. Exactly what the vehicle on the left was designed to do is not clear: can any readers help?

ways based on the 109-inch Station Wagon. Mobile Cinema conversions were done by British Films Ltd of Shaftesbury Avenue in London, and by Cintec of West Norwood, also in London. Filming and sound reproduction units were also available.

FIRE APPLIANCES were always a popular Land-Rover conversion, and there were several types, on both the 88-inch and 109-inch chassis. The manufacturers were Carmichael and Sons of Worcester, HCB-Angus of Southampton, Sun Engineering of Feltham, and Foamite, also of Feltham.

HYDRAULIC PLATFORMS came in two types. Western Engineering of Delabole in Cornwall made a fixed-base type, which elevated to a maximum height of 15 feet and was designed for tree lopping or fruit picking. Simon Engineering of Dudley made the second type, which came on a rotating base and extended to a maximum height of 25 feet. This type was recommended for inspection and maintenance work or bridges, street lamps, and the like.

LUBRICATION TENDERS were made by Tecalemit of Euston Road, London (later in Plymouth). They were based on the 109-inch chassis and consisted of a self-contained lubrication set which fitted into the load bed. The idea was to provide a mobile oil, grease and air dispensary for vehicles working onsite.

MOBILE WORKSHOPS were offered by

Tooley Electro Mechanical of Earl Shilton, Leicester. These were probably custom-built and would therefore have come in a variety of different forms. Tooley's also provided other specialist hydraulic equipment for Land-Rover conversions.

PRE-HEATERS, which warmed up the engine coolant and the interior of the vehicle, were available from Bahco Condrup Ltd of London EC1. They were petrol-powered and could be preset to switch on at the time required.

POWERED AXLE TRAILERS which converted the Land-Rover into a 6x6 coupled unit were manufactured by Dixon-Bate of Chester. The one-ton trailers came in cargo or tanker forms, and were driven by a propellor shaft from an additional gearbox mounted at the rear of the towing Land-Rover. They were marketed as "Bushmaster" trailers and were made by Scottorn of New Malden in Surrey.

RADIO TRANSMITTER/RECEIVER UNITS were made by Pye Telecommunications of Cambridge. A wide range of different types was available.

RAILWAY ENGINE conversions for light shunting and inspection duties could be manufactured by Heenan and Froude of Gloucester. However, it is unlikely that very many found buyers.

RECOVERY VEHICLES were generally on long-wheelbase chassis, and were fitted

with a manually-operated crane in the load bed. The crane and other vehicle breakdown and recovery accessories were made by Harvey Frost Ltd., of Bishop's Stortford.

REFUSE TRUCKS were made by Eagle Engineering of Warwick on the 109-inch chassis. They had a 3 cubic foot tipping body with sliding side hatches for loading and a swinging tailgate for discharge.

ROAD SPEED LIMITERS for petrol engined models only could be bought from Iso-Speedic Ltd., of Warwick.

SHOCK ABSORBING SEATS were made by Bostrom Manufacturing Ltd., of Northampton, and were marketed as the Saxon Thinline seat. They were probably designed only to replace the standard seats in the front of a Land-Rover; no shock-absorbing rear bench or inward-facing Station Wagon seat replacements seem to have been offered.

SNOWPLOUGHS came in several different forms, for fitment to either 88-inch or 109-inch Land-Rovers. The demountable blades could be raised manually or hydraulically, and came as either straight or V-shaped types. The makers were Atkinsons of Clitheroe and Cuthbertsons of Biggar. In addition, there was a snow blower attachment, made by Rolba in Switzerland.

SPRING ASSISTERS for fitting above the

The MD gets down to business: the smartly-dressed gentleman trying out a power saw driven by an English Electric-converted Land Rover is William Martin-Hurst, who had just bought the Buick V8 for Rover when this picture was taken.

rear axle of semi-permanently or permanently laden vehicles came in the shape of hollow rubber springs. They were made by Aeon Products of London N1.
STAKE SIDE BODIES could be had on the 109-inch chassis, and were made by P.D. Stevens and Sons Ltd. of Market Drayton.
VACUUM BRAKES for use with trailers were made by Feeny and Johnson of Wembley, in Middlesex.
WELDERS had been a feature of Land-Rover approved equipment since the earliest days, and Lincoln Electric Ltd., of Welwyn Garden City offered tailboard-mounted welding sets which were driven from the rear PTO. A cab-mounted welder, which replaced the centre seat and was driven from the centre PTO, was offered by Hayters Ltd., of Spellbrook, Bishop's Stortford.
WINCHES were made by M.A.P.

(Mayflower Automotive Products) of Tavistock, who offered a 5,000lb mechanically-operated front-mounted type, and by Fuller Lucas and Company, who sold a capstan type called the Plumett.

Thanks to Vin Hammersley at Land Rover for pictures. Some of these conversions will be covered in more detail in the "Rare Rovers" series, and I would be very pleased to hear from anyone who can supply further information about those listed here.

A Reader's help

The following is typical of the information which readers supplied in response to queries raised in *The Land Rover Story*. It relates to the vehicle pictured on the opposite page and came from Andreas Salmen, who lies in Menden, Germany.

The vehicle was designed for logging work, and specifically for dragging logs up steep slopes. First, the Land Rover would be parked at the top of the slope. Then the two long posts carried on the roof and attached to the H-frame at the front would be lowered into position until they stood vertically in front of the vehicle. A wire line would then be run down the slope from the top of these posts and secured high up on a convenient tree (or possibly another post) at the bottom to form an overhead "railway".

A trolley would be attached to the winch cable and would run down to the bottom of the slope along the overhead line. Logs would then be chained to the trolley, which would be winched back up the slope, bringing the suspended logs with it. The whole process could then be repeated.

North American Series IIs and IIAs

Rover attracted some useful publicity in the USA when Land Rovers featured among the support vehicles for Donald Campbell's record attempts with Bluebird in 1960.

James Taylor takes a look at the Land Rovers sold in North America between 1958 and 1971.

BEFORE 1958, Rover had no real presence in the USA, but sold its products through Rootes Motors Inc, the North American arm of the British Rootes Group which owned marque names like Hillman, Humber and Sunbeam. Both Rover saloons and Land Rovers entered the US market in 1949, although the first documented public showing of Land Rovers in the USA was at the British Automobile and Motorcycle Show in April 1950.

Rootes Motors in fact held Rover and Land Rover franchises not only for the USA, but also for Canada and the Caribbean. It was an arrangement which suited Rover, because the small Solihull company could simply not afford to establish its own dealer network in such a vast territory. However, Rootes Motors were understandably more keen to promote large Humbers than rival Rovers, and sales even of Land Rovers were never numerous. In the USA, they were very slow indeed, although Canadian and Caribbean sales were healthy. One source puts the total Land Rover sales in Rootes' three territories at around 200 a month, while noting that Land Rover sales in the USA were more like 100 a year. In a country which had invented the Jeep and the term built-in obsolescence, Land Rovers which looked the same from year to year stood little chance except as novelties.

By the late 1950s, however, sales of imported cars were improving dramatically in the USA. Rover was just about to introduce its new 3-litre (P5) saloon, and the company no doubt entertained hopes of cashing in on the vogue for imported cars with this model. It therefore terminated its

agreement with Rootes in 1958 and established its own North American subsidiary, sending out H. Gordon Munro to run the operation. The first headquarters of the new Rover Motor Company of North America were in Canada, at Mobile Drive on the edge of Toronto's Golden Mile, and there was a subsidiary office at 26-12 37th Street on Long Island, New York. Parts depots were set up in Vancouver, New York and San Francisco, and there was an additional sales office in Montreal.

It took some time to establish a dealer network in such a large territory, and most of 1958 was taken up in doing so. The first of the new North American dealerships to open was Concours Motors of Springfield, Massachusetts, early in 1959. Still touting for dealers as well as custom, Rover took a stand at the annual Sportsmen's Show in Toronto during March 1959 and another at the New York Automobile Show in April. Among the attractions at both were examples of the 90 and 105 saloons and a highly-polished unpainted aluminium Series II 88-inch Land Rover Station Wagon. As the company was not slow to point out, all the aluminium which then went into a Land Rover's body panels was actually Canadian in origin.

However, Rover had not yet understood its market. When the 3-litre saloon arrived in the USA during the second half of 1959, RMCNA discovered the hard way that a big car without power steering was almost unsaleable in North America, and as late as November 1960 the Rover Board was discussing a retro-fit programme under which power steering could be fitted to unsold cars which had already been shipped across the Atlantic. On the Land Rover front, canvas cabs did not go down well, and only when truck cab models were introduced did sales pick up a little. Similarly, any sober analysis of the US market in the late 1950s would have recognised that diesel engines were unlikely to be popular. And yet Rover considered it worthwhile to catalogue both petrol and diesel 88-inch and 109-inch Series II models. It would be interesting to know just how many diesel-powered Land Rovers they did manage to sell.

Over the next few years, RMCNA did try hard, although they never again equalled the publicity attracted when they provided the support vehicles for Donald Campbell's World Land Speed Record attempt at Bonneville salt flats during September 1960. Pictures show that four 88-inch and two 109-inch Land Rovers were on the strength, together with a fleet of six 3-litre saloons and three P4 saloons. One of the 88s had been fitted out as a fire tender by Minimax; one other Land Rover had telemetry equipment which enabled the support crew to monitor component temperatures on board the Bluebird record car while it was making its record attempts; one had been equipped in Canada as a mobile workshop; and the other two contained starting motors for the record car and air compressors to power its jacking system and to provide a blast of cold air to cool its brakes down in between record runs.

Presumably, RMCNA did succeed in doing something about the £5,000 a week loss they were making at the time of their involvement with the Bluebird run, and which was discussed by a concerned Rover Board in November 1960. They certainly did feel able

to move their headquarters into New York, where they established themselves in the Chrysler Building on 42nd Street and Third Avenue. The Toronto address was kept on as a Canadian regional office, and a second regional office (which covered 14 western states) was established on the West Coast at 373 Shaw Road South in San Francisco. By 1962, they had moved their New York headquarters to a more prestigious address at 405 Lexington Avenue.

This Series II was built in Canada at the Toronto headquarters as a parade vehicle for the 1959 Royal Tour

By 1962, however, the new P6 2000 saloon was in the final stages of its pre-production development, and Solihull was gearing up to launch it into the US market during 1964. In preparation for this, there was a management shake-up at RMCNA, and a new man was put in charge at 405 Lexington Avenue. This was J. Bruce McWilliams, who had spent 10 years as a UN official in New York before joining first Saab in the USA and then the Mercedes-Benz division of Studebaker (which sold the German cars in the US until the late 1950s). With McWilliams came his wife Gertrude, an Englishwoman who took charge of RMCNA's new and greatly enlarged advertising budget.

Under the McWilliamses, RMCNA expanded its dealer network greatly and established a very much higher profile in the

USA. Mainly instrumental in this were the strange but memorable advertisements which soon became characteristic of the company. When the Great Train Robbers were found to have used a pair of Land Rovers as getaway vehicles, RMCNA put out a series of humourous and highly effective advertisements which capitalised on the vehicles new-found notoriety. Sales catalogues reflected the same attention-grabbing philosophy, and few showroom visitors could have failed to remember the colourful egg-shaped brochures for the 3-litre saloon and coupé models which were issued for Easter 1963, even if most of them did fail to buy the cars.

In addition, the McWilliamses arranged for RMCNA to replace the feeble heater then standard on Land Rovers with a more powerful, locally-sourced Kodiak unit, and they persuaded Solihull to paint Land Rovers for the USA in a wider range of colours than were available elsewhere. A selection of the factory's standard colours were offered in the USA, but that market remained for many years the only one where a red Land Rover could be bought. It also looks as if it was the McWilliamses who took the decision to drop all the utility models of the Land Rover from the US range and to concentrate exclusively on Station Wagon variants.

These changes had the desired effect on sales. Although no figures are available for years earlier than 1964, there can be no doubt that year's total of 952 Land Rover sales in the USA was very much greater than the totals achieved in the earlier 1960s; 1965 was even better with nearly double that figure, although 1966 saw sales falling off again for reasons which are not clear at present.

Things had certainly started to look up. Solihull sent Graham Bannock out to the USA to carry out a proper market survey and to report back on how best Rover could meet American motorists' requirements. From the report he submitted in 1964 came the idea for the vehicle which became the Range Rover six years later, but in the meantime the company was able to change its model mix in order to achieve better sales. One result was that the single-carburettor 2000 saloon was replaced on the American market by the

The all-aluminium body panels of the Land Rover were demonstrated during 1959 by this unpainted Show vehicle.

The 1968 Federal Land Rovers had their headlamps mounted on the front wings. A year later, all Series IIA models would receive a new front end treatment with the headlamps in a styled recess in the wings. This vehicle appears to be an early try-out, and lacks the side marker lamps demanded by the new Federal laws.

more powerful 2000TC and by the 2000 Automatic in 1966.

However, RMCNA soon became more than a little frustrated with the speed at which Solihull worked. They knew what their customers wanted, and they knew, after Bannock had reported back, that Solihull could no longer be in any doubt. But they found it hard to understand why the new models they needed took so long to prepare. Two things in particular had always hindered US sales of Land Rovers: one was the vehicles' tiny fuel tanks (Americans tend to travel much greater distances than Europeans), and the other was their poor road performance. Bruce McWilliams now began to press Solihull very hard to do something about these shortcomings.

McWilliams never did get the bigger fuel tank he wanted, but he did get a more powerful Land Rover, which Solihull hoped would meet American demands for more road performance. This was a US-only variant of the 109 Station Wagon with the high-compression, Weslake-head six-cylinder engine (see Rare Rover in the

October issue of LRO), and it replaced all other versions of the 109 Station Wagon in the USA when it was announced in September 1966.

The six-cylinder 109 was a step in the right direction, but McWilliams wanted more. He knew that Rover's Managing Director, William Martin-Hurst, had secured the manufacturing rights to the 3.5-litre Buick V8 engine, and so during May and June 1966 he had his own engineers install a Buick V8 into an 88-inch Station Wagon which he then had shipped over to Solihull to demonstrate what was wanted. Project Golden Rod was more fully described by Michael Green in the May 1989 issue of LRO, and there can be little doubt that a production version of this vehicle would have given Land Rover sales in the USA a major boost. It was not to be, however. Some sources suggest that the Solihull engineers simply could not understand why anyone should want a Land Rover which was capable of 85mph or more and, because the Engineering Department was heavily preoccupied with other things in 1966-67, Golden Rod was returned to RMCNA with a polite "thanks, but no

thanks".

A major preoccupation for all British car manufacturers at this time was the new safety and emissions control regulations which were going to come into force in the US market during 1968. At Solihull, a special Emissions control section was set up in the Engineering Department to adapt Rover's existing engines. Top priorities were the 2-litre engines in the P6 saloons, the 3.5-litre V8 which was due to appear in a special US-market P6 model during 1969, and the 2.25-litre petrol engine which still powered most Land Rovers sold in the USA. As work on these was expected to take up all the time available before the new regulations came into effect, Rover decided against even trying to adapt the six-cylinder engine. As a result, the six-cylinder 109 Station Wagon was withdrawn from the US market during 1967, before it had really had a chance to make its mark. For 1968, the only Land Rover which remained available on the US market was the 88-inch DeLuxe Station Wagon with 2.25-litre petrol engine.

Rover was very proud of the fact that it was the first non-US manufacturer to introduce emissions-controlled vehicles into

LAND-ROVER

GET-AWAY VERSION!

(Left behind by an owner.)

We are strictly on the side of law and order. Let that be understood straight away. But can you blame us for feeling a certain warm glow when we read that the perpetrators of England's latest great robbery also chose a Land-Rover to do the job? For some time now we have been pointing out that the armed services of 26 countries use the Land-Rover, the police forces of 37, veritable legions of country squires, desert chieftains, titled persons, oil and gold prospectors, not to mention sportsmen and all sorts of nice families who use them for skiing, beach buggying and other pleasant things —in some 160 countries, in fact. But what a marvelously splendid "proof of the pudding" it is that the chaps who pulled off both The Great Train Robbery and, now, the Longfield, Kent, job were equally discerning.

If you'd like to check one out for some purpose you have in mind drop us a card and we'll send you a list of our dealers.

We told you that big door was great for loading things!

THE ROVER MOTOR COMPANY
OF NORTH AMERICA LIMITED
405 LEXINGTON AVE NEW YORK 17 NY USA

the USA, and was no doubt also quite proud that the emissions control equipment did not harm the performance of the Land Rover's 2.25-litre petrol engine too greatly. However, in other respects the 1968 "Federal" 88 Station Wagon had a number of very noticeable differences from its equivalents sold in other markets, and it is strange that it was not given a unique chassis numbering system like the "Federalised" Rover saloons.

The 1968 Federal 88 Station Wagon was the first normal-control Land Rover to have its headlights mounted in the wing fronts (initially without the styled recess introduced a year later and carried over for Series III models). US lighting regulations also demanded side marker lights in the wings and amber front running lights instead of the white sidelamps standard until then. In addition, the new regulations demanded a dual braking system with a tandem master cylinder, and some smaller revisions to dashboard and switchgear.

US Land Rover sales actually went up for 1969, but in 1970 they were down again and in 1971 still further. One reason must have been that the engines were gradually losing power as they were adapted to meet tightening emissions laws; another was probably that Rover was getting some very bad press in the USA as a result of poor quality control and lackadaisical dealer service. Finally, British Leyland (which had appointed Bruce McWilliams to head its entire US operation) was now in charge and was putting all its effort into selling sports cars and Jaguar luxury saloons. Land Rovers came a very long way down the priorities list and were essentially left to fend for themselves.

By the time Series IIA Land Rover

production came to an end in 1971, Land Rover sales in the USA were slipping badly. Rover car sales were also in a bad way, and the company pulled its saloons out of the US market that year. BL did manage to sell a few thousand Series III 88-inch Station Wagons over the next few years – in fact sales took an upturn in the early 1970s – but the cost of meeting increasingly tight emissions control regulations persuaded them to stop selling Land Rovers in the USA in the autumn of 1974.

Many readers responded to my appeal for information and provided material used in this episode of the Land Rover Story. My thanks go to Jim Allen, Dick Green, Michael Green, John Hanna, Jim Joss and the PR staff of Land Rover North America. In spite of their best efforts, however, there are still many gaps in the story of Land Rover in the USA, and I would be very pleased to hear from anyone who can help to fill them.

SALES FIGURES

Note: no sales figures are available prior to 1964.

1964	952	1968	N/A
1965	1840	1969	1222
1966	1137	1970	873
1967	415	1971	756

There were 811 109 six-cylinder Station Wagons built in 1966-1967. These all had a special chassis numbering sequence beginning 343...Other US models were numbered within the appropriate sequence for LHD export models.

LAND ROVER OFFICIAL FACTORY PUBLICATIONS

Land Rover Ser. 1 Workshop Manual	4291
Land Rover Ser. 1 1948/53 Parts Catalogue	4051
Land Rover Ser. 1 1954/58 Parts Catalogue	4107
Land Rover Ser. 1 Instruction Manual	4277
Land Rover Ser. 1 & II diesel Instruction Manual	4343
Land Rover Ser.II & IIA Workshop Manual (part 1 engine)	AKM8159
Land Rover Ser.II & IIA Workshop Manual (part 2 chassis)	AKM8159
Land Rover II/IIA bonneted control Parts Catalogue	605957
Land Rover Ser. IIA Parts Catalogue	RTC9840CC
Land Rover IIA/IIB Instruction Manual	LSM641M
Land Rover Ser. III Workshop Manual	AKM3648
Land Rover Ser. III Workshop Manual V8 Supplement (edn. 2)	AKM8022
Land Rover Ser. III Parts Catalogue	RTC9841CE
Land Rover Ser. III Owners' Manual (1971-81)	607324B
Land Rover Ser. III Owners' Manual (1981-85)	AKM8155
Land Rover 90/110 & Defender Workshop Manual	SLR621ENWM
Land Rover 90/110 Owners' Manual	LSM0054
Land Rover Discovery Workshop Manual	SJR900ENWM
Land Rover Military (Lightweight) Ser. III Parts Catalogue	
Land Rover Military (Lightweight) Ser. III User Manual	608180B
Land Rover 101 1 tonne forward control Workshop Manual (soft & hard cover)	RTC9120B
Land Rover 101 1 tonne forward control Parts Catalogue	6082943
Land Rover 101 1 tonne forward control User Manual	608239
Range Rover Workshop Manual (edn. 7) 1970-85	AKM3630
Range Rover Workshop Manual 1986 on (includes LSM 180WM)	SRR660EN WM
Range Rover (up to 1985) Parts Catalogue	RTC9846CH
Range Rover (2 door) Owners' Handbook	606917
Range Rover Owners Handbook (1981 on)	AKM 3193
Range Rover Owners Handbook (1983 on)	LSM 0001HB

Owners' Workshop Manuals
Land Rover 2/2A/3 1959-83 Owners' Workshop Manual
Land Rover 90,110 & Defender Owners' Workshop Manual

From: LRO Mail Order Ltd. Anglian House, Chapel Lane, Botesdale, Diss, Norfolk, IP22 1DT Phone: 01379 890056

Or in case of difficulty direct from the distributors

Brooklands Books Ltd., PO Box 146, Cobham, Surrey KT11 1LG, England.
Phone: 01932 865051 Fax: 01932 868803
Brooklands Books Ltd., 1/81 Darley St., PO Box 199, Mona Vale, NSW 2103, Australia.
Phone: 2 999 78428 Fax: 2 979 5799
Car Tech, 11481 Kost Dam Road, North Branch, MN 55056, USA
Phone: 800 551 4754 & 612 583 3471 Fax: 612 583 2023

Printed in Hong Kong